ADOLESCENT
SUICIDE

ADOLESCENT SUICIDE

An Integrated Approach
to the Assessment of Risk
and Protective Factors

Peter M. Gutierrez, Ph.D., and

Augustine Osman, Ph.D.

Northern Illinois University Press

DeKalb, IL

Library of Congress Cataloging-in-Publication Data

Gutierrez, Peter M.

Adolescent suicide : an integrated approach to the assessment of risk and protective factors / Peter M. Gutierrez and Augustine Osman.

p.   cm.

Includes bibliographical references and index.

ISBN 978-0-87580-616-7 (alk. paper)

1.   Teenagers--Suicidal behavior.

2.   Suicide--Prevention.

I. Osman, Augustine. II. Title.

HV6546.G87 2007

362.280835--dc22

2007024578

Contents

Acknowledgments

The list of individuals who provided support, encouragement, and interest in this book throughout the process is quite long, and I don't want to risk accidentally omitting anyone. Therefore, I will simply say thanks to my family, friends, colleagues at NIU and in AAS, and my students for all you've done for me. But I'd be remiss if I didn't specifically thank my colleague, friend, and co-author, Augustine, for sharing my vision for this book and helping make the daunting process of actually writing a book seem possible. I couldn't have done it without you. We would also like to thank our colleague Dr. Jim Mazza for providing extensive feedback on the final draft of the manuscript and pointing out numerous places where we needed to be clearer. Finally, I'd like to dedicate this book to the parents, family, and friends of the teens who have died by suicide. I hope that our efforts on this project will contribute to a decrease in suicides in the future.

Peter M. Gutierrez, Ph.D.

This book in part represents a summary of some of the papers that Peter and I have presented at professional conferences or published in peer-reviewed journals in recent years. I remain thankful for the opportunity to continue to collaborate with a colleague and close friend; thank you, Peter. We are indeed thankful for the encouragement and multiple prompts of our editor, Melody Herr. In particular, we acknowledge Melody's patience in answering the host of questions we had for our first book. We would also like to thank the staff at the Mental Health Institute, Independence, IA, for help with the data collection procedures for our projects. Next, I remain indebted to a number of close friends, mentors at West Virginia University, students and colleagues at the University of Northern Iowa and UTSA, and all the members of my family. Finally, Peter and I hope that all health care professionals will find this work useful for clinical and/or research-related activities. We hope that this work will reflect new ways in which suicide-related behavior could be conceptualized, as a balance of risk and protective factors.

Augustine Osman, Ph.D.

We would like to thank our co-authors and the publishers listed below for graciously allowing us to reprint portions of these previously published articles. Copyright agreements and/or permission letters are on file for the following:

Guilford Press

Gutierrez, P. M. (2006). Integratively assessing risk and protective factors for adolescent suicide. *Suicide and Life-Threatening Behavior, 36*(2), 129-135.

Gutierrez, P. M., Watkins, R., & Collura, D. (2004). Suicide risk screening in an urban high school. *Suicide and Life-Threatening Behavior, 34*(4), 421-428.

Lawrence Erlbaum Associates, Inc.

Gutierrez, P. M., Osman, A., Barrios, F. X., & Kopper, B. A. (2001). Development and initial validation of the Self-Harm Behavior Questionnaire. *Journal of Personality Assessment, 77*(3), 475-490.

Gutierrez, P. M., Osman, A., Kopper, B. A., & Barrios, F. X. (2000). Why young people do not kill themselves: The Reasons for Living Inventory for Adolescents. *Journal of Clinical Child Psychology, 29*(2), 177-187.

Sage Publications

Gutierrez, P. M., Osman, A., Kopper, B. A., & Barrios, F. X. (2004). Appropriateness of the Multi-Attitude Suicide Tendency Scale for non-white individuals. *Assessment, 11*(1), 73-84.

Taylor and Francis Group, LLC

Gutierrez, P. M., Muehlenkamp, J. J., Konick, L. C., & Osman, A. (2005). What role does race play in adolescent suicidal ideation? *Archives of Suicide Research, 9*(2), 177-192.

ADOLESCENT SUICIDE

Part I

Theoretical and Empirical Issues

Related to Adolescent Suicide

Introduction to the Assessment of
Risk and Protective Factors

It is widely accepted that suicide and suicide-related behaviors (e.g., suicide attempts, threats, and ideation) are significant public health problems, and adolescents in particular are at high risk of engaging in nonlethal suicide-related behaviors (Grunbaum et al., 2002). It is also well established that the best predictor of future behaviors is a history of past behaviors (Pinto, Whisman, & McCoy, 1997). Therefore identifying adolescents who are at greatest risk of engaging in suicide-related behaviors before those behaviors become serious should reduce the incidence of suicide. Additionally, providing appropriate interventions for at-risk teens should improve their overall quality of life and increase the chances that they will lead long, healthy, and productive lives. The challenge is determining how best to identify at-risk teens.

Multiple approaches can be taken to assess for adolescent suicide risk. For example, the American Medical Association has recommended that physicians regularly ask about suicide during appointments with their adolescent patients (Kuchar & DiGuiseppi, 2003). Many schools have annual screening days at which students are asked about a variety of health risk related problems, including suicide (Reynolds, 1991a). In addition, school personnel are often trained to note suicide risk markers in their students and to follow up as necessary (Gould & Kramer, 2001). Mental health professionals working with adolescents should be attuned to indications of change in suicide risk and should know how to determine the level of risk.

Our goal is to present a theoretically and empirically based approach to adolescent suicide risk assessment that acknowledges the developmental differences between adolescents and other age groups. This approach is founded in the belief, backed by research evidence, that the combination of risk and protective factors affecting each adolescent best determines the probability of engaging in suicide-related behaviors at any given time (Gutierrez, Osman, Kopper, & Barrios, 2000). Most established assessment tools (e.g., self-report measures, structured clinical interviews) focus solely on risk factors. We believe that it is necessary to put together the appropriate battery of instruments to assess risk in any given setting, but it is also important to note that suicide risk assessment is only one component of clinical assessment.

We see assessment as the process of gathering as much information as possible from as many sources as possible about a given adolescent so that well informed decisions can be made about diagnosis and treatment. Such sources include structured diagnostic interviews, semi-structured clinical interviews, personality or intelligence testing, and review of records (e.g., school, medical). In addition, the individual adolescent, parents/caretakers, schoolteachers, and other important adults may all serve as sources of information. The nature of the setting in which assessments are performed, specific referral questions, and the theoretical orientation of the professional conducting the assessment will dictate how the assessment is conducted. We also believe that assessment is an ongoing process, and it is necessary to frequently update the data upon which clinical decisions are made. In this book we will explain the importance of assessing risk and protective factors for adolescent suicide as an integral component of clinical assessment.

Before providing an overview of the structure of this book, it is necessary to define the key terms we will be using throughout. Adolescents are defined as individuals between the ages of 12 and 18. This age range spans the typical onset of puberty through the age at which most individuals graduate from high school and are considered by societal norms to be young adults capable of independent living. Our definitions of suicide-related behaviors are based on O'Carroll et al.'s (1996) nomenclature. A suicide is defined as any death resulting from intentional self-inflicted injury. A suicide attempt is any potentially self-injurious behavior in which there is evidence that the individual intended, at some level, to die. Suicide threats stop short of action but are meant to give the impression that the individual intended self-harm. Suicidal ideation is defined as self-reported thoughts of engaging in suicide-related behaviors (i.e., any of the above behaviors). When referring to the spectrum of these behaviors, we will use the broad term suicide-related behaviors. We will refer to the fatal outcome of these behaviors either as a suicide or death by suicide. Terms such as failed attempt and committed suicide will not be used due to the implication that death is either a successful outcome or that the act of dying is pejorative. As Shneidman (1993) has been so eloquently teaching us for years, suicide results when the psychological pain one is suffering overwhelms one's resources to continue coping with that pain, and death is seen as the only possible way to end the pain. Therefore referring to suicide as a choice made by an individual seems to miss the point. Suicide is a decision a person makes, but we believe it is the decision after all other possibilities have been exhausted, or when the pain the individual suffers does not allow that person to make any other decision. We view suicide as a preventable problem and therefore will focus on the complexity of its multiply determined nature rather than pointing blame at the individual engaging in suicide-related behaviors.

This book is intended to be of use to a broad range of professionals working with adolescents and to be accessible to nonprofessionals with a serious interest in the problem of adolescent suicide. It should be useful for experienced researchers branching in this new direction as well as graduate students wishing to supplement their assessment training or conduct suicide research. We intend to help answer the question, "How can I tell if this individual is likely to engage in suicide-related behaviors?" Because there is no simple answer to that question, our response is, "It depends on the setting in which you work." To adequately answer this question, we have organized the book into three sections.

The first section addresses the theoretical issues related to assessing risk and protective factors in an integrated fashion, specific target variables in each domain, weaknesses in the existing adolescent suicide assessment literature, and the psychometric issues underlying the creation and evaluation of appropriate measures. The second section contains separate chapters on self-report instruments to assess risk factors, protective factors, or the combination of both simultaneously. In each chapter, significant attention is given to the psychometric qualities of assessment tools we have created over the years. Information is also summarized from the published literature on relevant measures we have found useful in our work. The third section is devoted to discussing comprehensive assessment packages to use in a variety of settings (e.g., clinical, schools) and with special populations (e.g., minority adolescents). Because the resources and needs vary from one setting to the next, we take into consideration administration time, feasibility of administering the measures in more than one sitting, cost of producing the package, demands on staff time for scoring and interpretation, and possible sources of collateral data. To the extent the data are available, we also provide information on gender, racial, and ethnic differences useful in interpreting scores. Finally, we discuss the differences between assessment for research versus clinical purposes. Because we are both active researchers and graduate faculty members, we are sensitive to the challenges of conducting adolescent suicide research. We have developed a variety of ways to reduce these challenges, which we share with readers preparing to embark on careers as suicidologists.

Ours is not the only book to address the issue of adolescent suicide risk assessment, but it is one of the few to focus solely on adolescents. Many books contain a chapter on the topic or include chapters on intervention and other related topics, but by focusing solely on assessment, we can provide significantly more depth and address key theoretical, methodological, and psychometric issues frequently overlooked by others. All assessment tools presented in this book were developed specifically for use with adolescents. A great many tools have been developed over the years to assess thoughts related to suicide, probability of engaging in suicide-related behaviors, and other known risk factors. Most of these scales were originally intended for use with adults. Unfortunately researchers and clinicians regularly use these scales when assessing adolescents, often with little to no empirical evidence that this approach is appropriate. Knowing that a scale is valid and reliable when administered to adults is no guarantee the same will be true when it is completed by adolescents. Young people have more limited life experience and are less emotionally and cognitively developed than adults. These differences may influence how they interpret and respond to questions about their thoughts, feelings, and behaviors. Unless firm evidence exists that a scale is developmentally appropriate, valid, and reliable when used with adolescents, it should not be used for something as serious as suicide risk assessment.

The quality we believe distinguishes our book is our integrated approach to assessing risk and protective factors simultaneously. We view suicide risk as a fluid construct, affected by many factors that may change dramatically from moment to moment. A frequently made statement in the aftermath of an adolescent suicide is, "I don't know why he did it; he had so much to live for." Conversely, clinicians are sometimes amazed that their clients are not suicidal, given the magnitude of problems with which they grapple. We believe that the same process can explain both situations. It is neither the number of reasons one has to live, nor the number of problems one faces that determines who will or will not die by suicide; rather, it is the combined effect of both. The ambivalence often observed in suicidal individuals can also be explained by the interaction of risk and protective factors. At times when the risk factors are stronger, the individual is more attracted to death and appears more suicidal. An increase in protective factors (e.g., receiving positive social feedback) or a decrease in risk factors (e.g., effective treatment for depression) may fairly rapidly tip the scales toward more attraction to life and the appearance of being less suicidal.

Our theoretical orientation is based primarily on the work of Orbach (e.g., 1997) and Linehan (e.g., Linehan, Goodstein, Nielsen, & Chiles, 1983). We also believe that work by Jobes and his colleagues (e.g., Jobes & Drozd, 2004; Jobes & Mann, 1999) with college-age individuals is developing along parallel lines. Orbach (1988) proposed the existence of a set of interrelated positive and negative factors influencing adolescent suicidality. He argued that all individuals possess feelings of attraction to and repulsion by life and death. Furthermore, he proposed that suicidal adolescents could be distinguished by their overall pattern of these attitudes toward life and death. Numerous studies have since supported this basic premise (e.g., Gutierrez, King, & Ghaziuddin, 1996; Orbach et al., 1991; Osman et al., 1994). Generally speaking, suicidal adolescents tend to be more attracted to death and repulsed by life while also being weakly attracted to life and repulsed by death than nonsuicidal adolescents (Gutierrez, 1999). Linehan and colleagues (1983) concluded that assessing protective factors against suicide is both possible and practical. They determined that individuals can report both strong reasons to want to die and strong reasons to stay alive. Although that work has focused on adults, we believe the general theory applies to adolescents as well and is supported by our research (e.g., Gutierrez, Osman, Kopper, & Barrios, 2000).

We will provide readers with the tools to sample a range of risk and protective factors that have been empirically determined to be strongly linked to suicide. Following the recommendations in this book is no guarantee of correctly identifying all at-risk adolescents with whom you work; however, using the assessment packages we recommend should increase the probability of accurate identification of high risk adolescents and provide a broad range of information on which to base clinical decision-making. As we have said, clinical assessment is a complex and ongoing process. We hope to make the process easier by illustrating how to gather data on suicide risk and protective factors for the adolescents with whom you work.

All of the measures recommended in the assessment packages discussed are self-report. We have decided to focus on self-report measures in this book for several reasons. Kaplan et al. (1994) reported that, like the clinical interview, self-report instruments are useful in assessing several risk factors, including frequency of ideation, previous attempts, and threats of future attempts. In addition, self-report instruments have the advantage of obtaining reliable information about recent suicidal ideation and risk factors that the individual may not openly communicate. Self report measures allow for simple and direct evaluation of symptom severity, especially when the chosen instruments have well-established norms and cut-off scores and are administered at multiple points in time (Kendall, Cantwell, & Kazdin, 1989).

When the variables of interest in a clinical assessment or research project are primarily internal affective states and cognitions, one must rely on the individual's subjective evaluations of these states. While there are reasons to question self report data, especially from adolescents, there are few viable alternatives. Youth are certainly capable of providing valid self report data, but they tend to endorse fewer symptoms than do either parents or clinicians (Kendall et al., 1989). There is also the risk of questions being misunderstood, not taken seriously, or intentionally answered inaccurately. Youth may fear that their answers will lead to an undesirable outcome, such as hospitalization or other types of mandatory treatment. In research settings, the concern might be their parents being informed, despite assurances of confidentiality. Benefits of self report measures include standardized administration, wording, and ordering of questions. In addition, participants may be more comfortable divulging information about topics related to suicide through the relative anonymity of a self report scale than by speaking face to face with an interviewer (Erdman, Greist, Gustafson, Taves, & Klein, 1987; Greist et al., 1973). In most cases, self report questionnaires are preferable to interviews as they are faster to administer and more efficient because in nonclinical settings they can be completed in groups (Eyman & Eyman, 1990). This is not to say that self-report measures are a replacement for structured and semi-structured clinical interviews, but they are a crucial component of a comprehensive assessment and are invaluable for purposes of ongoing case management.

Besides the practical considerations of self report methodologies, some argue that the quality of data produced may be comparable to that obtained through clinical interviews. Shain, Naylor, and Alessi (1990) compared self report of depressive symptoms for a group of adolescent psychiatric inpatients. They found correlations between clinician rating and self report ranging from .73 to .87, supporting the contention that self report data are both more efficient to gather and are adequate for research and clinical purposes. Correlations between parent and child reports of depressive symptoms, by contrast, tend to be quite low (i.e., r below .25) (Kendall et al., 1989; Moretti, Fine, Haley, & Marriage, 1985), suggesting that the youth themselves are a better source of information.

Similar findings support the use of self report of additional variables related to suicide risk. A group of outpatients with a history of prior ideation, past suicide attempts, or current suicidal ideation completed the Harkavy Asnis Suicide Survey (Harkavy-Friedman & Asnis, 1989) and were interviewed face to face regarding suicidal thoughts and behaviors (Kaplan et al., 1994). The authors calculated the Kappa coefficients between the two data sources for a variety of suicide related behaviors. Kappas ranged between .63 for suicidal thoughts in the past week to 1.0 for family history of suicide deaths. Twice as many participants endorsed current ideation on the self report measure than they had during the interview. The authors concluded that self report of suicide related behavior is valuable in clinical settings, where clients may be more comfortable with the response format, and nonclinically for screening purposes.

Data from a longitudinal study indicated that agreement between child and mother report for both suicidal ideation and attempts was quite low (Klimes Dougan, 1998). Of note, children's lifetime self report of suicidality at the final assessment point failed to agree with a previous report for 19% of the sample. Children who only endorsed suicidality through one mode (i.e., self report or interview) most often did so on the self report measure. Similar results were obtained in a community sample of children and adolescents (Kashani, Goddard, & Reid, 1989). Finally, a study of families with children between the ages of 9 and 18 found child report of both current ideation and lifetime history of ideation to be twice that of parent report (Velez & Cohen, 1988).

Now that the reader knows the theoretical orientation driving our work and the evidence supporting the use of self-report measures, we can move on to the issue of determining suicide risk. We begin with an overview of the known risk and protective factors and a discussion of important psychometric considerations when developing scales before proceeding to a detailed discussion of individual measures. We conclude the book with a guide to assessing adolescent suicide risk in a variety of settings and with select special populations. Finally, all of the measures we have developed that are discussed in the book appear in the Appendix. Readers have permission to reproduce any of these measures for research or clinical purposes by virtue of having purchased this book.

Summary of Clinical Practice Implications

- Assessing adolescent suicide risk is complicated and understandably stressful for professionals.

- The setting in which the assessment is performed determines how best to structure it.

- Both risk and protective factors must be assessed simultaneously.

- Adolescent self-report is valid, reliable, and appropriate for assessing risk and protective factors.

Empirically Supported Risk Factors

Volumes have been written on the topic of risk factors for adolescent suicide and suicide-related behaviors. Rather than summarizing the broad range of theories and those explored in studies, we will focus only on those for which there is strong empirical support. In the second half of the chapter, we will critique methods used to assess these risk factors in adolescents and make recommendations for future research.

Individual Risk Factors

By far the strongest evidence exists for adolescents who have made a prior suicide attempt to be at risk of future attempts (e.g., Lewinsohn, Rohde, & Seeley, 1994; McKeown et al., 1998); however, our aim is to help identify youth whose risk levels are elevated by other factors but who have not made a suicide attempt. We will focus on these factors in this chapter. The presence of serious psychopathology is also well supported as significantly elevating risk. Most of the research focuses on adolescents suffering from an affective disorder (Allison Pearce, Martin, Miller, & Long, 1995; Andrews & Lewinsohn, 1992; Pearce & Martin, 1994; Reinherz et al., 1995), such as major depression or anxiety disorders. Hopelessness, although not a diagnosable disorder, is commonly found in adolescents with psychiatric disorders and has consistently been found to be related to suicide risk (see Maris, 1991b; Maris, Berman, Maltsberger, & Yufit, 1992). Other less frequently studied but related risk factors have included problem-solving deficits (Rotheram-Borus, Trautman, Dopkins, & Shrout, 1990; Sadowiski & Kelley, 1993), escape from negative emotional life stressors (Baumeister & Scher, 1988), personality characteristics (Kashden, Fremouw, Callahan, & Franzen, 1993), substance use disorders (Beautrais, Joyce, & Mulder, 1996; Fowler, Rich, & Young, 1986), and low self-esteem (Overholser, Adams, Lehnert, & Brinkman, 1995). Velting, Rathus, and

Miller (2000) reported that adolescent attempters could be distinguished from psychiatric patient nonattempters based on their personality profiles. Specifically, attempters demonstrated more forceful and borderline tendencies and less submissive and conforming tendencies. Lewinsohn, Rohde, and Seeley (1994) found both history of past suicide attempts and functional impairment due to illness/injury to be risk factors uniquely predictive of future suicide attempts.

The risk of serious suicide-related behavior is much higher in clinical populations than adolescents in general. For example, Kovacs, Goldston, and Gatsonis (1993) presented data from a longitudinal study of depressed children and nondepressed clinical controls. At study entry, 58% of the clinical sample had a history of suicidal ideation, and 9% had made at least one attempt. They reported that ideation was 2.5 times and suicide attempts 11 times more likely in the depressed group. Rates of ideation remained fairly stable during the follow up period (62%), but attempt rates doubled (18%). Ideation remained more common in the depressed group but was higher in girls than boys (74% v. 52%). Suicide attempts were also more likely in the depressed group, with more girls (26%) than boys (12%) having made an attempt by the end of the study. Kovacs and colleagues concluded that the risk of suicide attempts for adolescents with an affective disorder is 4 to 5 times higher than for those with a nonaffective disorder.

Additional support for the links between serious mental illness and suicide risk comes from treatment follow up studies. A six month follow up study of adolescent inpatients determined that risk of attempt was increased by major depressive disorder ($OR = 4.7$), death of a relative ($OR = 3.5$), and family financial problems ($OR = 2.9$) (Brent, Kolko, et al., 1993). King, Hovey, Brand, and Ghaziuddin (1997) concluded that only depressive symptoms and ideation combined to predict subsequent attempts in their follow up of adolescent inpatients.

Gender Differences

Rich, Kirkpatrick-Smith, Bonner, and Jans (1992) found that the combination of scores on hopelessness, depression, substance use, and reasons for living (i.e., protective factor) scales accounted for 46% of the variance in ideation for males and 57% for females. Mazza and Reynolds (1998) also found gender differences in their longitudinal study of high school students. Significant gender differences in time one variables associated with time two suicidal ideation were found. For males, the number of daily hassles and negative life events were the best predictors. Low social support and number of depressive symptoms were the best predictors of ideation for females.

Family Risk Factors

In addition to individual risk factors, several familial factors have been found to influence whether an adolescent engages in suicide related behavior.

For example, Adams, Overholser, and Lehnert (1994) found that adolescents most frequently attributed suicide attempts to feeling detached from parents, inability to talk effectively with family members, and interpersonal conflicts. Kosky, Silburn, and Zubrick (1990) reported that approximately 82% of their suicidal sample had hostile home environments and had also experienced persistent interpersonal conflicts within the family. Other familial factors contributing to serious suicide attempts include recent parental loss (Marano, Cisler, & Lemerond, 1993), exposure to frequent family violence (Kosky, 1983), suicide related behavior by family members or a close friend (Sorenson & Rutter, 1991), and physical and sexual abuse (de Wilde, Kienhorst, Diekstra, & Wolters, 1992). Marano et al. (1993) observed that combinations of insufficient family support and loss were the strongest sociodemographic predictors of adolescent suicide.

Psychopathology within the family must also be considered as potentially contributing to adolescent suicide risk. For example, Pfeffer, Normandi, and Kakuma (1994) reported significant differences between families of suicide ideators, attempters, and nonclinical controls on measures of alcohol abuse, mood disorders, and antisocial characteristics. More suicide attempts occurred among first-degree relatives of the attempters than in both clinical and normal control groups. More first-degree relatives of attempters and ideators had a history of psychiatric hospitalization than did the controls. In addition, these authors found that approximately 50% of the mothers of the suicide attempter group had also attempted suicide. Adam, Bouckoms, and Streiner (1982) observed that there was a higher incidence of family psychopathology in a suicide attempter group than in nonclinical controls.

A final family-related factor, the role of parenting in suicide risk, also has been examined (Allison et al., 1995). Suicide related behavior was found to be correlated with low parental care, high parental overprotection, and high parental criticism. The authors concluded that parenting style has a greater direct effect on suicidality than does hopelessness, but the impact is mediated by feelings of hopelessness in the youth. In a separate study, children of depressed mothers and controls participating in a longitudinal study were assessed for possible risk of suicidal ideation and attempt (Klimes-Dougan et al., 1999). By adolescence, 20% of the offspring of nondepressed mothers, compared to 50% with bipolar mothers and 57% with unipolar mothers, reported suicidal ideation. Twenty one percent of sibling pairs of mothers with unipolar depression had a history of ideation, compared to 6% of sibling pairs of mothers without an affective disorder diagnosis. Of those who eventually made a suicide attempt, 77% had reported ideation three or more years prior to the attempt. It appears that when parents' ability to adequately care for their children is compromised by their own psychopathology, there is a significant impact on suicide risk for the children; however, the possibility of genetic transmission of risk cannot be overlooked.

To summarize this somewhat dizzying array of research findings, it appears that factors contributing to adolescent suicide risk can be broadly grouped into three categories: psychological disorders, individual variables, and interpersonal variables. In the remainder of this chapter, we will discuss the methods that have been used to assess risk factors in these domains. As will be highlighted, much of the confusion surrounding what are and are not risk factors, and which factors are more or less predictive of future behavior, results from the methods employed when studying these constructs.

Review of Methods

One challenge in studying risk factors for adolescent suicide is their link to a low probability behavior (i.e., death by suicide). Many researchers choose less lethal but more common proxy variables as their outcome measure. For example, almost 17% of adolescents said they had seriously thought about attempting suicide at least once during the prior year (Grunbaum et al., 2004). Almost as many (i.e., 16.5%) said they had made a specific plan for how they would try to kill themselves, and 8.5% made a suicide attempt. As a result, suicidal ideation and suicide attempts are the variables of interest in most risk research.

Psychological Autopsies

There is no direct way to study adolescent suicide, because the only individuals who can explain why they did what they did are deceased; however, psychological autopsy data from completed adolescent suicides may provide useful clues for distinguishing between suicidal and nonsuicidal youth. This technique requires conducting very careful and thorough interviews with the surviving family members, friends, peers, and others in the social network of a suicide victim (Shneidman, 1981; Werlang & Botega, 2003) and is used by researchers as well as the legal system (Jacobs & Klein-Benheim, 1995). Ideally multiple informants are used along with other sources of data, such as medical records and police reports, in order to increase the reliability and validity of the final conclusions (Hawton et al., 1998). As with a medical autopsy, the information gathered is carefully analyzed to identify the most likely contributing factors to the death. Combining the results of multiple psychological autopsies can establish common patterns of risk factors. One such study compared adolescents who had died by suicide to suicide attempters and ideators who made a plan, threat, or suicide gesture (Brent et al., 1988). The only demographic differences across the three groups were that those who died by suicide were older and more often male. Interpersonal conflicts were common in all three groups, with the highest rates of parental conflict reported by the attempters. Attempters and those who died by suicide had high rates (90%) of psychological disorders. Adolescents who completed suicide had higher rates of bipolar disorder and any comorbid diagnosis. Most (83%) of the adolescents who completed suicide made some statement about it within a week of their death. Half of them made their statements to only a friend or sibling.

Psychological autopsy data from 67 adolescents' suicides were compared with data from 67 matched community controls (Brent, Perper, Moritz, Baugher, & Allman, 1993). Seven of the completed suicides had no psychiatric history, compared with 38 of the controls. Although the adolescents with no psychiatric history showed more suicidal ideation in the week prior to death than seen in controls, their impulsivity did not differ. The group with no psychiatric history showed less ideation and was assessed to be less depressed than the completed suicides with a psychiatric history. Compared to the completed suicides with diagnosed disorders, the group without a psychiatric history had fewer prior episodes of ideation and suicide attempts and less severe suicide episodes. Both groups of completers were distinguishable from controls on these variables. Completers without psychiatric history of attempts had fewer interpersonal conflicts and stressful life events than did the other completers in the year prior to death. Family variables also helped discriminate between groups. Completers with a psychiatric history came from families with more incidences of major depression and substance abuse. There were no differences in family history of completed suicide across groups, but completers with no psychiatric history came from families with more incidences of psychopathology than had the controls.

Psychiatric Patient Studies

Much also can be learned by studying adolescents who are currently suicidal. Because the most seriously suicidal adolescents are often patients in psychiatric facilities, research conducted with these populations tends to have small samples. A great deal of information is often available about these adolescents from multiple sources. For example, interview data from parents, other family members, and the adolescent can often be combined with medical chart data to form a fairly detailed picture of the individual's psychological functioning. It is also common to collect psychological test data (e.g., intelligence, personality) and to administer a variety of self-report measures as part of the intake process. From a research perspective, the challenge is how to combine qualitative and quantitative information in order to allow for statistical analyses and hypothesis testing. In addition, even when all data is quantitative, differences in how measures are scored complicates statistical analyses. Gaps in the information are also common due to different lengths of stay, availability of informants, and level of impairment of the patient.

The issue is not that these challenges make clinical inpatient data useless —quite the opposite, in fact. We have learned a great deal about suicide-related behavior in adolescents from research conducted with these young people; however, we must not lose sight of the fact that these youth make up a very small percentage of the overall adolescent population and are likely not representative of all adolescents. As a result, generalizing from these findings to attempt to understand adolescent suicide risk in broad terms may not be appropriate. It also may not be appropriate to try to generalize from one clinical population to another for the same reasons.

Longitudinal research, which attempts to test specific hypotheses about risk factors by following adolescents over a long enough period of time for subsequent suicide-related behaviors to become manifest, is most appropriately conducted with clinical populations. Because these young people's level of risk is high to begin with and many have a history of prior suicide-related behaviors, the probability of them engaging in these behaviors in the future is greater. Rather than gathering a huge random sample (i.e., 1000+) from the population of all adolescents in order to have enough participants likely to engage in the behaviors of interest, much smaller samples can be used. This makes clinical research more cost-effective in many ways and increases the chances of statistically significant findings.

But the question still remains about the extent to which clinical research findings can be applied to nonclinical adolescents. In an ideal world, no adolescent would ever become so seriously suicidal that he or she would need to be hospitalized. For that to become a reality, we need to determine which risk factors are identifiable in nonclinical adolescents. It is within this area of research that methodological problems are the most troublesome.

Nonclinical Studies

Perez (2005) took an interesting approach to attempting to determine how much can be learned about adolescent suicide risk from large-scale cross-sectional research. Using data from the 1999 Youth Risk Behavior Survey (YRBS), published by the Centers for Disease Control and Prevention, he used statistical techniques to construct and test various trajectories of suicide-related behaviors. He hypothesized that a developmental progression exists from seriously thinking about suicide to making an attempt that requires medical attention. In addition, he examined the relationship between the hypothesized trajectory and other serious risk behaviors, such as substance use. Both hypotheses were generally supported; thus Perez concluded that adolescents' responses to the suicide risk items on the YRBS are valid measures of their level of risk and relate to suicide intent, as most students endorsing more serious risk behaviors (e.g., suicide attempt) also endorsed all less serious behaviors (e.g., planning a suicide). A small percentage of adolescents deviated from the normative trajectory, indicating that caution should be exercised in interpreting level of risk when a nonnormative pattern of responses is found. To guard against potentially missing at-risk youth, Perez suggested that screening questions should always be asked about a range of suicide-related risk behaviors, even if the adolescent initially denies lower risk behaviors, such as thoughts of suicide or making suicide plans. Finally, he cautioned that given the nature of the YRBS questions, the derived trajectory is most likely valid only within a one year time frame. But this may be less of a concern given that any longer time frame would make examination of predictive validity all but impossible. The results of this study are promising because they were based on a nationally representative sample of nonclinical adolescents. Not only do the findings support the existence of serious suicide risk in the general population but also that group administered self-report measures are a valid and reliable means of assessing risk.

Problems with Existing Methodologies

Sampling Issues

Perez's (2005) study highlights one of the major concerns we have with much of the existing research on adolescent suicide risk: the use of measures not specifically designed to study the problem and data extracted from studies conducted for other purposes. While a valuable source of data, the YRBS only contains four questions specific to suicide-related behaviors. In addition, the questions are all categorical (e.g., yes/no), which limits what can be done statistically with the data. As we have already discussed, adolescent suicide is a complex problem, and the same holds true for the nature of factors contributing to risk. Caution must be exercised in placing too much weight on findings based on a limited number of questions, especially those extracted from a larger data set focusing on a broader issue than adolescent suicide risk. These types of studies may not be the best source of information for gaining an in-depth understanding of the problem.

The most rigorous research designs utilize random samples in which every member of the population of interest has an equal probability of being selected for participation (Kazdin, 2003). Studies such as the YRBS come close to achieving this goal but fall short because only students enrolled in public high schools who are present on the day of survey administration are eligible to participate. At the opposite end of the random selection continuum are the studies conducted on a single inpatient unit. These types of samples are used because they are convenient, but there is rarely much random about their makeup. The closer a study comes to truly random sampling, the more confident we can be about generalizing from the findings. In other words, most researchers would be comfortable concluding that the rates of suicidal ideation found in the YRBS come pretty close to approximating the true rates in nonclinical adolescents. But almost every study based on a convenience sample sounds a cautionary note about applying the results to other segments of the adolescent population. Many suicide risk factor studies did not utilize random samples and should be interpreted cautiously.

A closely related and, unfortunately, quite common problem is the result of nonrepresentative samples. The racial, ethnic, gender, age, social class, and sexual orientation composition of a study's sample should as closely match the percentages of these characteristics in the population as possible. As with the issue of random selection, the less representative a sample, the less appropriate it is to generalize from the findings. Few studies achieve representativeness on the entire set of participant characteristics listed, in part because of issues related to determining such things as social class or sexual orientation. Far too many studies are nonrepresentative across the entire range of characteristics. As a result, we do not know the extent to which widely accepted risk factors affect adolescents who are not Caucasian or straight. Certainly an argument can be made that some risk factors (e.g., major depression) should be universal, but as good empiricists, it is difficult to accept this assertion without first seeing the data to support it.

Measurement Issues

Although more researchers are choosing measures specifically designed and validated for use with adolescents, studies are still being conducted, particularly with older adolescents, relying on primarily adult measures. The most common examples are studies using the Beck Depression Inventory-II (BDI-II; Beck et al., 1996) as the only measure of depressive symptoms. While this practice is common, the BDI-II is not the most appropriate choice and may not yield the best data for adolescent suicide risk research. Without first knowing whether the measures used are developmentally appropriate for the chosen sample, drawing conclusions based on the resulting data is potentially problematic. For example, adolescents might overendorse a particular item not because they experience the symptom asked about at high levels but because they misunderstand the wording of the question. Of equal concern are studies that either create measures specifically for the study, without first demonstrating the reliability and validity of them, or rely on measures with weak psychometric properties. A final issue is the all too common practice of relying on a single risk indicator rather than multidimensional measures. We have read and reviewed an alarming number of studies in which the suicide risk measure is a single question along the lines of, "Have you ever thought about killing yourself?" This approach is psychometrically unsound and is particularly problematic when studying serious issues such as adolescent suicide. But new research should not suffer from these flaws. As will be discussed in Chapter 5, adequate options of valid and reliable measures appropriate for use with adolescents are available.

Concluding Thoughts

In this chapter, we have provided readers with an overview of the methodological weaknesses in the existing literature. Ideally researchers should begin with random samples and, when that is not possible, strive for representative samples. Carefully select measures that were developed for use with adolescents and have published reliability, validity, and normative data specific to your population of interest and designed for use in suicide research. Whenever possible, rely on multiple indicators of risk constructs. Additionally, anyone reviewing the existing literature on suicide risk should carefully scrutinize the methods used to determine how closely they conform to these recommendations. The further a study deviates from these standards, the less confidence should be placed in the findings.

Summary of Clinical Practice Implications

- Risk factors for adolescent suicide generally fall into the domains of psychological disorders, individual variables, and interpersonal variables.

- When asking adolescents screening questions, the entire set should be completed even if initial responses deny suicidality.

- When choosing measures for assessment protocols, the same cautions apply as when conducting research—look for comprehensive measures specifically designed for use with adolescents that possess evidence of reliability and validity.

Empirically Supported Protective Factors

Although there have been some findings about the role of protective factors in adolescent suicide-related behaviors, a critical or integrated review of the evidence has not been assessed in the extant literature. In this chapter, we attempt to critically examine the literature on the protective factor construct. Following the introduction section, we list a number of advantages for focusing research on protective factors in the suicide literature. We also offer an expanded definition of the protective factor construct. Next, we review representative studies that have examined the relations between protective factors and adolescent suicide-related behaviors. We then discuss self-report instruments of the protective factor construct. We conclude by listing a number of potential protective factors that may be linked to adolescent suicide-related behaviors.

Empirically Supported Protective Factors for Adolescent Suicide

Adolescent suicide-related behavior continues to be an important public health concern. Recent research suggests that youth suicide rates will continue to increase as they have for the past several decades (Clark, 1993; Diekstra, Kienhorst, & DeWilde, 1995; NCHS, 2000). Many other studies have confirmed the high rates of adolescent suicide-related behaviors, such as severe suicidal ideation and attempts (Andrews & Lewinsohn, 1992; Kann et al., 2000; Lewinsohn, Rohde, & Seeley, 1996; Weissman, Bruce, Leaf, Florio, & Holzer, 1991). Nearly 8.3% of 9th- through 12th-grade students have reported attempting suicide one or more times in the 12 months prior to participating in a national survey (Kann et al., 2000). Among these youth, 2.6% reported making a suicide attempt that resulted in serious injury or self-harm requiring medical attention. In addition, 19.3% of the students surveyed reported seriously thinking about killing themselves during the study period.

Prevalence rates of suicide-related behavior appear to be even higher in clinical adolescent populations (Diekstra et al., 1995; Gould & Kramer, 2001; Klimes-Dougan, 1998).

A major challenge in developing new and effective approaches to the prevention or management of adolescent suicide-related behaviors, such as suicidal ideation and suicide attempts, is the lack of empirically established representative sets of factors that serve as independent determinants (e.g., antecedents), mediating or maintaining factors for adolescent suicide-related behaviors. In recent years, both risk and protective factors have been recognized in developing suicide prevention and management strategies for adolescent self-harmful behaviors (e.g., Eggert, Thompson, Herting, & Nicholas, 1995; Randell, Eggert, & Pike, 2001). Suicide risk factors are those antecedent conditions that trigger or increase the opportunity for a youth to engage in intentional suicide-related behaviors. Examples of suicide risk factors include depression, hopelessness, and past suicide attempts (see Gould & Kramer, 2001; Tanney, 1992). There are now numerous well-validated self-report instruments that have been designed for assessing risk factors that are associated with adolescent suicidal behavior (e.g., see Chapters 2 and 5). To date, progress in the conceptualization and assessment of protective factors continues to lag behind.

In this chapter, we examine the relations between protective factors and adolescent suicide-related behaviors with the intent of highlighting the importance of the protective factor construct for the assessment of suicide-related behaviors. As noted previously, despite the clinical importance of protective factors to the assessment and effective management of adolescent and adult suicide-related behaviors (see Heisel & Flett, 2004; Linehan, Goodstein, Nielsen, & Chiles, 1983; Osman et al., 1999), less attention has been devoted to the topic of protective factors and related domains in adolescent suicidality. As a result, a limited number of self-report instruments have been developed and validated empirically for use in assessing protective factors that are linked with adolescent suicidal behaviors. Our observation shows that at least two major issues have dampened the interest of researchers for evaluating the links between protective factors and suicide-related behaviors. The first issue is the lack of a clear conceptual or integrated theoretical model of the protective factor construct in the suicide literature. To date, limited attempts have been made to redress this problem (e.g., Frankl, 1959; Linehan et al., 1983; Rudd, 1990). The second issue is whether existing self-report measures of protective factors have well-established theoretical foundations and psychometric characteristics, such as predictive and incremental validity estimates.

We examined the literature for those protective factors that have been investigated in the assessment of adolescent suicide-related behaviors. First, we offer a provisional operational definition of the protective factor construct that might be useful for identifying important domains of this construct. In addition, we list some clinical advantages for studying a number of protective factors in the suicide literature. Second, we review studies that have evaluated links between protective factors and suicidal behavior. We also identify a set of reliable and valid self-report measures that might be useful for assessing several protective factors and related domains. Third, we list a number of potentially useful protective factors that may be of interest to other researchers in this area. In Chapters 6 and 7, we will explore similar types of issues for well-established self-report instruments including the Reasons for Living Inventory for Adolescents (RFL-A; Osman et al., 1998) and the Multi-Attitude Suicide Tendency (MAST; Orbach et al. 1991) scale that have been developed and validated specifically for evaluating adolescent-specific protective factors.

Conceptualization of Protective Factors

In numerous research involving both risk and protective factors, data related to protective factors have generally been conceptualized in terms of low scores on self-report risk assessment instruments rather than scores on self-report instruments validated specifically as protective measures. To identify the relations between specific protective factors and suicide-related behaviors, it is important to show empirically that protective factors are seen as more than simply the opposite or absence of factors on risk self-report instruments (Felix-Ortiz & Newcomb, 1992; Stouthamer-Loeber et al., 1993).

In this chapter, we focus most of our attention on those protective factors, or variables, that have been linked empirically (e.g., as mediators or moderators) to decreased risk for adolescent suicide-related behaviors. Accordingly we conceptualize protective factors as those supportive resources (e.g., structural or functional variables that act as direct, moderating or mediating factors) that serve as buffers for, or safeguards against (a) adolescent suicide-related behaviors (e.g., Osman, Gutierrez, Muehlenkamp, et al., 2004) or (b) *direct and significant risk factors*, such as depression and hopelessness, for suicidal behavior. Like risk factors, protective factors can be defined by single or multiple dimensions or facets. For example, functional social support could be considered a viable multidimensional protective construct to the extent that: (a) multiple domains of this construct (e.g., the functional supports of peers, school, and family) can be identified as clinically relevant to adolescent suicidality, and (b) scores on well-developed self-report measures of the target domains can be linked empirically to decreased risk for adolescent suicide-related behaviors in the extant literature. Indeed, for protective factors to have clinical or research utility, it is important that self-report instruments designed to assess relevant variables are grounded in strong theoretical foundations and have good psychometric characteristics (see Chapter 11). Accordingly, we will discuss most of these psychometric issues in Chapter 4. In this chapter, we review only those studies that used self-report instruments with some established psychometric characteristics with adolescents ages 12 to 19 years.

Some Advantages to Studying Protective Factors

There are several potentially good reasons for developing interest in the conceptualization and assessment of protective factors. We will list briefly some of the key advantages. We note, however, that because there are no clear data supporting these perspectives, we offer these advantages only as potential areas for future clinical and/or research investigations.

1. It might advance the ability of mental health professionals to gain a comprehensive rather than a biased understanding of an array of both protective *and* risk events that serve as antecedents to the development of adolescent suicide-related behaviors.

2. It might increase research focus on protective factors as potential mediators or moderators for adolescent suicide-related behaviors. Currently, protective factors are underrepresented as clinically relevant variables in the suicide literature.

3. It might lead to the development and validation of clinically useful multidimensional screening and assessment instruments for adolescent suicide-related behaviors. The limited number of evidence-based self-report measures of protective factors remains a great and legitimate concern in the suicide literature.

4. It might provide the foundation for developing new and effective models of approaches to the comprehensive assessment and management of suicide-related events. For example, we have conceptualized protective factors in part as those functional resources that buffer against direct risk factors for suicide.

5. It might offer positive messages to youths at various stages in the assessment, treatment, and follow-up contact periods. For example, youth and family members might be more likely to undertake follow-up assessments if they can have positive perceptions of the initial assessment procedures that include protective variables.

6. Focus on the early identification of protective factors might provide unique opportunities for mapping out individual resources (e.g., relative strengths) that could be integrated into planning suicide preventive programs and effective interventions.

7. Protective factors tend to serve as meaningful outcomes for several suicide-related intervention programs. Efforts to focus on protective factors at intake assessments might enhance *consistency* in both the treatment and follow-up periods of youth with suicide-related behaviors.

8. Clearly, the assessment of protective factors can be undertaken on multiple occasions because of the *high base rates* of these factors in the general population. Thus schools and clinics could conduct periodic screenings to highlight the importance of protective factors. We remain gravely concerned that annual screening opportunities have not been extended to a number of protective factors in suicide-related behaviors.

9. When assessed using evidence-based self-report instruments, protective factors could serve as effective predictors of clinically relevant outcomes (see Chapter 11). In particular, data from protective measures might have the potential to identify youth at risk for suicide-related behaviors.

10. It might advance research designed to explore common features of risk and protective factors for adults and adolescents.

Research on Protective Factors Associated With Adolescent Suicide-Related Behaviors

As we noted previously, there has been little empirical evidence linking protective factors with specific suicide-related behaviors such as suicidal ideation and suicide attempts. Moreover, only recently have researchers proposed clear functional definitions of suicide-related behaviors. For purposes of this review, we used the O'Carroll et al.'s (1996) nomenclature to select suicide ideation and suicide attempts as empirically relevant *suicide outcome* measures (see Table 3.1).

We conducted several computer and manual (e.g., reference sections of key journal articles) searches of the suicide literature to identify protective factors that have been linked empirically to these two suicide-related outcomes as well as to any other relevant type of protective factor such as attraction to life. Some of the major databases we searched for empirical publications included PsycINFO, PsycARTICLES, LexisNexis, and Ingenta. We specified at least *four* criteria for identifying potential studies for inclusion in this review. Specifically, to be included in this review, the study had to meet the following criteria:

1. The study had to include detailed sociodemographic information including age (ages 12 to 19 years), gender, and ethnicity for clinical or nonclinical youth. We note, however, that we did not review studies that focused only on evaluating the links between these sociodemographic variables and the prespecified outcome measures.

2. The study had to include at least one self-report assessment instrument (see Chapter 4) designed to tap the domain(s) of a protective factor construct. Given the demands for accuracy in the screening for suicide-related behaviors, we expected the potential self-report instrument to have coefficient α estimate of at least .70. We did not include studies in which a single or a few items were simply combined to create an index for assessing a protective factor, such as religiosity and family interactions (e.g., Flouri & Buchanan, 2002; O'Donnell, Stueve, Wardlow, & O'Donnell, 2003; Stack & Wasserman, 1992). As noted repeatedly in our work, the reliable and valid measurements of our constructs depend heavily upon the use of empirically supported assessment instruments with well-established theoretical foundations.

3. Given that recommendations for developing and validating protective self-report instruments emerged with the introduction of the Linehan's Reasons for Living Inventory (RFL; Linehan et al., 1983), we included only studies published in English between 1986 and 2005.

4. Finally, it was important that (a) the study included at least one of the prespecified outcome measures and (b) statistically significant findings were reported by the authors that involved at least group comparisons, correlation analyses, or regression analyses.

Some of the search terms we used were as follows: *suicide protective factors, protective resources, adolescent adaptive factors, resilience.*

Results of Comprehensive Review

Results of the review identified a limited number of methodologically well-designed studies that have explored the relations between protective factors, such as problem solving, reasons for living, resilience, and the risk for adolescent suicide-related behaviors. Thus we report on a few representative studies that utilized psychometrically reliable and valid self-report instruments (see Table 3.1). In line with recent work in this area (e.g., Osman, Gutierrez, Muehlenkamp, et al., 2004), we grouped these factors into two primary categories: (a) Personal Protective Factors and (b) Environmental Protective Factors. Each category is represented by selected subcategories and related studies.

Personal Protective Factors
Bodily Experiences and Investment

Support for the links between bodily experiences and specific suicide-related behaviors have been examined in only two methodologically sound investigations. The first study was based on Orbach and Mikulincer's (1998) body investment model that personal feelings and attitudes toward the body including (a) bodily image, feelings, and attitudes, (b) body protection, (c) comfort in physical touch, and (d) body care are linked directly with adolescent suicidal tendencies. In studies with Israeli suicidal inpatient and community youth (Study 4; $n = 148$), multivariate regression analyses by the authors showed that scores on scales designed to assess (a) body image, feelings, and attitudes and body care were significantly linked with scores on an attraction to life (AL) scale, and (b) the body image, feelings, and attitudes and comfort with touch scale scores were linked positively with the repulsion by death (RD) scale scores.

In a follow-up study, Orbach, Stein, Shani-Sela and Har-Even (2001) compared the responses of inpatient adolescent suicide attempters ($n = 37$), appropriate inpatient adolescent controls ($n = 30$), and a community sample of

Table 3.1

Protective Factors—Personal

Study	Study Samples	Protective Variable Measured	Measure (Self-Report)	Suicide Outcome(s)

A. Personal Protective

1. BODY EXPERIENCES/INVESTMENT

Study	Study Samples	Protective Variable Measured	Measure (Self-Report)	Suicide Outcome(s)
Orbach & Mikulincer (1998). Israel	57 suicide attempters 45 inpatient controls 46 community controls	Body image feelings Body care Comfort with touch	Body Investment Scale(BIS; Orbach & Mikulincer, 1998)	Attraction to Life (AL) Repulsion by Death (RD)
Orbach, Stein, et al. (2001). Israel	37 suicide attempters 30 inpatient controls 30 community controls	All 4 BIS scale scores Body feelings and body care	BIS (Orbach & Mikulincer, 1998)	Attraction to Life (AL) Repulsion by Death (RD)

2. SOCIAL PROBLEM SOLVING

Study	Study Samples	Protective Variable Measured	Measure (Self-Report)	Suicide Outcome(s)
Sadowski & Kelley (1993). USA	30 suicide attempters 30 psychiatric controls 30 normal controls	Social Problem Solving	Social Problem-Solving Inventory (D'Zurilla & Nezu, 1990)	Suicide Attempts Problem Orientation Problem-Solving Skills
Reinecke, DuBois, et al. (2001). USA	53 suicide attempters 52 inpatient controls	Social Problem Solving	Social Problem-Solving Inventory-Revised (SPS-R; D'Zurilla, Nezu, & Maydeu-Olivares, 1994)	Suicide Ideation Problem-Solving Orientation
Chang (2002). USA	121 boys and 185 girls—high school	Social Problem Solving	SPS-R (D'Zurilla, Nezu, & Maydeu-Olivares, 1994)	Suicide Ideation

3. SELF-ESTEEM

Study	Study Samples	Protective Variable Measured	Measure (Self-Report)	Suicide Outcome(s)
Marciano & Kazdin (1994). USA	42 suicide attempters 39 suicide ideators 42 inpatient controls	Self-Esteem	Self-Esteem Inventory (SEI; Coopersmith, 1967)	Suicide Attempt Suicide Ideation
Overholser, Adams, et al. (1995). USA	254 psychiatric inpatients 288 high school controls	Self-Esteem	Rosenberg Self-Esteem Scale (RSE; Rosenberg, 1965)	Suicide Ideation
De Man & Leduc (1995). Canada	129 boys and 117 girls—high school	Self-Esteem	RSE (Rosenberg, 1965)	Suicide Attempt

Study	Study Samples	Protective Variable Measured	Measure (Self-Report)	Suicide Outcome(s)
		3. SELF-ESTEEM *(continued)*		
Dori & Overholser (1999). USA	32 repeat attempters 24 single attempters 34 inpatient controls	Self-Esteem	RSE (Rosenberg, 1965)	Suicide Attempt
Kelly, Lynch, et al. (2001). USA	210 inpatients 96 outpatients 65 residential programs 111 community controls	Self-Esteem	Interpersonal Support Evaluation (ISE; Cohen & Hoberman, 1983) questionnaire	Suicide Attempt Suicide Ideation
Wild, Flisher, et al. (2004). South Africa	939 public school boys and girls	Self-Esteem	Self-Esteem Questionnaire (SEQ; DuBois, Felner et al., 1996)	Suicide Attempt Suicide Ideation
Yoder & Hoyt (2005). USA	226 boys and 243 girls—community youth	Self-Esteem	RSE (Rosenberg, 1965)	Suicide Ideation

adolescent volunteers ($n = 30$) on a number of risk and protective measures. They found that the two control groups reported stronger attitudes and feelings, as well as body protection, than the suicide attempters (all p values $< .05$). In addition, the authors observed that all subscale scores of the Body Investment Scale (BIS) were correlated positively and significantly with the attraction to life (AL) scale scores. The body image feelings and body care scale scores were linked negatively and significantly with scores on the repulsion by death (RD) scale scores. It should be noted, however, that these analyses used smaller sample sizes (range = 45 to 57) that limit the extent to which the findings can be generalized to other non-Israeli samples.

MEASURES OF BODY INVESTMENT

To date, only one study has developed and validated a self-report measure of bodily experiences for use with adolescents. The Body Investment Scale (BIS; Orbach & Mikulincer, 1998) has a strong theoretical foundation and is composed of 24 items assessing emotional investment in the body. Respondents rate each item on a 5-point Likert-type scale ranging from 1 *(I do not agree at all)* to 5 *(Strongly agree)*. Nine of the 24 items are scored in the reverse direction, and subscale scores are derived by summing items within a subscale. Psychometric analyses of the BIS have been conducted with Israeli youth in four studies. In the initial factor analysis with Varimax rotation (accounting for 55% of the variance), four factors were extracted that tap positive emotional investment in body image feelings and attitudes, body touch, body care, and body protection. Each scale is composed of six items. Estimates of internal consistency and validity are adequate. For example, in a series of regression analyses, scores on the Rosenberg Self-Esteem Scale (RSE; Rosenberg, 1965) were linked positively with body image feelings and attitudes (coefficient = .58, $p < .01$), body touch (coefficient = .22, $p < .01$), and body care (coefficient = .42, $p < .01$). Body protection was weakly linked with maternal care (coefficient = .21, $p < .01$). Overall, preliminary findings suggest that this scale shows promise as a brief screening instrument in the area of adolescent suicidality. Some limitations of the BIS as an evidence-based screening instrument include (a) the lack of test-retest reliability data and (b) limited validity data regarding performance indicators in clinical and nonclinical populations in the U.S.

Social Problem Solving and Coping

Previous research has shown that the ability to use a range of problem-solving strategies is linked with decreased risk for intentional suicide attempts. We identified three representative studies that have examined the links between social problem solving as a protective factor and a number of adolescent suicide-related behaviors. In 1993, Sadowski and Kelley reported that normal adolescent controls ($n = 30$) had greater ease in generating meaningful alternative solutions to social problem situations than did the psychiatric suicide attempters ($n = 30$). In addition, the normal controls reported better decision-making skills than both the suicide attempters and psychiatric controls ($n = 30$). Regarding the implementation of solutions, the normal controls were more confident than the suicide attempters in implementing effective solutions to problem situations (all p values $< .05$). Overall, the normal youth were found to use better problem-solving and coping skills compared to the suicide attempters and psychiatric controls.

Reinecke, DuBois, and Schultz (2001) examined the link between social problem-solving orientation and the risk for suicidality in a sample of 69 boys and 36 girls admitted to a psychiatric inpatient unit. Results of the analyses indicated that the nonsuicidal inpatient controls reported lower levels of negative problem-solving orientation strategies; that is, the nonsuicidal inpatients ($n = 52$) used fewer negative problem-solving strategies than the suicidal inpatients ($n = 53$). Additionally, high scores on the positive problem-solving scale were linked with low scores on a measure of suicidal ideation ($r = -.32$, $p < .05$) and other psychological distress measures. In a sample of 306 high school students in 2002, Chang found that both life stress and social problem-solving skills accounted for an additional 10% of the variance in suicidal ideation over and beyond risk factors such as demographic variables and history of suicidal behavior. In addition, scores on the problem-solving inventory were found to be negatively linked with scores on a measure of suicidal ideation ($r = -.25, p \leq .001$). Limited support was found for the role of social problem solving as a mediator (partial) for the influence of stress on suicidal ideation.

MEASURES OF SOCIAL PROBLEM SOLVING

The measures of problem solving have varied substantially in studies of adolescent suicidal behavior (see Table 3.1); however, this review identified one measure that has been used frequently to tap social problem solving in adults and adolescents. In particular, the Social Problem-Solving Inventory-Revised (SPSI-R; D'Zurilla, Nezu, & Maydeu-Olivares, 1994) is a short version of the frequently used 70-item Social Problem Solving Inventory (SPSI; D'Zurilla & Nezu, 1990). D'Zurilla and Maydeu-Olivares (1995) have conducted an excellent review of the psychometric properties of the SPSI as well as other self-report measures of (a) problem solving and (b) social problem solving (see also a comprehensive review by Speckens & Hawton, 2005). Although the factor structure and initial psychometric properties of the SPSI-R were established with nonclinical adults, this instrument is gathering satisfactory properties for use with adolescents. It is also important to note that the instrument has a well-developed theoretical foundation.

The SPSI-R is composed of 52 items; each item is rated on a 5-point Likert-type scale that ranges from 0 (*not at all true of me*) to 4 (*extremely true of me*). Unrestricted exploratory factor analysis (see Maydeu-Olivers & D'Zurilla, 1996) extracted five factors: positive problem orientation (ppo), negative problem orientation (npo), rational problem solving (rps; composed of 4 subscales), impulsivity/carelessness style (ics), and avoidance style (as). The intercorrelations among the factor scales were reported to range from low (npo v. rps; $r = -.20$) to high (npo v. as; $r = .75$).

Sadowski, Moore, and Kelley (1994) evaluated the fit of the five-factor solution of the SPSI-R in a large sample of high school students ($n = 708$) ages 13-17 years. A small sample of adolescent inpatients ($n = 63$) was included to explore other reliability and validity estimates of the SPSI-R. The five-factor model provided moderate fit of the sample data (e.g., goodness-of-fit index = .88, and root mean square residual = .05). Estimates of reliability for the factor scale scores and concurrent validity were good. For example, the total SPSI-R score correlated moderately and significantly with ratings of social skills ($r = .42, p < .001$); it also correlated low and negatively with depression severity ($r = -.36, p < .001$) in the high school sample. In addition, the total SPSI-R score for the high school sample ($M = 114.47, SD = 25.20$) was significantly higher than for the clinical inpatient sample ($M = 91.83, SD = 32.39$), $t(769) = 6.66, p < .001$, Cohen's $d = .87$. Based upon the current data, the SPSI-R appears to be appropriate for use with adolescents. Additional normative and psychometric data, however, are needed to help redress concerns about the use of this instrument as an evidence-based measure of the social problem-solving construct for children and adolescents.

Self-Esteem

Another protective factor that has received extensive attention in the literature is self-esteem. We identified seven representative studies that have examined the links between self-esteem (self-evaluation) and suicide-related behaviors in adolescent samples.

Marciano and Kazdin (1994) reported a negative and significant link between self-esteem and hopelessness (r = -.33) responses, a major risk factor for adolescent suicidal behavior, for samples of nonsuicidal inpatient controls (n = 42). Scores on the Coopersmith (1967) Self-Esteem Inventory were used to tap self-esteem. Results of independent correlation analyses showed that the link between hopelessness and self-esteem was higher for suicidal children (r = -.72) than for the nonsuicidal youth (n = 42; r = -.33), z = 2.64, p < .01. Further discriminant analyses of the data showed that self-esteem scores accounted for approximately 11.8% of the variance in assessing the risk for the severity of suicidal thoughts. The authors identified self-esteem as an important positive variable in the assessment of suicide-related behaviors.

In the first well-designed study of self-esteem, using the Rosenberg Self-Esteem Scale (RSE; Rosenberg, 1965), Overholser, Adams, Lehnert, and Brinkman (1995) found that nonclinical high school controls (M = 30.64, SD = 5.44) obtained significantly higher scores than the psychiatric inpatients (M = 29.43, SD = 6.81) on the total RSE score, $t(540)$ = 2.27, p < .02, d = .20 (small effect size). In addition, Pearson correlation analyses showed that self-esteem scores were significantly and negatively linked with scores on both the suicidal ideation (r = -.61, p < .001) and suicide attempts (r = -.30, p < .001) self-report measures in the psychiatric inpatient sample. Likewise, self-esteem scores were linked significantly and negatively with scores on the suicide ideation (r = -.50, p < .001) and suicide attempts (r = -.48, p < .001) measures in the high school samples. De Man and Leduc (1995) reported a similar link between scores on the RSE and a well-validated measure of suicide ideation (r = -.44, p < .001) in a sample of 246 (129 boys and 117 girls) Canadian high school students. Dori and Overholser (1999) examined the associations among scores on measures of hopelessness, depression, and self-esteem in a small sample of adolescent psychiatric inpatients with a range of suicide-related behaviors (i.e., multiple and single suicide repeaters v. clinical nonsuicidal). Self-esteem responses were also assessed with the RSE. The data indicated that self-esteem responses had a protective link with suicide-related behaviors. In particular, self-esteem scores were negatively and highly associated with major depressive responses (r = -.76, p < .001), major risk symptoms for adolescent suicidal behavior. In discriminant analyses that included total scores on the study measures, the authors concluded that scores on each measure were useful in classifying the study participants (e.g., self-esteem = 38.9%), although the unique contributions of gender, depression, and hopelessness variables were most useful in group classifications.

Kelly, Lynch, Donovan, and Clark (2001) used hierarchical logistic regression analyses to examine the relations between a range of potential predictor variables, including self-esteem and suicide ideation and attempts in separate samples of boys (n = 228) and girls (n = 254). Self-esteem was assessed with the 12-item self-esteem subscale of the Interpersonal Support Evaluation (ISE; Cohen & Hoberman, 1983) self-report instrument. Unlike the RSE, low scores on the ISE suggest high levels of self-esteem. The results showed that although self-esteem was not predictive of both suicidal ideation and suicide attempts in boys, self-esteem was predictive of both suicidal ideation (OR = 1.70, p < .001) and suicide attempts (OR = 1.40, p < .05) in girls. Wild, Flisher, and Lombard (2004) examined the links between suicidal behaviors and psychological factors, including depression and six domains of self-esteem, in a large sample of public high school students. They used the Self-Esteem Questionnaire (SEQ; DuBois, Felner, Brand, Phillips, & Lease, 1996); the SEQ taps self-esteem areas that include peers, school, family, sports, and the body. In multinomial logistic regression analyses, global self-esteem (i.e., total SEQ score) was a significant factor in differentiating (a) suicidal ideators and normal controls (*Relative Risk Ratio* = 2.41, p < .001) and (b) suicide attempters and normal controls (*Relative Risk Ratio* = 3.65, p < .001). In addition, low family self-esteem was uniquely linked with suicidal ideation and suicide attempts for all the comparison groups, all p values < .01. In terms of unique contributions to the equation, both high levels of depression and low family self-esteem showed significant links with increased likelihood for suicidal ideation and suicide attempts. The authors noted correctly that these later findings had been reported previously in the suicide literature (e.g., Lewinsohn et al., 1994).

In a comprehensive family stress model developed to understand the links between family economic pressure and adolescent suicidal behaviors, Yoder and Hoyt (2005) recently found that self-esteem had negative and moderate links with suicidal ideation (coefficient = -.34, p < .01) and adolescent depression (coefficient = -0.23, p < .01), indicating that self-esteem is an important variable in evaluating adolescent suicidal ideation and related variables, such as depression and hopelessness. The overall structural model had good goodness-of-fit estimates to the sample data (e.g., CFI = 1.00, RMSEA = 0.069).

MEASURES OF SELF-ESTEEM

The most widely used self-report instrument for assessing global self-esteem in clinical and nonclinical populations is the Rosenberg Self-Esteem (RSE; Rosenberg, 1965) scale. The 10-item version is composed of five positively worded and five negatively worded items. Respondents are asked to rate each item on a 4-point Likert-type scale ranging from 1 (*strongly agree*) to 4 (*strongly disagree*). Scoring is performed by reverse scoring the negatively worded items and summing the ratings to obtain a global positive self-esteem score. The RSE has shown good reliability and validity estimates in the clinical literature (e.g., Corwyn, 2000; Lewinsohn, Seely, & Gotlib, 1997). In most studies with the RSE, however, it has been observed that self-esteem scores make only moderate contributions to the prediction of suicide-related behaviors when depressive symptoms are controlled statistically.

The normative data (means and standard deviations) presented in Table 3.2 show some of the difficulties with efforts to compare findings across studies with this instrument. More specifically, the reverse scoring procedure for the RSE has not been carried out consistently across studies. A self-esteem measure that is designed specifically for use with children and adolescents but continues to be used less often in investigations of suicide-related behaviors is the Coopersmith Self-Esteem Inventory (SEI; Coopersmith, 1967). Regardless of the performance of any of these measures, we note that most of these self-report instruments were developed in the 1960s; there is the need for constructing contemporary instruments with adequate psychometric properties that could be used to assess dimensions of this very important protective construct.

Table 3.2

Normative Data (Means and Standard Deviations)— Rosenberg Self-Esteem Scale

Study	Study Samples	Mean	Standard Deviation
Rosenberg Self-Esteem Scale (RSE; Rosenberg, 1965)			
Overholser, Adams, et al. (1995)	Psychiatric Inpatients ($n = 254$)	29.43	6.81
	High School Students ($n = 288$)	30.64	5.44
De Man & Leduc (1995)[a]	High School Students ($n = 246$)	7.80	2.22
Dori & Overholser (1999)	Repeat Attempters ($n = 32$)	25.53	7.76
	Single Attempter ($n = 24$)	24.46	6.87
	Inpatient Controls ($n = 34$)	26.12	8.82
Yoder & Hoyt (2005)[a]	Boys ($n = 243$)	4.01	0.49
	Girls ($n = 226$)	4.01	0.50

[a] Items coded such that low scores suggest higher levels of self-esteem.

Environmental Protective Factors

We searched for studies that have examined the links between suicide-related behaviors and (a) social support and (b) religiosity; however, findings from five of the religiosity investigations were mixed (Evans, Hawton, & Rodham, 2004; Kandel, Raveis, & Davies, 1991; Maris, Berman, Maltsberger, & Yufit, 1992; Perkins & Hartless, 2002; Wagman, Resnick, Ireland, & Blum, 1999). In particular, the link between religiosity and adolescent suicidality has not been well established in the literature and may relate in part to the fact that existing measures of religiosity do not have both clear conceptual foundations (e.g., church attendance, religious beliefs, frequency of prayers) and satisfactory psychometric properties. Thus our review of the literature focused on only the social support construct.

Social Supportive Patterns

The protective effects of family and friends have been studied extensively in the adolescent literature. For example, the quality and patterns of support within families have been found to serve as protective factors for youth who may be at increased risk for suicide-related behaviors (D'Attilio, Campbell, Lubold, Jacobson, & Richard, 1992; Kandel, Raveis, & Davies, 1991; King, Segal, Naylor, & Evans, 1993; Rudd, 1990; Stewart, Lam, Betson, & Chung, 1999). We identified seven representative studies that examined the relations between family supportive resources and adolescent suicidal behaviors.

In one of the first early investigations in this area, Rubenstein, Heeren, Housman, Rubin, and Stechler (1989) examined the links between familial factors of cohesion and adaptability and the risk for adolescent suicidal behavior. Most of the analyses carried out by the authors were with data from a high school sample of 204 girls and 96 boys ages 13 to 19 years. Scores on the Family Adaptability and Family Cohesion measure (FACES-II; Olson, Portner, & Bell, 1982) were used to tap family adaptability and cohesion, respectively. Self-reported suicide attempt in the previous year was adopted as the measure of suicidality. In the initial correlation analyses, high scores on the self-reported suicide measure were linked significantly with low scores on both the Family Cohesion ($r = -.36, p < .001$) and Family Adaptability ($r = -.28, p < .001$) subscales. In a step-wise logistic regression analysis that included scores on the cohesion and stress measures as predictors, family cohesion was identified as an independent predictor of adolescent suicidal behavior ($\chi^2 = 11.67, p < .0006$). Overall, the authors concluded that high levels of family cohesion and low levels of stress are most characteristic of youth who may be at minimal risk for suicidal behavior.

Additional studies with the FACES-II were carried out by Fremouw and colleagues (1993) using adolescent inpatient and high school samples. In addition to a number of psychological risk and problem-solving variables, these

Table 3.3

Protective Factors—Environmental

Study	Study Samples	Protective Variable Measured	Measure (Self-Report)	Suicide Outcome(s)
		B. Environmental Protective		
		SOCIAL SUPPORTIVE PATTERNS		
Rubenstein, Heeren, et al. (1989). USA	60 suicidal 240 non-suicidal Public high schools	Family cohesion Family adaptation	Family Adaptability and Family Cohesion Scale (FACES-II; Olson et al. 1982)	Self-reported suicide attempts
Fremouw et al. (1993). USA	30 suicide risk 21 inpatient controls 89 high school controls	Family cohesion.	15-item Subscale of the FACES-II instrument	Suicidal ideation and attempts
Yuen, Andrade, et al. (1996). Hawaii, USA	77 suicide attempters 1,702 non-attempters	Family support Friend support	Perceived Social Support from Friends (PSS-Fr) and Family (PSS-Fa; Procidano & Heller, 1983)	Suicide Attempts
Greening & Stoppelbein (2002). USA	1,098 High school 28% African American 72% Caucasian	Family support Friend support	Perceived Social Support from Friends (PSS-Fr) and Family (PSS-Fa; Procidano & Heller, 1983)	Perceived Suicide Risk
Perkins & Hartless (2002). USA	3,895 African American 11,027 Caucasian	Family support	Search Institute's Profiles of Student Life: Attitude and Behavior Questionnaire (ABQ; Benson, 1990)	Suicide Ideation Suicide Attempts
Esposito & Clum (2003). USA	10 Internalizers 22 Externalizers 22 Co-morbid conditions 19 Other controls	Perceived Social support	Survey of Children's Social Support (SOCSS; Dubow & Ullman, 1989)—Short-form	Suicide Ideation
Thompson, Mazza, et al. (2005). USA	690 boys 597 girls	Family support	High School Questionnaire: Profile of experiences (Eggert et al., 1994)	Suicide Ideation

researchers examined the relations between scores on the 15-item family cohesion subscale of the FACES-II measure (Olson et al., 1982) and suicide risk. The participants included 33 inpatient youth at risk for suicide, 21 psychiatric controls, and 89 high school nonclinical controls ages 12 to 18 years. In several preliminary pair-wise comparison analyses, the suicide-risk group had significantly lower family cohesion scores (M = 11.5, SD = 6.0) than the high school (M = 17.4, SD = 6.5) control sample, Cohen's d = .93. Results of subsequent logistic regression discriminant analyses showed that in the comparison involving the psychiatric suicide-risk and high school youth, scores on the family cohesion subscale were most useful in differentiating between these groups, coefficient = .11, p < .05.

Yuen and colleagues (1996) examined the links between family support and adolescent suicidal behavior in a Native Hawaiian high school sample. In their longitudinal investigation, these researchers asked a large sample (N = 1,779) of adolescents to complete self-report instruments that included the Perceived Social Support from Friends and Family (PSS-Fr, PSS-Fa; Procidano & Heller, 1983). Self-reported suicide attempts were assessed using a 14-item validated scale. Of the original study participants, 4.3% reported having made at least one suicide attempt within 6 months of the survey. The authors found that the nonattempters (M = 3.72, SD = 0.92) obtained significantly higher scores than the attempters (M = 2.74, SD = 0.94) on the family support subscale score, Cohen's d = 1.06. Results of the correlation analyses showed negative and significant relations between scores on measures of suicide attempts and family support, r = -.22, p < .001. Likewise, logistic regression analytic results showed that the family support subscale score was a significant predictor of suicide attempts in the previous 6 months of questionnaire administration, χ^2 = 19.72; OR = 0.56, p < .0001.

In a large sample of African American and Caucasian community samples (N = 1,098), Greening and Stoppelbein (2002) examined relations between family support and perceived risk for suicide-related behaviors. Scores on the PSS-Fr and PSS-Fa (Procidano & Heller, 1983) were also used to tap social supportive resources. Perceived suicide risk was assessed with ratings on a 7-point scale. The mean age of the study participants was 15.90 years (SD = 1.21). The authors found that, following the Bonferroni correction procedure, perceived risk for suicide was associated significantly with family support (r = -.18, p < .0001) but not with peer support. Although both family support and support from friends may serve as protective factors, data from existing measures continue to suggest that family support alone may be specific to low risk for adolescent suicide-related behaviors when both of these variables are included in the analyses (also, see Prinstein, Boergers, Spirito, Little, & Grapentine, 2000).

In another state-wide investigation that included African American (n = 3,895) and Caucasian (n = 11,027) adolescents (ages 12–17 years; M age = 14.5 year, SD = 1.56), Perkins and Hartless (2002) examined the links between family support and suicide-related behaviors. Participants completed the Search Institute's Profiles of Student Life: Attitude and Behavior Questionnaire

(ABQ; Benson, 1990) in a number of group testing situations. A 5-item subscale of the ABQ was used to assess family support; single items were used to assess suicidal ideation and suicide attempts. Logistic regression analyses were conducted to identify potential predictors of suicidal ideation and attempts after controlling for other risk factors, such as alcohol use and hopelessness. For the combined sample, family support was identified as a significant predictor of suicidal ideation, $\beta = -.66$, $p < .0001$. Likewise, family support was retained as a significant predictor of suicide attempts, $\beta = -.41$, $p < .011$. Finally, in an ecological risk-factor assessment model, the authors noted that the risk for suicide tends to be significantly lessened when the family is perceived as supportive and enjoyable.

Esposito and Clum (2003) evaluated the relative contributions of a number of psychiatric disorders and psychosocial factors in the prediction of adolescent suicidality. In particular, the authors examined the role of perceived social support as a moderator variable interacting with internalizing disorders. There were 10 internalizers (i.e., youth with diagnoses of major depression, dysthymia, and generalized anxiety disorder), 22 externalizers (i.e., youth with diagnoses of oppositional defiant disorder, conduct disorder, and substance-related disorders), 22 youth with comorbid disorders (i.e., youth with both internalizing and externalizing disorders) and 19 other control participants ages 14 to 18 years (M age = 16.0, SD = 1.28). Scores on a short form of the Survey of Children's Social Support Scale (SOCSS; Dubow & Ullman, 1989) were used to assess perceived social support; scores on the Modified Scale for Suicidal Ideation (MSSI; Miller, Norman, Bishop, & Dow, 1986) were used to assess suicide ideation.

Results of the partial correlation analyses (controlling for gender) showed that scores on the perceived scale were negatively and significantly linked with scores on a suicidal ideation measure ($r = -.56$, $p < .01$). In a series of hierarchical regression analyses, the authors found in the initial steps that perceived social support was a significant predictor of suicidal ideation (coefficient = $-.47$, $p < .01$). Further analyses of the interaction terms showed that, for the comorbid disorders, perceived support served as a buffer to reduce the link between comorbid conditions and suicide ideation (coefficient = $-.37$, $p < .01$). In a more recent investigation, Thompson, Mazza, Herting, Randell, and Eggert (2005) evaluated the links between levels of family support and suicidal behavior. The High School Questionnaire (Eggert, Herting, & Thompson, 1994) was completed by 690 boys and 597 girls (M age = 15.9 years, SD = 1.4; range = 14–18 years). Results of this path-analytic study showed that lack of family support had a significant direct effect on adolescent suicidal behavior for the boys (coefficient = 0.5, t = 1.98, $p < .05$), but not for the girls, $p > .05$. These findings suggest that deficits in perceived social support may have differential impacts within certain samples (also see Mazza & Reynolds, 1998).

MEASURES OF SOCIAL SUPPORT

Two common self-report instruments used in most of the studies we reviewed are the Family Adaptability and Cohesion Evaluation Scales-II (FACES-II; Olson et al., 1983) and the Perceived Social Support from Friends (PSS-Fr) and Family (PSS-Fa; Procidano & Heller, 1983). Each instrument was used in two of the seven studies reviewed. The FACES-II and the PSS are described briefly below.

FACES-II (Olson et al., 1983). To date, four versions of the FACES have been reported in the literature, although studies that examined the links between adolescent suicide and social support adopted either the original version or the second edition (i.e., FACES-II). The FACES is built on Olson's Circumplex Model, which suggests that functional families tend to maintain adequate balance between cohesion and adaptability. The frequently used 30 items of the FACES-II are rated on a 5-point scale (14 adaptability and 16 cohesion items) that ranges from *almost never* to *almost always*. Little research has examined the factor structure of the FACES-II (also see the revised version, FACES-III; Crowley, 1998) in diverse samples of adolescent populations. Olson et al. reported satisfactory coefficient α estimates of .78 and .87 for the Adaptability and Cohesion subscales, respectively. Likewise, satisfactory test-retest reliability estimates of .83 (Cohesion) and .80 (Adaptability) were reported for the subscales. Doherty-Schmid, Rosenthal, and Brown (1988) reported strong evidence for the convergent validity of scores on the FACES-II.

Normative data for the FACES-II are limited for youth with suicide-related behavior and diverse samples of nonclinical youth (see Olson & Tiesel, 1991; Rubestein et al., 1989). The relative strength of the FACES-II and related versions is its strong conceptual foundation; however, the psychometric properties of all versions of this measure are limited. In particular, studies are needed to address estimates of discriminant validity, normative data for clinical populations, and reliable factor structure.

Perceived Social Support from Family and Friends (Procidano & Heller, 1983). Each subscale of the Perceived Social Support from Family (PSS-Fr) and the Perceived Social Support from Friends (PSS-Fr) is composed of 20 items designed to assess the extent to which an individual perceives the need for support from family and friends. The scales are based on Procidano and Heller's hypothesis that perceived availability of a support network from family and peers can serve as important buffers to a number of distress and problem behaviors. Items on the instrument are rated as *yes*, *no*, or *I don't know*. Higher scores on the scales suggest greater levels of perceived support from family and friends.

Procidano and Heller (1983) reported good test-retest correlation on the PSS (r = .83) over a one-month interval. These authors also obtained high internal consistency reliability estimates for the PSS-Fr (α = .84) and PSS-Fa

(α = .90) in their instrument development sample. In a small clinical sample (n = 35 boys, 25 girls) of adolescents ages 11–18 years, Gavazzi (1994) reported mean levels of 10.2 (SD = 4.9) and 13.8 (SD = 4.6) for the PSS-Fa and PSS-Fr, respectively. The coefficient α estimates of the PSS-Fa (.85) and PSS-Fr (.86) for their clinical samples were also adequate. We identified only one study that examined the factor structure of the PSS-Fa in a sample of nonclinical adolescents. In particular, Windle and Miller-Tutzauer (1992) identified a 3-factor solution in an unrestricted exploratory analysis for the PSS-Fa in sub-samples of 147 boys and 153 girls recruited from three suburban high schools. Both Gavazzi (1994) and Greening and Stoppelbein (2002) provided adequate estimates of concurrent validity for scores on this instrument. Gavazzi reported scores on the PSS-Fa and PSS-Fr as strong predictors of psychosocial maturity (R^2 = .50, p < .001). Greening and Stoppelbein reported low to moderate correlations between scores on a self-report measure of depression and scores on the PSS-Fa (r = -.53, p < .30, p < .001) and the PSS-Fr (r = -.30, p < .001). Similarly, scores on a measure of hopelessness were linked moderately and significantly with scores on the PSS-Fa (r = -.35, p < .001) and the PSS-Fr (r = -.21, p < .001).

Although scores on the PSS have been shown to have some clinical utility, additional studies are needed to address other psychometric issues including test performance indicators of sensitivity and specificity and the stability of factor solutions across diverse populations. Normative data are available for a number of nonclinical populations (e.g., Canetti, Bachar, Galili-Weisstub, De-Nour, & Shalev, 1997; Lyons, Perrotta, & Hancher-Kvam, 1988; Rudd, 1990) but not for clinical adolescents with a range of suicide-related behaviors.

Other Potential Protective Factors

Although we have focused in this chapter only on protective factors with evidence-based self-report instruments, we are aware of other potential protective factors that could be linked with adolescent suicidal behaviors. In particular, investigations that used 2 to 3 self-report indices have found protective factors, such as life satisfaction, to be associated with higher reasons for living. Support for these types of exploratory investigations would be strengthened with the development and validation of related self-report instruments. We list a number of those potential protective factors that might be of interest to researchers in future investigations:

1. Purpose in Life (Ryff, 1989).

2. Satisfaction with Life (Diener et al., 1985).

3. Positive Emotion (Joiner et al., 2001).

4. Spiritual Well-being (Paloutzain & Ellison, 1982).

5. Stability on Family Routine and Activities (Markson & Fiese, 2000).

Concluding Thoughts

In summary, there is undoubtedly a range of possible protective factors to consider when studying suicide-related behaviors. In this chapter, we limited our review of the literature to those protective factors that are assessed with psychometrically well-established self-report instruments. We have identified potential benefits for developing instruments that might be useful in assessing a number of other potential protective factors. Overall, given that there is never a clear time frame when risk or protective factors could serve as proximal factors for suicidal ideation or suicide attempts, we continue to argue that it is important to consider a combination of both risk and protective factors in the screening or assessment of adolescent potential for suicide (see Chapter 7). Finally, we encourage the development of integrated multidimensional theoretical models to guide research and clinical practice. None of the studies we examined in this chapter focused on adopting all the contemporary recommendations for developing and validating self-report instruments (see Chapter 4).

Summary of Clinical Practice Implications

- Protective factors are supporting resources that serve as buffers for adolescent suicide-related behaviors or significant suicide risk factors, such as depression and hopelessness.

- Protective factors can generally be grouped into personal protective factors and environmental protective factors.

- Assessing protective factors should help in treatment planning by identifying relative strengths that can be further bolstered.

- Protective factors can be regularly reassessed as an indicator of treatment effectiveness.

- Empirically supported factors to assess include body investment, social problem solving, coping skills, self-esteem, and family support.

- Other potentially useful factors to assess include purpose in life, satisfaction with life, positive emotion, spiritual well-being, and stability of family routine and activities.

Guidelines for the Development and Validation of Suicide-Related Behavior Instruments

Psychometric Considerations

This chapter will be of most interest to readers with a strong background in statistics and research design, or as we sometimes affectionately refer to this group (ourselves included)—serious research geeks. We hope that the information presented here will be practically useful for those engaged in scale construction and validation work. We also believe that individuals evaluating measures for use in clinical practice and research will be able to apply what they learn here to make sound decisions about the appropriateness, utility, and psychometric quality of scales under consideration. Finally, we hope that all readers will come away with a better appreciation of the statistical side of assessment work.

Instruments—*Psychometric Considerations*

In the past few decades, clinical researchers have recommended a wide variety of strategies for developing and validating clinically relevant assessment and research instruments (e.g., DeVellis, 2003; Kline, 1993; Smith & McCarthy, 1995). Some of these strategies have been implemented systematically in the development and evaluation of a number of self-report instruments in areas such as mood disorders (Beck, Steer, & Brown, 1996; Dozois, 2003), disability application (Sayer, Spoont, Nelson, & Nugent, 2004), and perfectionism (Hill et al., 2004). Unfortunately there have been limited attempts to extend these contemporary measurement strategies to the development and validation of self-report instruments in the area of adolescent suicidality. For example, most manuals developed for use with suicide-related behavior instruments do not contain comprehensive information about content validity estimates, although these estimates have been recognized to be preliminary for establishing other indices of validity, such as concurrent and predictive (Haynes, Richard, & Kubany, 1995).

In this chapter, we discuss several basic psychometric guidelines for developing and evaluating scores on self-report instruments that are specific to the assessment of adolescent suicide-related behavior. The guidelines discussed here are based on contemporary psychometric approaches to instrument development and validation (e.g., Cicchetti, 1994; Clark & Watson, 1995; DeVellis, 2003; Floyd & Widaman, 1995; Haynes et al., 1995; Nunnally & Bernstein, 1994). We acknowledge that most of the instrument development and validation strategies we discuss could be extended easily to other assessment methods, including semi-structured interviews, behavior rating scales, and direct observation approaches. We also recognize that the list of guidelines we describe and recommend is not exhaustive; indeed, a variety of approaches to instrument development and validation strategies could be identified in the psychometric literature (see DeVellis, 2003; Goldberg, 1972; Golden, Sawicki, & Franzen, 1984; Kline, 1993). Our major purpose in this chapter is to discuss guidelines for extending contemporary psychometric strategies to the development and evaluation of scores on adolescent-specific suicide-related self-report questionnaires.

The Role of Self-Report Questionnaires in Psychological Assessment

Many dimensions of adolescent internalizing disorders (e.g., frequency of suicidal ideation) cannot be observed and assessed directly; they also tend to vary frequently (e.g., Eyman & Eyman, 1990). Self-report questionnaires present specific advantages to the assessment of a number of dimensions of internalizing disorders, such as depression, suicidal ideation, and feelings of anxiety (see Chapter 1). Specifically, in addition to their cost-effectiveness and simplicity in administration and scoring, self-report instruments allow for reasonable evaluation of multiple dimensions of internalizing disorders, such as the frequency, duration, and severity of the target construct. In clinical settings, for example, the use of well-validated self-report questionnaires can contribute empirically based information to the clinical treatment planning, monitoring, and outcome evaluations of a number of internalizing disorders. As discussed more fully in the first chapter, there is strong empirical support for the advantages of self-report questionnaires in the assessment of internalizing disorders (e.g., Kaplan et al., 1994; Shain et al., 1990).

Some of the major drawbacks of self-report measures, however, relate to the potential for the overreporting or underreporting of sensitive internalizing symptoms, especially when the assessment processes involve (a) the use of self-report questionnaires with limited normative, reliability, and validity data and (b) limited opportunity for the mental health care professional to conduct follow-up queries of independent informants, such as parents, close friends, and teachers. In Chapter 5, we introduce and discuss the Self-Harm Behavior Questionnaire (SHBQ; Gutierrez, Osman, Barrios, & Kopper, 2001) as a self-report or an interview-based instrument that could be used to maximize self-reported suicide-related behaviors. Additional strategies for minimizing the error rate (e.g., false positive identifications) in self-report instruments are discussed in more detail in Chapters 8 and 9. In this chapter, we focus discussion on strategies for developing and evaluating scores on self-report instruments of suicide-related behaviors to help minimize measurement errors. Despite the potential problems, it is important to keep in mind that self-report questionnaires can and should be designed to help obtain valuable assessment or screening information that could not be obtained from methods such as ratings by others.

Development and Validation of Self-Report Measures of Suicidal Behavior—*Conceptual Foundations*

Standard nomenclatures or theories in instrument development and validation facilitate operational definitions of targeted constructs, improve clarity of domains or facets of the construct, and serve organizing functions of the findings regarding the construct (DeVellis, 2003; Murphy & Davidshofer, 1994; Rudd & Joiner, 1998). One standard that psychometricians have considered recently for developing self-report instruments is the *Diagnostic and Statistical Manual of Mental Disorders* and revised editions (e.g., *DSM-IV-TR;* American Psychiatric Association, 2000). This standard, however, provides only brief descriptions of suicide-related behaviors within the classifications of psychological disorders, such as the mood and Axis II disorders (e.g., borderline personality). Suicide has not been formally recognized as an independent disorder in the *DSM*.

A number of other perspectives or theories of suicide and suicide-related behavior have been proposed to help guide the conceptualization of suicide-related thoughts and behaviors. Some of these include the escape (Baumeister, 1990; Dean & Range, 1996), developmental (Blumenthal & Kupfer, 1990; Maris, 1991a), and sociological (Durkheim, 1951). To date there are as many perspectives of suicide-related thoughts and behaviors as there are types of suicide deaths (e.g., Beck et al., 1973; Rudd, 1990). To the extent that most of these perspectives have offered instrument developers well-defined standards that could systematically guide instrument development, the lack of specified conceptual or theoretical foundations of most target instruments continue to be elusive.

Suicide-Specific Self-Report Instruments

In the absence of a well-integrated theoretical model of suicidality, O'Carroll and colleagues (1996) have proposed a standard nosologic (nomenclature) system that might provide instrument developers with an adequate conceptual foundation for developing content-relevant self-report measures of suicide-related behavior. Briefly, O'Carroll et al.'s nomenclature identifies a number of constructs (i.e., domains) that are specific to adolescent suicidal behavior. These domains include suicidal ideation, suicide threat, and suicide attempts (with or without injuries). Suicidal ideation, for example, is defined as "any self-reported thoughts of engaging in suicide-related behavior" (p. 247). In developing self-report questionnaires for adolescents, the specific contents of the target domain (e.g., suicidal ideation) must be clearly specified. For example, the domain of suicidal ideation should be specified further to include *frequency of thoughts triggered by a number of life events* identified by expert raters, theory, and clinical research (see below). A summary of some key components of this nomenclature has been given in the first chapter of this book.

Rudd and Joiner (1998) discussed several advantages to clinical practice and research for adopting this proposed nomenclature. We recommend that instrument developers select *relevant variables* within this nomenclature as potential target constructs when developing adolescent-specific self-report measures of suicide-related behavior. Overall, the specific objective is to specify and adopt a construct that has a well-integrated conceptual foundation that will guide instrument development, validation, and clinically meaningful interpretations of scores from the potential instrument.

Nonspecific Self-Report Inventories

Clinical researchers have adopted the practice of using broad spectrum, nonspecific, self-report instruments (i.e., suicide-specific set of items or subscales that are typically embedded in measures of other constructs, such as depression) to assess suicide-related thoughts and behaviors (see Goldston, 2003, for a brief discussion of this issue). In this book, we conceptualize broad spectrum inventories to include those standardized self-report instruments of other-internalizing or other-externalizing constructs, such as depression and anger, that (a) contain either a single suicide-specific item or subscale *and* (b) were not designed specifically for the assessment of suicide-related behaviors. For example, we consider the Beck Depression Inventory-II (Beck et al., 1996), a broad spectrum instrument because it contains a single item measure (Item 9: Suicidal thoughts or wishes) of suicide-specific behavior (i.e., "I would kill myself if I had the chance"). In addition, it was not designed for the assessment of suicide-specific behaviors. Our concern is that when responses to these broad spectrum instruments are summed to obtain a total score, it is difficult to interpret the obtained score as a *true* representation of a suicide-related behavior of interest.

Furthermore, in psychopathology research, there are concerns among some psychometricians that a number of basic psychometric issues (e.g., content validity and internal consistency reliability) are not being addressed adequately whenever specific items (e.g., suicide-related) are dropped from broad spectrum self-report instruments for questionnaire administrations (see Smith & McCarthy, 1995). Dropping items from a previously validated instrument can alter substantially its psychometric properties. To then rely on the modified (i.e., nonvalidated) version of the instrument without updated normative and psychometric data can raise a number of concerns about what is being assessed and how results should be interpreted. Because of the frequent use of these broad spectrum assessment instruments, clinical researchers have not paid adequate attention to the processes of scale construction and validation in this area; thus, we do not recommend the use of broad spectrum assessment inventories as suicide-specific measures in clinical and research settings.

As discussed in Chapters 2 and 3, it is important to make clear distinctions between suicide-specific risk and protective factors and factors that may not be linked directly with suicidal behaviors (i.e., nonspecific factors). Specifically, although factors *associated* with suicidal behaviors (e.g., risk factors such as depression and problem solving deficits) provide important information to the assessment processes on a range of suicide-related behaviors, most existing self-report instruments are not designed specifically to tap these factors. In Chapter 5, we will discuss two well-established self-report instruments that are specific to the assessment of suicide-related thoughts and behaviors. In Chapters 6 and 7, we review additional research related to those instruments that are specific and appropriate for use in assessing factors that are linked directly to adolescent suicidal behaviors. Future investigations are needed to develop and evaluate the psychometric adequacy of self-report measures that are specific (i.e., in terms of content) to the assessment of suicide risk or protective factors. For example, we need content-relevant suicidal ideation and attempt measures that we can use to evaluate other related psychological responses, such as social and interpersonal relationships.

Professional Training Considerations

Because a series of studies are generally conducted to address instrument development and evaluation issues, instrument developers are expected to have strong background knowledge of (a) current legal and ethical guidelines in working with at-risk youth and (b) basic psychometric information that includes reliability and validity concepts. In addition, it is useful to have practical problem-solving skills related to a number of project implementation issues. For example, instrument developers would find it useful to consider answers to the following questions:

1. What types of interpersonal skills are helpful in working with youth who may be at greatest risk for suicidal behavior? What types of strategies or resources are needed to make effective referrals of youth who are determined to be at greatest risk for suicide-related behaviors?

2. What are the characteristics of youth who are at greatest risk for suicide-related behaviors? Has the instrument developer shown sufficient sensitivity to cultural, ethnic, and gender issues as well as the social stigma associated with self-harmful behaviors?

3. Is the instrument developer familiar with a number of social service agencies in the community where data are being collected that provide services for youth who are at greatest risk for self-harmful behaviors? What specific strategies are useful for working with these agencies?

4. To what extent are all the relevant professional and paraprofessional staffs at a targeted agency or setting willing to support the purposes and procedures of projects that are being conducted by the instrument developer? What are potential costs (e.g., resources, staff involvement) to a targeted agency or facility for conducting suicide-related projects?

5. What specific strategies are needed for resolving unexpected suicide-related problems during project implementation?

6. Is the instrument developer familiar with strategies for obtaining Ethical Committee approvals for conducting suicide-related projects?

We recognize that these questions may not be relevant for all potential instrument-development settings, and a full discussion of these issues is beyond the scope of this book; however, the scales we have developed, which will be discussed in more detail in subsequent chapters, grew out of our efforts to answer these questions. Regardless of their clinical or research orientations, instrument developers need to have good problem-solving skills when they attempt to develop and validate scores on self-report questionnaires in multiple settings. This list should sensitize readers to the types of issues to consider before trying to develop new measures.

Instrument Development—*Methodological Strategies*

Specify the Construct and Related Domains

The initial steps in developing a clinically relevant self-report instrument for assessing adolescent suicide-related behavior involve (a) specifying the target construct (i.e., what to measure), (b) operationally defining the related construct domains to be measured, and (c) specifying the purpose of the instrument (DeVellis, 2003; Fabrigar, Wegener, MacCallum, & Strahan, 1999; Fitzpatrick, 1983; Haynes et al., 1995; Murphy & Davidshofer, 1994). As noted earlier, we recommend that instrument developers adopt O'Carroll et al.'s (1996) proposed nomenclature to guide the empirical rationale for selecting a suicide-specific construct. This nomenclature identifies and offers objective definitions of several distinct constructs that should facilitate (a) the generation of a content-relevant and representative set of suicide-related behavior items, (b) comparisons of research findings across investigations, and (c) future plans for refining the target instrument.

In addition to specifying the target construct, the question of whether the structure of the construct should be represented by a single or multiple domains (i.e., a multidimensional instrument) should be addressed *before* beginning the item generation processes (DeVellis, 2003). Alternatively, the potential instrument could be conceptualized to tap multiple modalities of the same target construct (e.g., cognitive and behavioral domains of the *suicide attempt* construct). Consistent with the conceptual approach that we adopt in this book, we recommend that instrument developers specify at least two measurable dimensions, such as risk and protective, of a target construct (e.g., Orbach et al., 1991; Osman, Gutierrez, Kopper, Barrios, & Chiros, 1998). It is important to note that youth at risk for suicide-related behaviors frequently present with a range of risk and protective factors (e.g., Gutierrez, Osman, Kopper, & Barrios, 2000; Heisel & Flett, 2004).

Specification of the major purposes for which scores from an assessment instrument are to be used is almost always an essential part of instrument construction. There are at least three major advantages to specifying the purposes of a new assessment instrument. First, it enhances the context (e.g., target population) in which the instrument can be administered and scored appropriately. Second, it helps in developing meaningful operational definitions for the domains related to the target construct. Third, it frequently helps direct the selection of a range of specific or relevant items for the prespecified target domains or facets. Traditionally, most self-report instruments of suicidality have been designed for the purposes of (a) screening for the parameters of suicide-related behaviors (e.g., frequency of suicidal ideation), (b) monitoring of changes in a target construct (during or after an intervention), and (c) conducting clinical research. In addition to these traditional objectives, we restate our recommendation for developing self-report questionnaires that focus on the assessment of both risk and protective factors (i.e., multidimensional instruments). Additionally, we encourage the development and validation of scores on highly specific measures of suicidality (e.g., suicide ideation within the context of academic stress) that would contribute to the differential diagnostic processes of most internalizing suicide-related behaviors.

Generate Construct-Relevant and Representative Items

The specific focus at this stage should be on generating a large representative set of suicide-specific items that are *relevant to* and have *direct correspondence* with the actual domains of the targeted suicide-related behavior construct (Haynes et al., 1995). It is important to emphasize that the content of the items generated should be (a) developmentally suitable or appropriate for use with a well-defined target population, (b) representative and relevant to each domain of a targeted suicide-related behavior construct, and (c) socially appropriate for a targeted population. Additionally, it is important to attend to specific item characteristics, such as clarity and conciseness (DeVellis, 2003).

Following the methodology of Haynes et al. (1995), we recommend that instrument developers use multiple sources to generate a range of items that *adequately represent each* prespecified domain or facet of the targeted suicide-related behavior construct. Examples of potential sources that could be useful for generating the initial set or pool of items include:

1. *Conduct Detailed Semi-Structured Clinical Interviews with Target Populations.* Youth with histories (past and present) of multiple suicide attempts and those thinking about engaging in suicide-related behaviors, for example, could be asked to provide valuable information related to the content and parameters of a target construct, such as frequency of suicidal ideation (e.g., within interpersonal relationships). Although this approach frequently yields a clinically relevant and representative set of items, it is important for instrument developers to become familiar with, as well as comply with, a number of privacy and legal issues related to instrument development, such as protection of the rights and well-being of the potential individual research participant (Fisher, 2003).

2. *Conduct Comprehensive Reviews of Relevant Empirical and Theoretical Literature.* Instrument developers should be knowledgeable in basic scale development strategies, population(s) of interest, structural components of the target construct, and relevant psychological literature. We recommend conducting systematic reviews of a variety of adolescent-specific suicide assessment instruments with established reliability and validity estimates. A number of major journals, such as *Suicide and Life-Threatening Behavior, Death Studies, Crisis, Journal of Clinical Child and Adolescent Psychology, Psychological Assessment,* and *Journal of Personality Assessment,* should be utilized as valuable resources for generating potential items. The specific goals should be to identify two or more domains or facets of the target construct and to generate a number of items that correspond to each domain of the construct for youth ages 12 to 18 years.

3. *Consult with Other Professionals and Nonprofessionals.* Consultation with a number of health and mental health care professionals (such as psychologists with various theoretical orientations, psychiatrists, emergency room physicians, social workers, and schoolteachers) who work closely with at-risk youth may provide relevant information about the target construct. Questioning a number of others, including parents, other caregivers, and peers, may also reveal relevant information about related constructs.

4. *Assess Environmental Contexts.* The psychosocial contexts in which suicide-related behaviors occur or persist can provide valuable information about items to include in a suicide-related behavior self-report questionnaire. For example, conducting small informal community group discussions can provide clinically relevant information related to cultural or religious beliefs about life and death. Furthermore, we believe that direct observation of behavioral incidents in clinic settings can provide relevant information about target constructs, such as suicide threat, suicide attempts with injuries, and methods of suicide attempts. It is clinically useful to develop instruments that give us information about specific contexts in which suicide-related behaviors occur. Overall, we agree with DeVellis (2003) that instrument developers should plan to generate three or four times the number of items that they intend to retain in the final version of the potential instrument using multiple sources.

Develop Instrument Instructions, Response Formats, and Scoring Procedures

Questions regarding the instructions and response format for completing the potential questionnaire items should be addressed concurrently as new items are being generated for the instrument (DeVellis, 2003). In general, instructions for completing the questionnaire items should be short, clearly worded, and represent the reading level of the population of interest. Additionally, the time period for rating the items should be specified. Because most suicide-related constructs are conceptualized as *state* conditions (i.e., temporary functioning of an individual), it is important that the period for rating items is less than six months. We recommend shorter intervals (within one to two weeks) to address concerns related to the rapidly developing changes observed in adolescents.

Self-report questionnaires generally use a range of response-format procedures. We recommend that self-report questionnaires designed for routine use or repeated administrations and scoring consider using either the binary-type (e.g., *true* and *false* format) or the traditional Likert-type (e.g., a 5-point response format: 0 = *almost never* to 4 = *almost always*) rating scale format. We note, however, that instrument developers who choose the binary-type format should ensure that the final versions of their questionnaires contain at least five items within each specified domain to allow for variability in the respondents' responses.

Finally, we are in agreement with DeVellis (2003) that instrument developers should avoid the use of reverse-worded items in self-report questionnaires in order to minimize respondents' confusion. Barnette (2000) observed that reverse-worded statements in self-report questionnaires are not considered exact opposites of directly worded statements. We believe that, like structured interview methods of assessment, questionnaire items should be designed to tap direct contents of a target construct. Regardless of the instructions and response format for completing questionnaires, we recommend that instrument developers write brief manuals describing steps in administering, scoring, and interpreting scores on their instruments (e.g., see Chapter 8); such manuals help enhance familiarity with and appropriate use of the instrument. Following Haynes et al. (1995), inferences made by users of an instrument from obtained scores should be consistent with the specific purposes for which the instrument was originally developed.

To summarize, the final item pool for a new questionnaire should be (a) generated using multiple sources, (b) relevant to the target construct and related domains, and (c) three to four times the number of items expected in the final version of the questionnaire. Adequate attention should be paid to the clarity of the instructions and appropriateness of the response options. In addition, a brief manual should be developed describing instructions for administering, completing, scoring, and interpreting scores on the final version of the instrument.

Instrument Validation—*Empirical Strategies*

During the empirical evaluation of scores on the potential instrument, the specific aims are to (a) explore expert confirmation for adequacy of the dimensions of the target construct and related items, (b) establish estimates of reliability of scores, and (c) explore a number of relevant validity estimates (i.e., inferences that could be made) for scores on the instrument. In general, these processes may require dropping items, adding new items, revising the original item wordings and sentence structures, and so on.

Empirical Validation I—Conduct Content Validity Ratings

Following the methodology of Haynes et al. (1995), instrument developers should recruit independent expert raters to conduct a number of content validity evaluations of the new questionnaire *quantitatively and qualitatively*. For example, as in Osman, Kopper, Barrios, Gutierrez, and Bagge (2004), at least three individuals with extensive experience with the target construct (major depressive disorder in adolescents) were asked to rate each depression item in the questionnaire along a number of dimensions such as:

a. *relevancy*—the extent to which each set of items identified by the instrument developer is relevant to the target construct (e.g., ratings of 1 = *not at all relevant* to 5 = *extremely relevant*);

b. *representativeness*—the extent to which each domain of the target construct is composed of a representative number (i.e., 4 or more) of items (e.g., ratings of 1 = *not at all representative* to 5 = *adequately representative*). Although there is no agreement in the extant literature regarding the actual number of items that should be included in each instrument, it is important to point out that the content of the items should be taken into consideration when making such a decision. Items that are similar in content may require a fewer number of items to attain adequate reliability estimates;

c. *specificity*—the extent to which each domain contains only items that are specific to the prespecified construct, as operationally defined by the instrument developer (e.g., ratings of 1 = *not at all specific* to 5 = *extremely specific*); and

d. *clarity*—the extent to which the potential respondents find each item easy to read and understand (e.g., ratings of 1 = *not at all easy* to 5 = *extremely easy*).

In addition, expert ratings should be conducted to include clarity of the instructions for completing the instrument, questionnaire length, social acceptability, clinical utility, and information about other critical dimensions of the construct not specified by the instrument developer. In establishing content validity estimates for the BDI-II items, for example, Osman, Kopper, et al. (2004) reported ratings of relevancy and specificity conducted by seven experts with extensive experience with the BDI-II.

Expert raters were also asked to make comments regarding the adequacy of the BDI-II for use with adolescents.

In summary, Haynes et al. (1995) have discussed extensively the importance of content validity analysis to the clinical utility of an assessment instrument. As they concluded, "clinical inferences from assessment instruments with unsatisfactory content validity will be suspect, even when other indices of validity [e.g., concurrent] are satisfactory" (p. 240). To date, because most self-report measures of suicide-related behaviors lack well-developed content validity estimates, scores from these instruments may not represent adequately important dimensions and aspects of adolescent suicidality.

Empirical Validation II—Conduct Initial Psychometric Analyses of the Items

ADDRESS SAMPLE SIZE CONSIDERATIONS.

Because sample size requirements do vary from study to study (e.g., factor analysis v. reliability analysis), it is important to compute and report both effect size and power estimates for each validation study whenever possible. In addition, we recommend that instrument developers provide an adequate rationale for the representativeness of the sample of interest for each investigation (see Kazdin, 1995). When conducting suicide-related research, instrument developers should be aware of problems related to recruiting large sample sizes for constructs with low base rates by maximizing estimates of content and internal consistency reliability of their instruments. For example, we have found that with high internal consistency reliability estimates of scores on our self-report instruments, sample sizes as small as 150 have been adequate when we conduct a number of multivariate analyses, such as confirmatory factor analyses.

CONDUCT PILOT ANALYSES OF THE ITEMS

Following the content-validity analyses, the initial set of questionnaire items should be evaluated empirically with a number of statistical procedures. Specifically, we recommend the following steps for the initial analyses. First, using a large representative sample (e.g., $N \geq 200$), the data should be submitted to a series of exploratory principal components analysis (PCA; a data reduction procedure) with both promax and direct oblimin rotations. Consistency across the scree plot from the reduced correlation matrix, parallel analysis (95%, PA), and minimum average partial (MAP) results (i.e., multiple criteria) should guide consideration in determining the number of dimensions (factors) to specify for extraction (Cattell, 1966; Fabrigar et al., 1999; Horn, 1965; Zwick & Velicer, 1986). In addition, the common factors (i.e., factor loadings) and related communalities should be examined in evaluating *the set of items* for retention within each dimension (i.e., scale).

Table 4.1

Computer Programs for Performing Factor Analysis

and Reliability Analysis

Comprehensive Exploratory Factor Analysis (CEFA)
URL: http://quantrm2.psy.ohio-state.edu/browne/software.htm

Mplus for Windows
Muthén & Muthén
11965 Venice Blvd.
Los Angeles, CA 90066

SAS System for Windows
SAS Institute Inc.
Cary, NC 27513

Systat for Windows
Systat Software Inc. (SSI)
501 Canal Blvd, Suite E233
Point Richmond, CA 94804-2028

SPSS for Windows
SPSS Inc.
S. Wacker Drive, 11th Floor
Chicago, IL 60606-6307

To attain simple structure of the rotated common components, we recommend retaining only items that (a) load $\geq .40$ on a primary factor and .25 on a secondary factor and (b) have at least moderate communality estimates $\geq .40$ (see Comrey & Lee, 1992; Fabrigar et al., 1999). Second, internal consistency reliability analyses (i.e., examination of coefficient α and corrected item-total scale correlations) should be conducted for the components or factor scales. Specifically, items should have corrected item-total scale correlations of .30 or higher (Nunnally & Bernstein, 1994). Third, the distribution of responses to each item should be evaluated for substantial departures of scores from normality (i.e., items with skewness value = 3 and kurtosis value = 10 should be dropped; Kline, 1998). Together, the components retained should account for at least 80% of the estimated variance in the sample data. These steps should be repeated at least twice before switching to an exploratory common factor analytic procedure.

Guidelines for conducting exploratory common factor analyses and internal consistency reliability estimates are discussed below. A number of statistical programs that describe step-by-step procedures for conducting the PCA procedure may include *Comprehensive Exploratory Factor Analysis (CEFA), Mplus for Windows, Statistical Package for the Social Sciences (SPSS) for Windows, SAS for Windows,* and *SYSTAT for Windows* (see Table 4.1). Floyd and Widaman (1995) have provided a detailed guideline for reporting the results of exploratory (and confirmatory) factor analytic investigations.

Instrument developers can also find a number of well-written textbooks and journal articles that offer extensive discussions of the steps and processes of factor analyses, reliability analyses, and item analyses (e.g., Browne, 2001; DeVellis, 2003; Fabrigar et al., 1999; Kline, 1993). It is important to maintain our focus in this chapter on summarizing only those basic procedural guidelines that have been reported in the psychometric literature for conducting and interpreting a number of reliability and validity analyses. Furthermore, we note that we will maintain focus of our discussions on classical test theory approaches, although we are cognizant of the advantages of item response theory (IRT) procedures in the construction and validation of assessment instruments (e.g., Bock, Gibbons, & Muraki, 1988; Hoijtink, Rooks, & Wilmink, 1999; Lord, 1980; Takane & de Leeuw, 1987).

USE EXPLORATORY COMMON FACTOR ANALYSIS
FOR THE FINAL SET OF ITEMS

Exploratory common factor analysis (EFA) includes a family of statistical procedures that are used frequently to explore and identify empirically a subset of items from the final item pool. The derived subsets generally represent multiple and specific dimensions (i.e., scales or subscales for the instrument) of the target construct. Specifically, following the PCA data reduction procedures noted previously, we recommend submitting the final item pool to an exploratory common factor analytic procedure, such as principal-axis factoring (see Floyd & Widaman, 1995). We recommend the use of the *Mplus* program when the instrument of interest contains a categorical (binary) response format or the distributions of the derived item scores are observed to be nonnormal (see Floyd & Widaman, 1995; Muthén & Muthén, 2004). An additional advantage of the *Mplus* program is that it can be used for the proper extraction of factor solutions when the item pool is composed of items with continuous *and* categorical response formats. Furthermore, this program offers appropriate rotation methods when (a) all variables are continuous or (b) when at least one of the variables is binary or ordered categorical.

Descriptive fit estimates, such as the Root Mean Square Error of Approximation and related confidence intervals (RMSEA; Steiger & Lind, 1980) from a range of rotated factor solutions, can also be used to guide decisions regarding the appropriate number of factors to retain. Regardless of the procedure adopted for determining the number of factors to retain, the final rotated solutions should be parsimonious, interpretable, and relevant to the theory of interest. In particular, the final version of the questionnaire should be composed of at least two dimensions (corresponding to the construct of interest), each defined by a minimum of four items. Additionally, an oblique rotation should be carried out to allow scores on the factor scales to be moderately correlated.

CONDUCT RELIABILITY ANALYSES

Unlike factor analysis, which is used to evaluate multiple dimensions of a new inventory, reliability is used to assess the consistency of scores on an instrument. Specifically, reliability is generally considered the degree to which items on a questionnaire consistently measure the target construct. It is also a measure of the degree of error associated with the instrument. The overall aim in constructing a self-report instrument is to *minimize* different sources of error. Some of these sources are linked to the instrument, the respondents, and the method used to compute the reliability estimate. Scores from newly developed self-report instruments should demonstrate adequate evidence of internal consistency *before* attempting to establish estimates of validity.

There are several different ways of estimating reliability of scores on an instrument, such as (a) internal consistency reliability, (b) test-retest reliability, (c) split-half reliability, and (d) alternate form reliability. In this chapter, we focus on two common ways of assessing reliability for most self-report measures of suicidality: internal consistency and test-retest reliability.

INTERNAL CONSISTENCY RELIABILITY

This approach involves administering the questionnaire once to the same sample of interest. Cronbach's coefficient α (Cronbach, 1951; α coefficient) is generally used to estimate reliability of scores on scales with Likert-type (5 or more response options) response format and the Kuder-Richardson 20 (KR-20, a special form of coefficient α) formula is used for evaluating scores on scales with dichotomous-type response formats. It should be noted, however, that both procedures are designed to evaluate the homogeneity of the content of items within a scale (or subscale).

Cicchetti and Sparrow (1990) have provided empirical guidelines for reporting and interpreting coefficient α estimates. Estimates below .70 are considered unacceptable; those between .70 and .79 are interpreted as fair. Estimates between .80 and .89 are considered good, and estimates $\geq$ .90 are interpreted as excellent. To maximize generalizability of scores on scales (or subscales), we also encourage instrument developers to report two additional estimates: (a) mean inter-item correlations (estimates between .40 and .50) for narrow band instruments (for broad spectrum instruments, values should range from .15 to .20) and (b) confidence intervals (CIs of at least 90%) around the α estimate (Cicchetti, 1994; Clark & Watson, 1995; Fan & Thompson, 2001).

As we noted earlier, it is important for scales to be composed of at least four content-relevant or valid items. With an average inter-item correlation of .40 (minimum estimate expected of narrow band instruments), a 4-item scale on a new instrument might yield a coefficient α estimate of only .73. For instruments designed to tap clinical at-risk behaviors, estimates of reliability are expected to range between good (.80) and high (.90 or higher). Consequently, suicide-related self-report instruments should be composed of scales (or subscales) with at least five content-valid items; scores on the total and subscales should be at least .80.

TEST-RETEST RELIABILITY ESTIMATE

This approach involves the repeated administration of the newly developed questionnaire to the same group of adolescents on well-defined occasions (e.g., two-week intervals). The correlation between scores from any two administrations (typically a correlation coefficient) represents the test-retest (Time 1 and Time 2) coefficient. The magnitudes of these estimates can range from 0 to 1.0, with higher values indicating stable estimates of test-retest reliability. The shorter period we recommended earlier for state measures can allow for (a) multiple instrument administrations, (b) addressing concerns in the adolescent literature related to developmental changes (e.g., the way adolescents think about the world is affected by normal cognitive development), and (c) monitoring the extent of attrition.

Empirical (Construct) Validity Analyses III— Relationships with Other Relevant Measures

The specific purpose of an instrument, in general, determines the types of validity estimates that should be established for the targeted construct. In this chapter, we have defined and discussed the nature of content validity in instrument construction and validation. Next, we will discuss briefly two estimates of validity that are established frequently for self-report questionnaires in the psychometric literature: criterion-related validity and incremental validity or utility.

CRITERION-RELATED VALIDITY

Criterion-related validity evaluates the *strength* of the relationship between scores on a new instrument (as the predictor) and a well-established criterion measure (as the criterion). There are two major subtypes of criterion-related validity, each defined by the time during which scores are obtained on the predictor and criterion measures. *Concurrent validity* is evaluated when scores on a new (the predictor) and criterion measures are obtained at about the same time. For example, scores on the Suicide Ideation Questionnaire (SIQ; Reynolds, 1988) are obtained as important criteria against which to assess the validity of scores on a new instrument.

It should be clarified further that, when evaluating evidence for concurrent validity, the criterion measure may (convergent) or may not (discriminant) be theoretically related to the predictor (i.e., the new measure). Specifically, *convergent validity* (a subtype of concurrent validity) is established when scores from a newly developed instrument (predictor) correlate moderately (e.g., range, r = .40 to .60) and significantly with scores from the same or similar well-established criterion measure. *Discriminant validity* (another subtype of concurrent validity) is established when scores from a newly developed instrument (predictor) correlate low (e.g., range, r = .01 to .39) and nonsignificantly with scores from a theoretically unrelated criterion measure. For example, scores on a newly developed measure of suicidal ideation might be expected to correlate higher with scores on the SIQ (convergent validity) than with scores from a measure of an unrelated construct (discriminant validity), such as pain catastrophizing. We note that there are a number of other ways (e.g., known-groups) of establishing evidence for concurrent validity (see additional comments below).

Predictive validity, a subtype of criterion-related validity, is evaluated when scores on a newly developed measure (predictor) are obtained at one time and scores on the criterion measure are obtained at a subsequent or future time. Evidence for predictive validity is established, for example, when scores from a newly developed measure of suicidal ideation accurately predict the future risk behaviors of adolescents, such as physical aggression, self-harm, suicide threats, and so on. To date, the majority of suicide-related self-report instruments lack evidence for predictive validity and may relate, in part, to factors such as low base rate (i.e., proportion of actual positives) of suicide-related behaviors, such as suicide deaths, difficulties recruiting representative or large sample sizes in validation studies, ethical concerns related to some research protocols, and the ephemeral nature of some state or internalizing variables.

Overall, criterion variables serve as *gold standards* against which scores on the new instrument are evaluated. As clinically valuable standards, scores on criterion measures are expected to be valid, relevant, and not contaminated with the predictor variable. When conceptualized as categorical or dichotomous variables (see Chapter 11), criterion measures with specific cut-off scores can be useful as benchmarks for evaluating discriminative efficacy (i.e., errors in prediction) of scores on a newly developed predictor measure. Evidence for the performance of an instrument is frequently expressed in conditional probability terms, such as *sensitivity, specificity, positive predictive value (ppv),* and *negative predictive value (npv)*. These estimates are discussed in detail in Chapters 5 and 11.

INCREMENTAL VALIDITY

Incremental validity is considered the extent to which scores on an assessment instrument (e.g., a newly developed self-report measure) contribute to the measurement or assessment of a well-defined criterion (e.g., suicide attempt) measure. In evaluating evidence for incremental validity, it is important for all potential predictor measures to have established reliability and criterion-related validity. Second, stronger evidence for the incremental validity of the newly developed instrument would be demonstrated if alternate instruments with established incremental validity are included among the predictor variables. Third, the relations (i.e., correlations) among the predictor measures should not be high (i.e., values $\leq$ .61 are adequate). Specifically, an incrementally valid measure should provide clinically useful information about the criterion measure that is not already obtained from the predictor measures.

Multiple regression and receiver operating characteristic (ROC) curve analytic procedures are generally used to evaluate the incremental validity of potential predictor measures. When using the multiple regression procedure, a two-step process is typically adopted for establishing incremental validity of scores on an instrument. First, zero-order (or biserial) correlations among scores on the predictor and criterion measures are examined. These correlations should not be high or else the measures are likely redundant. Second, hierarchical linear regression analysis is carried out to identify the single or set of predictors that are statistically significant (e.g., looking at R^2_{diff} values as initial estimates) in predicting scores on the established criterion variable (e.g., Haynes & Lench, 2003). Multivariate logistic regression is generally used when the criterion variable is dichotomous. In Chapter 11, for example, we used both the ROC and simultaneous regression analytic procedures to establish predictive validity estimates for risk and protective self-report instruments.

Descriptive/Normative Statistics

In addition to reliability and validity estimates, instrument developers should report a number of descriptive statistics including *the means, standard deviations, confidence intervals around the obtained mean scores,* and so on for the inventory's total and subscale scores. Note that it is important to evaluate the reliability and validity of all derived subscale scores, not just the total score, of a newly developed instrument. To maximize use of the instrument, it is also important to provide full demographic information (e.g., age, geographic region, ethnicity, gender) for the instrument development and validation samples.

Concluding Thoughts

In summary, a psychometrically well-developed self-report questionnaire can provide scores that have clinical utility in the assessment, planning, and management of adolescents at risk for suicide-related behaviors. In this chapter, we have identified and discussed a number of instrument construction and validation strategies useful to individuals interested in constructing or selecting self-report instruments for use in clinical or research settings. For example, we highlighted the importance of an integrated perspective for guiding the various content validation processes. Most of the emphases were on identifying sets of items that are relevant and representative of well-defined suicide-specific construct domains. In addition, we discussed a number of empirical strategies for evaluating scores on self-report instruments. For example, we discussed principal components analysis as a data reduction procedure. Cronbach α estimates and mean inter-item correlation estimates were introduced as indexes for evaluating the internal consistency reliability of scores on a derived scale. Other psychometric issues we discussed included sample size and professional training considerations. Finally, we introduced and discussed briefly two major validity estimates and related subtypes: criterion-related and incremental.

Because of the importance of validity estimates to the construction and validation of self-report instruments, we decided to use existing data sets from clinical and nonclinical adolescent samples to illustrate in greater detail several procedures for calculating validity estimates on some of our self-report instruments. For example, in Chapters 5 and 6, we illustrate the use of confirmatory factor analysis (CFA) as a powerful statistical strategy for evaluating the structure of a self-report instrument. Data from clinical and nonclinical adolescents were also used to report estimates of internal consistency reliability. In Chapter 7, we use data from clinical and high school youth to illustrate a range of validity estimates, such as concurrent and incremental. We also highlight the need for using multiple measures in the assessment of adolescent suicide-related behaviors. In Chapter 11, we use data from adolescent psychiatric inpatients to illustrate evidence for the predictive or discriminative validity of scores on several risk and protective self-report instruments. We also discuss and illustrate strategies for establishing several conditional probabilities including sensitivity, specificity, positive predictive value, and negative predictive value.

In conclusion, it is our hope that readers planning to undertake scale development projects will use the information in this chapter as a guide and will review in particular the data presented in Chapters 6, 7, and 11 as illustrations of these points. Those readers who would rather have a root canal without anesthesia than have to create and evaluate a new scale but who want to ensure that they are using the best possible measures for their specific research or clinical purposes should now have a better idea of the types of information to review. In other words, before adopting a measure, search the literature to determine how many of the analyses discussed in this chapter have been conducted, then compare the results to the benchmarks we provide. If no such information can be found, contact the developer of the measure to determine if it exists in unpublished form or if studies are underway to generate it. The more published (i.e., peer reviewed) data that exists regarding a scale's reliability and validity the better.

Summary of Clinical Practice Implications

- Self-report instruments are uniquely appropriate for assessing multiple dimensions of internalizing disorders.

- Self-report data adds empirical information to treatment planning, monitoring, and outcome evaluation.

- Good measures are based on clear operational definitions of the construct being assessed.

- The most useful measures are focused on specific domains (e.g., suicidal thoughts) of clinical interest rather than broad spectrum measures or measures modified to assess something other than their original intent.

- Good measures are developed through a systematic, multistage process and result in empirical support for appropriateness of item content, clarity of instructions, specific scoring instructions, reliability, and validity.

- Normative data for all subscales and total scores for a wide range of individuals is also a sign of a well-developed measure.

Part II

Empirically Based Self-Report Instruments

The Suicidal Ideation Questionnaire
and the Self-Harm Behavior Questionnaire

In Chapter 4, we offered specific guidelines for developing and validating scores on self-report instruments for use with adolescents. In this chapter, we identify and illustrate a set of criteria that we consider empirically useful for judging self-report instruments as evidence-based (*EB*) for screening purposes in clinical practice and research. In addition, we present psychometric data on two self-report instruments that would support their use as EB screening instruments of suicidal behavior. To orient the reader to these instruments, we first provide brief descriptions of each. Information related to the administration and scoring procedures of the instruments can be found either in Chapter 8 or in related manuals. In particular, we will focus on applying the criteria we develop to the following self-report instruments: The Suicidal Ideation Questionnaire (SIQ; Reynolds, 1988) and the Self-Harm Behavior Questionnaire (SHBQ; Gutierrez, 1998; Gutierrez, Osman, Barrios & Kopper, 2001).

Criteria for Evidence-Based Screening Self-Report Instruments

Clinical researchers and psychometricians have undertaken systematic investigations to identify a number of psychometric properties of reliability and validity that are indicative of empirically based measures (e.g., see Hay, Hawes, Faught, & Hay, 2004; Klein, Dougherty, & Olino, 2005; Nezu, Ronan, Meadows, & McClure, 2000). To date, however, specific psychometric criteria have not been developed for recognizing and adopting suicide-related assessment instruments as evidence-based for screening purposes in clinical and nonclinical settings. Kazdin has shown that guidelines are important for selecting and using existing self-report instruments in clinical practice and research settings (2005), and in attempting to establish these guidelines, we were mindful of Kazdin's observation that "psychometric evaluation of any [self-report instrument] can be endless because in principle no finite number of studies can exhaust one type of validity . . . time (e.g., cohorts)" (Kazdin, pp. 549-550). Accordingly, we offer the following as *minimum criteria* for evaluating self-report instruments as evidence-based for screening purposes. We note that most of the psychometric issues presented below have been discussed extensively in Chapter 4. (For readers who do not have a strong background in psychometrics, it would be helpful to review the material presented in Chapter 4.) We suggest six criteria as follows:

1   The instrument must have a strong conceptual or empirical foundation to guide specifications of the (a) context and purposes for using the instrument and (b) specific target domains and related facets.

2   It is important for the instrument to have established normative data (e.g., means and standard deviations, local or national) for at least two well-defined groups (e.g., ethnicity and age groups) within the last 5 to 7 years that might be useful as reference points for interpreting scores from other adolescent samples.

3   The instrument should possess empirical evidence of reliability that includes an internal consistency coefficient of .80 or higher or estimates of test-retest reliability (see Cicchetti, 1994; Chapter 4).

4   The available criterion-validity estimates should include (a) known groups with empirically established levels of psychological distress (e.g., multiple suicide attempters versus nonattempters) and (b) instrument performance indicators, such as sensitivity, specificity, positive predictive values, and negative predictive values. In particular, in extending these indicator concepts to measures of suicide attempts, sensitivity refers to the percentage of adolescents with a history of suicide attempts who are correctly identified as suicide attempters. Specificity refers to the percentage of youth without history of suicide attempts (e.g., inpatient controls) who are correctly identified as nonattempters. Positive predictive power (ppp) refers to the percentage of youth who are predicted as suicide attempters who are actually suicide attempters. Negative predictive power (npp) refers to the percentage of youth who are predicted as nonsuicide attempters who are actually nonsuicide attempters. In screening for suicide-related behaviors, it is important to maximize both the sensitivity and negative predictive power of scores on a self-report screening instrument.

5   Related to the above issues, it is important for the instrument to have established cut-off scores to guide consistent interpretations of obtained scores from other groups.

6   To help incorporate screening data into routine practice or research activities, it is important for the instrument to be easily administered, scored, and interpreted within a 15-30 minute time frame.

Data from instruments meeting 5 to 6 of the criteria will be considered *high* evidence-based; those meeting 3 or 4 of the 6 criteria will be considered *moderate* evidence-based, and those meeting fewer than 3 of the 6 criteria will be considered *low* evidence-based for screening purposes. These criteria will also be applied to instruments that we present and discuss in Chapters 6 and 7. We note that these criteria are based on our clinical work with these instruments in the past 10 years; different researchers or clinicians might adopt different standards for selecting and using screening self-report instruments.

Suicidal Ideation Questionnaire

Description of the SIQ

The Suicidal Ideation Questionnaire (SIQ; Reynolds, 1988) is a 30-item self-report instrument designed to assess thoughts and ideas that are linked with suicidal behaviors in clinical and nonclinical populations. In particular, this 30-item version of the instrument is designed for use with adolescents and young adults (grades 10-12) to tap suicidal ideation. Each item is rated on a 7-point scale ranging in frequency from 0 *(I never had this thought)* to 6 *(almost every day)* during the past month. A 15-item version (SIQ-JR) appropriate for use with students in grades 7-9 is also available.

Theoretical Foundations of the SIQ

The content of the SIQ items range from general thoughts and wishes about death (e.g., Item 6, *Thought of death*) to serious and specific thoughts of suicide (e.g., Item 2, *Thought of killing self*), reflecting the *hierarchical model* of suicidal thoughts. Although not stated explicitly in the professional manual, it is important to note that the scoring format of the SIQ items is consistent with O'Carroll et al.'s (1996) conceptualization of suicidal ideation. As discussed in Chapter 2, the presence of suicidal ideation has been associated with a number of internalizing (e.g., depression and hopelessness) and externalizing (e.g., aggressiveness and substance abuse) problems. In particular, suicidal ideation is linked strongly with suicide attempts (Beautrais, Joyce, & Mulder, 1996; De Man & Leduc, 1995). Although some attempts have been made to explore dimensions of the SIQ, this instrument is best conceptualized as a measure of a unidimensional construct.

Instrument Development and Related Norms

Detailed information regarding the development and normative samples of the SIQ are reported in the professional test manual (see Reynolds, 1988). We provide only a brief review of this topic. The SIQ items were generated based on extensive semi-structured interviews with approximately 150 adolescents and young adults with severe disturbances in mood and suicide-related behaviors. Groups of items were also generated to match the predefined domains of the SIQ. The original 3-part response format was modified, the item descriptions refined, and the final items were evaluated for initial psychometric properties in a small sample of 100 high school adolescents ages 14 to19 years.

Normative information (i.e., means and standard deviations) for the SIQ are reported in the professional manual for grade level, ethnicity, and gender ($n = 2{,}180$). In particular, normative data of the SIQ ($M = 17.79$, $SD = 26.78$) is reported for a school-based sample of 890 adolescents; the mean age was 16.05 years ($SD = 0.99$). In addition, normative data for the SIQ are presented for a number of adolescents and young adults such as adolescent psychiatric ($M = 69.60$, $SD = 49.98$) suicide attempters ($n = 53$).

Research with the SIQ in several clinical and nonclinical settings have been reported in the extant literature (e.g., see Hewitt, Newton, Flett, & Callander, 1997; King, Hovey, Brand, & Ghaziuddin, 1997; Pinto, Whisman, & McCoy, 1997; Reinecke, DuBois, & Schultz, 2001). In particular, in the past 5 to 7 years, updated normative data have been reported on the SIQ for clinical and nonclinical youth in a number of studies; however, updated norms have not been reported in the professional manual. In 2001, Mazza and Reynolds reported a mean SIQ raw score of 22.24 ($SD = 27.47$) for a sample of 277 girls and a mean SIQ raw score of 14.04 ($SD = 22.38$) for a sample of 179 boys with a range of suicide-related behaviors. Likewise, in 2001, Reinecke et al. reported a mean SIQ raw score of 37.71 ($SD = 40.00$) for a small sample of 99 adolescent psychiatric inpatients ages 12 to 18 years (M age = 14.9, $SD = 1.4$ years). In 2002, Chang published a mean SIQ percentile score of 59.06 ($SD = 15.41$) for a large sample of 306 public high school students. It is important to point out that some studies have reported SIQ mean raw scores while others have included the mean percentile scores, making comparisons across some of the studies difficult.

Reliability Analyses

In the instrument development samples, Reynolds (1988) reported estimates of internal consistency (i.e., Cronbach α) and test-retest reliability for scores on the SIQ. In particular, estimates of internal consistency reported for the 10th-, 11th-, and 12th-graders were $\geq .96$ (range = .969 to .974). The manual also reported mean inter-item correlations of .53 and greater for the obtained coefficient α estimates.

Regarding test-retest reliability estimates over a 4-week time frame, the manual indicated an estimate of .72 in samples of 801 adolescents (Mean total SIQ score at Time 1 = 17.46, $SD = 20.76$; Mean total SIQ score at Time 2 = 17.49, $SD = 23.82$). As a unidimensional state measure, these reliability estimates are within the expected moderate to high ranges.

Validity Analyses

As we discussed in Chapter 4, validity estimates are important for ensuring that an assessment or screening instrument taps the construct it was designed to measure. Recall that we also discussed various types of validity estimates. In this chapter, we discuss the following types of validity estimates for the SIQ scores: known-groups, concurrent (convergent and discriminant) validity, and diagnostic utility. In addition, we examine potential cut-off scores for using this instrument as a screening measure.

KNOWN-GROUPS VALIDITY

Evidence for known-groups validity has been mixed for this instrument. Based on normative data in the manual, the mean SIQ score has been shown to be useful in differentiating the responses of the adolescent normative samples ($n = 890$; Mean = 17.79, $SD = 26.78$) from the responses of (a) hospitalized adolescent suicide attempters ($n = 53$; Mean = 69.60, $SD = 49.98$), $t(941) = 12.83$, Cohen's $d = 1.81$ and (b) college women with bulimia ($n = 52$; Mean = 36.70, $SD = 25.7$), $t(940) = 4.96$, $p < .001$, Cohen's $d = .71$. In addition, girls ($M = 20.79$, $SD = 29.19$) reported significantly higher levels of suicide ideation than did boys ($M = 13.43$, $SD = 20.05$), $t(877) = 4.35$, $p < .001$, Cohen's $d = .29$ in the instrument development samples. Although most studies involving clinical and nonclinical adolescents have provided support for group differences on the SIQ total score (e.g., see Colle, Belair, DiFeo, Weiss, & LaRoche, 1994; Harrington et al., 2000; Pinto et al., 1997), a number of analyses that have included clinical subgroups have not provided consistent support for evidence of known-groups validity (e.g., see Harrington et al., 1998; King et al., 1995; Mazza & Reynolds, 2001; Ritter, 1990).

CONCURRENT-CONVERGENT VALIDITY

Estimates of concurrent validity for the SIQ have received strong support in the extant literature. In particular, the manual reports moderate and positive links between scores on the SIQ and (a) the Reynolds Adolescent Depression Scale (RADS; Reynolds, 1987; $r = .58$, $p < .001$), (b) the Adolescent Hassles Inventory (Reynolds & Waltz, 1986; $r = .44$, $p < .001$), and the Children's Manifest Anxiety Scale-Revised (CMAS-R; Reynolds & Richmond, 1978; $r = .56$, $p < .001$) in the normative samples. In other investigations, scores on the SIQ have been shown to correlate moderately and significantly with scores on established measures of (a) suicide (King & Kowalchuk, 1994; King, Raskin, Gdowski, Butkus, & Opipari, 1990; Reinecke et al., 2001; Reynolds & Mazza, 1994), (b) depression (Mazza, 2000; Reinecke et al., 2001), and (c) hopelessness (Reinecke et al., 2001).

CONCURRENT-DISCRIMINANT VALIDITY

The SIQ manual does not report strong estimates of discriminant validity for the instrument development samples. Likewise, a limited number of studies have examined links between scores on the SIQ and variables that are not specific to suicide ideation. We found only one study that has reported low links between scores on the SIQ and a measure of rational problem-solving ($r = -.08$) in a sample of 105 adolescent psychiatric inpatients (Reinecke et al., 2001). While this is the type of result one would hope to see in a study of this nature, more evidence of discriminant validity is needed.

DIAGNOSTIC UTILITY/PERFORMANCE

The manual suggests a cut-off score of 41 as indicative of the need to make referral for further assessments for psychopathology and suicide risk. In addition, scores on any 3 of the 8 critical items are to be examined when determining the need for additional evaluation. Estimates of test performance such as sensitivity, specificity, and positive predictive values are not reported in the manual. Using logistic regression analyses, Pinto et al. (1997) reported a cut-off score of 20 as most useful for differentiating the responses of attempters and ideators from psychiatric controls. In particular, for the analyses involving the attempters and controls, sensitivity was 83%, specificity was 58%, positive predictive value was 71%, and negative predictive value was 73% for a cut-off score of 20. In the analyses involving ideators and controls, sensitivity was 82%, specificity was 58%, positive predictive value was 65%, and negative predictive value was 77%.

The Current Investigation—*Psychometric Properties of the Suicidal Ideation Questionnaire*

Data Sets

Using data we have collected in the past two to three years, we examined additional psychometric properties of the SIQ in high school and adolescent psychiatric inpatient samples.

Method

PARTICIPANTS

High School Sample   Data used in this study were collected over a three-year period as part of a Personal Adjustment Screening Survey (PASS) implemented at a Midwestern high school to identify potentially at-risk students for further evaluation. The sample consisted of 192 boys and 251 girls ranging in age from 14 to 18 years (*M* age = 15.68, *SD* = 1.15). Approximately 43.1% were Caucasian, 31.6% African American, 9.7% Hispanic American, and 1.6% other race/ethnicity; 14% did not specify their race/ethnicity.

Adolescent Psychiatric Inpatients   Data used in the study were obtained from consecutive admissions to two adolescent psychiatric inpatient units in the Midwest. The sample included 92 boys and 124 girls ranging in age from 14 to 17 years (*M* age = 15.50, *SD* = 0.98). Regarding ethnicity, 85.2% were Caucasian, 7.9% Hispanic American, 2.8% African American, 2.8% Asian American, and 2.7% other race/ethnicity. Review of the medical charts showed that approximately 30.1% had been diagnosed with major depressive disorder, 22.2% conduct disorder, 17.1% oppositional defiant disorder, 8.3% posttraumatic stress disorder, 7.9% attention-deficit hyperactivity disorder, and 14.4% other psychiatric diagnoses. Of these participants, 33 (15.3%) were first-time suicide attempters, 86 (39.8%) were multiple attempters, and 97 (44.9%) were psychiatric controls. The high school youth were similar in age with the psychiatric inpatients, $t(657) = 1.69, p = .092$.

MEASURES AND PROCEDURES

All the participants completed a brief demographic background information questionnaire and the SIQ. In addition, the adolescent psychiatric inpatients completed the *Suicidal Behaviors Questionnaire* (SBQ-R; Osman et al., 2001). The SBQ-R is composed of four items. Each item on this instrument is designed to tap a specific aspect of the suicide behavior construct including past suicide attempts (Item 1), frequency of suicide ideation (Item 2), suicide threat (Item 3), and suicide likelihood (Item 4). Estimates of reliability and validity of scores on the SBQ-R have been supported adequately in clinical and nonclinical samples. In this investigation, we used the SBQ-R items as independent variables in separate regression analyses.

Results

ESTIMATES OF INTERNAL CONSISTENCY

In the high school sample, the Cronbach α estimate for the SIQ was high, .96 (95% Confidence Interval [CI] = .96, .97; mean inter-item $r = .45$). Likewise, the coefficient α estimate in the psychiatric inpatient sample was high, .98 (95% CI = .98, .99; mean inter-item $r = .65$). These estimates are comparable to those reported in the manual for the instrument development samples. We have included both the confidence intervals and the mean inter-item correlations for these estimates.

COMPARISONS WITH NORMATIVE DATA

Independent samples t-tests indicated that (a) the normative sample ($n = 890$; $M = 17.79, SD = 26.78$) scored significantly higher on the mean SIQ score than did the current high school ($n = 443$; $M = 12.22, SD = 19.29$) sample, $t(1,331) = 3.92, p < .001, d = .23$, and (b) the psychiatric inpatients ($n = 216$; $M = 42.81, SD = 46.30$) had significantly higher mean SIQ score than did the normative sample, $t(1,104) = 10.45, p < .001, d = .79$. As expected, the psychiatric inpatients scored significantly higher on the SIQ mean score than did the current high school youth, $t(657) = 11.94, p < .001, d = .99$.

Analyses involving the current high school sample data showed that girls ($n = 251$; $M = 14.80, SD = 21.80$) obtained significantly higher scores on the SIQ than did boys ($n = 192$; $M = 8.85, SD = 14.80$), $t(441) = 3.25, p < .001, d = .31$.

Similarly, for the psychiatric inpatient sample data, girls (n = 124; M = 53.15, SD = 50.82) obtained significantly higher scores on the SIQ than did boys (n = 92; M = 28.89, SD = 35.12), $t(214)$ = 3.93, $p < .001$, d = .54.

DIAGNOSTIC PERFORMANCE

Using the receiver operating characteristic (ROC) curves analysis, we examined the psychometric performance of the SIQ mean raw score in differentiating between (a) multiple suicide attempters and psychiatric controls and (b) first-time suicide attempters and psychiatric controls. In the analyses involving psychiatric suicide attempters, ideators, and controls, Pinto and colleagues (1997) recommended a cut-off score of 20 as having the greatest clinical utility in differentiating the responses of well-defined subgroups. The SIQ manual recommends a cut-off score of 41 as having the greatest clinical utility.

Results of the SIQ at various cut-off scores are presented in Table 5.1. Using 22 as the optimal cut-off score, the sensitivity of the scale score was 86%, specificity was 83%, positive predictive value was 81%, and negative predictive value was 87% in differentiating the multiple attempters and

Table 5.1

Cut-off Scores on the Suicidal Ideation Questionnaire—Diagnostic Indicators

Cut-off Score	Sensitivity	Specificity	ppp	npp
Multiple Attempters v. Psychiatric Controls				
20	.87	.79	.79	.88
21	.86	.79	.79	.87
22*	.86	.83	.81	.87
35	.66	.90	.85	.75
40	.64	.92	.87	.74
First-time Attempters v. Psychiatric Controls				
20	.70	.79	.54	.89
21	.67	.79	.52	.88
22*	.64	.83	.55	.87
35	.55	.90	.64	.85
40	.48	.92	.67	.84

Note. ppp = positive predictive power, npp = negative predictive power.

* = optimal cut-off score

control groups. The area under the curve (AUC) attained medium accuracy, AUC = .895 (95% CI = .841, .935). Overall the cut-off score identified in this project is similar to the cut-off score of 20 suggested by Pinto et al. (1997), suggesting the need for using lower cut-off scores on this instrument for psychiatric inpatient samples.

USING THE SIQ TOTAL SCORE AS CRITERION VARIABLE

We conducted regression analyses to examine the utility of scores on the SIQ as a criterion measure in the combined samples of (a) multiple suicide attempters and psychiatric controls and (b) first-time suicide attempters and psychiatric controls. We used scores on the four SBQ-R items as predictors in the regression analyses. In the analysis involving the multiple attempters and psychiatric controls, scores on the frequency of suicide ideation (coefficient = .46, $p < .001$), suicide threat (coefficient = .21, $p < .001$), and self-reported suicide likelihood (coefficient = .26, $p < .001$) were linked as predictors of scores on the SIQ. Next, in the analysis that included first-attempters and psychiatric controls, only scores on the frequency of suicide ideation (coefficient = .55, $p < .001$) and the self-reported suicide likelihood (coefficient = .27, $p < .001$) were predictors of scores on the SIQ. It is important to note that scores on the past suicide attempts item (SBQ-R Item 1) were not linked with scores on the SIQ in these analyses.

Evaluation of the SIQ as a Screening Measure

The purpose of this investigation was to evaluate the SIQ as a screening self-report instrument. The findings suggest caution in the use of this instrument alone as a screening self-report instrument. First, updated normative data or information have not been reported in the professional manual. Second, the recommended cut-off scores for using this instrument remain controversial; studies have not replicated the proposed cut-off score of 41. Third, the SIQ does not tap a range of suicide-related behaviors. In particular, the findings of this investigation showed that scores on the SIQ were not linked with past suicide attempts. Regardless of these limitations, researchers continue to use the SIQ as a screening instrument because of its strong conceptual foundation, high estimates of reliability, and ability to differentiate the responses of a subgroup of adolescents. Using the preestablished criteria, we rate the SIQ, as a screening instrument, to be at the moderate level.

The Self-Harm Behavior Questionnaire

Description of the SHBQ

The SHBQ (Gutierrez et al., 2001) is a brief self-report instrument designed to provide detailed clinical information about nonlethal suicide-related behavior in clinical and nonclinical settings. This measure is intended for use with adolescents and adults ages 13 and older. It is composed of four specific parts assessing different facets of the suicide-related behavior construct: intentional self-harm, suicide attempts, suicide threat, and suicide ideation. In addition to the dichotomous (yes/no) response format, each section includes a free-response format that allows for the clarification of responses (i.e., behavior, thoughts, and verbalizations) that include intentionality and expected outcomes. Sample sections and sample items are as follows:

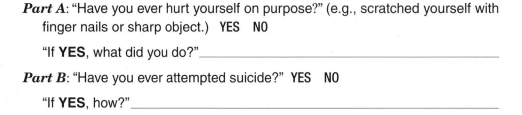

Part A: "Have you ever hurt yourself on purpose?" (e.g., scratched yourself with finger nails or sharp object.)   **YES   NO**

"If **YES**, what did you do?"_____

Part B: "Have you ever attempted suicide?"   **YES   NO**

"If **YES**, how?"_____

The SHBQ is given in the Appendix. The SHBQ administration and scoring procedures are presented in Chapter 8.

Theoretical Foundations of the SHBQ

The SHBQ items are based on results of several studies that included semi-structured interviews by well-trained researchers regarding suicidality in clinical and nonclinical settings. Items were also based on previous research and years of clinical work with adolescents and young adults. The dimensions of the SHBQ are consistent with O'Carroll et al.'s (1996) conceptualization of suicidal behavior. For example, the SHBQ is composed of a number of facets that include suicidal ideation, suicide threat, and suicide attempts. These constructs have been presented and discussed in Chapters 1 and 4. In light of our previous discussion regarding limitations of the SIQ (Reynolds, 1988), it is important to emphasize the need for self-report measures of suicidal behavior to tap multiple dimensions of the suicidality construct. At least one factor-analytic study has provided empirical support for the four structural dimensions of the SHBQ in a U.S. sample (see Gutierrez et al., 2001).

Instrument Development and Related Norms

A comprehensive description of the development of the SHBQ can be found in Gutierrez (1998). In brief, the interview format of this instrument was modified as a self-report instrument because of the observation that "people are more comfortable admitting to thoughts and behaviors related to suicide when they are asked to circle a response . . . instead of providing a verbal report" (see Gutierrez et al., 2001; p. 476).

The construct validity of the SHBQ was evaluated in a sample of 342 undergraduates. The mean age of the sample was 19.48 years (*SD* = 1.52). Preliminary norms were based on results of a factor-analytic and validation study sample of undergraduates. Results of an exploratory principal-axis factoring with varimax and promax rotations that used 22 SHBQ items showed low to moderate correlations among the four factors, consistent with the a priori conceptual formulation of the instrument.

Normative data (i.e., means and standard deviations) for the SHBQ were reported as follows: For men (n = 140), the mean score was 5.24 (SD = 8.26); for women (n = 202), the mean score was 6.74 (SD = 10.68). An independent samples t-test showed no significant difference between the genders on the SHBQ total score, $t(340)$ = 1.40, $p < .001$. However, significant gender differences were indicated on the subscales, with women scoring higher than men on the suicide attempts, suicide threat, and suicide ideation subscales. In addition, normative information data were reported for small sample sizes of nonsuicidal (n = 20) and severe suicidal ideation (n = 20) students on the SHBQ total and subscale scores. In particular, the mean score of the total SHBQ for the severe suicidal ideation students (M = 28.50, SD = 14.83) was significantly higher than those obtained for the nonsuicidal students (M = 0.65, SD = 2.16), $F(1, 38)$ = 69.03, $p < .001$. Cross-cultural normative data have been reported for a sample of 361 consecutive inpatients in Germany (M age = 41.9; range = 17 to 77 years) (Fliege et al., 2006). Normative data have not been reported extensively for adolescent high school and psychiatric inpatient samples.

Reliability Analyses

Cronbach α estimates for scores on all the SHBQ subscales were high in the normative samples: suicide attempts (.96, 95% CI = .95, .97), self-harm (.95, 95% CI = .94, .96), suicide threat (.94, 95% CI = .93, .95), and suicide ideation (.89, 95% CI = .87, .91).

Although test-retest reliability estimates were not reported for the SHBQ in the normative data analyses, Fliege et al. (2006) reported strong test-retest reliability estimates for each subscale over intervals of 7 to 150 days (mean = 68 days) as follows: suicide attempts (r_{tt} = .96), self-harm (r_{tt} = .98), suicide threat (r_{tt} = .93), and suicide ideation (r_{tt} = .93). The study participants included 242 women and 119 men ages 17 to 77 years. These authors also did not report reliability estimates for adolescent samples.

Validity Analyses

As with the SIQ, we examined the following validity estimates for scores on the SHBQ: known-groups, concurrent (convergent and discriminant) validity, and diagnostic utility. Unlike the SIQ, the SHBQ is a multidimensional self-report instrument. Accordingly, we examined findings related to the factor structure of this instrument.

KNOWN-GROUPS VALIDITY

Gutierrez et al. (2001) provided initial evidence for known-groups validity of the SHBQ in small samples of undergraduates screened for severe suicide ideation. As noted previously, students with severe suicide ideation had significantly higher SHBQ total scores than did the nonsuicidal students, Cohen's d = 2.63. Similarly, students with severe suicide ideation (n = 20) had significantly higher scores than did the nonsuicidal students (n = 20) on the self-harm (n = 4.85 v. 0.45; SD = 5.62 v. 2.01), suicide attempts (M = 5.90 v. 0.00; SD = 7.63 v. 0.00), suicide threat (M = 9.95 v. 0.00; SD = 6.19 v. 0.00), and suicide ideation (M = 7.80 v. 0.20; SD = 2.80 v. 0.89) subscale scores. Fliege et al. (2006) reported considerable evidence for known-groups estimates of the SHBQ for a large inpatient sample (n = 361) in Germany. In particular, patients with high scores on the SHBQ reported more severe symptoms of depression, anxiety, and perceived stress than those with low scores on the SHBQ (t = -3.2, -3.7, -4.4 respectively, all p values < .01). Estimates of known-groups validity have not been reported previously for adolescent samples.

CONCURRENT-CONVERGENT VALIDITY

Correlations between scores on the SHBQ and scores on a number of validation self-report instruments, such as the Adult Suicidal Ideation Questionnaire (ASIQ; Reynolds, 1991; r = .70), the Suicide Probability Scale (SPS; Cull & Gill, 1982; r = .57), the Suicidal Behaviors Questionnaire-Revised (SBQ-R; Osman et al., 2001; r = .77), and the Beck Depression Inventory-Second edition (BDI-II; Beck, Steer, & Brown, 1996; r = .58) provided strong evidence for the concurrent-convergent validity of this instrument in the normative samples. Likewise, moderate to high links were shown between the SHBQ subscale scores and all the concurrent validation self-report measures of suicide ideation, suicide probability, suicidal behavior, and depression severity. For example, for the SHBQ suicide ideation subscale, these estimates ranged from .48 (SPS) to .66 (SBQ-R), all p values < .01.

CONCURRENT-DISCRIMINANT VALIDITY

Discriminant validity estimates were not reported in Gutierrez et al. (2001) for the SHBQ in the normative samples. However, a reanalysis of the normative data utilizing dependent correlation analyses showed that scores on the SHBQ self-harm subscale are not as strongly linked with a measure of depression severity (i.e., BDI-II; Beck et al., 1996) as it is with a measure of suicide probability (i.e., SPS; Cull & Gill, 1982), $t(339)$ = 2.50, p < .01.

Although not included in our criteria for evaluating the adequacy of self-report measures as screening instruments, it is important to acknowledge data regarding the incremental validity of scores on the SHBQ in the normative sample. The extant literature suggests that newly established assessment and screening instruments should demonstrate adequate estimates of incremental validity (e.g., see Haynes & Lench, 2003; Mash & Hunsley, 2005). In a series of hierarchical multiple regression analyses, Gutierrez et al. (2001) showed that scores on the SHBQ suicide ideation subscale contributed adequate information to the prediction of scores on a measure of suicide probability (i.e., SPS; Cull & Gill, 1982) over and beyond those scores contributed by a well-established measure of depression severity.

DIAGNOSTIC UTILITY/PERFORMANCE

Gutierrez et al. (2001) did not report performance indicator scores of the SHBQ in the instrument development and validation samples; however, we found inter-rater agreement analyses in a study by Fliege et al. (2006) in a large clinical sample (n = 361). In particular, Fliege et al. reported substantial agreement between scores on the SHBQ and a validation self-report measure of self-harm (κ = .63). When we reanalyzed these data, we found strong estimates of specificity (97%) and negative predictive power (85%), with an overall classification rate of 86% with regard to self-harm behavior. In the comparison involving agreement between scores on the SHBQ and clinician ratings, Fliege et al. reported an overall κ estimate of .22 (low). A reanalysis of these data showed good estimates of specificity (84%) and negative predictive value (92%).

CONSTRUCT VALIDITY

Using data from the normative samples, Gutierrez et al. (2001) conducted principal-axis factor analyses with varimax and promax rotations on 22 of the 32 SHBQ items. They extracted a 4-factor solution that accounted for approximately 80.1% of the variance in the sample data. As expected, each item loaded adequately on its a priori factor; however, they did not attempt to replicate these solutions in samples of clinical and nonclinical adolescents.

Fliege et al. (2006) conducted exploratory (EFA) and confirmatory factor analyses (CFA) to determine the replicability of the 4-factor solution in an inpatient sample. A 4-factor solution, similar to that reported in Gutierrez et al. (2001) emerged from the EFA. The four factors accounted for approximately 85% of the variance in the German sample data. Furthermore, results of the CFA provided satisfactory fit of the 4-factor model to the clinic sample data (CFI = .96, TLI = .96). Thus, the SHBQ seems to tap four dimensions of the suicide-related behavior construct in adult samples.

Current Study—*Psychometric Properties of the Self-Harm Behavior Questionnaire in Adolescent Samples*

Data Sets

Recall that we have consistently pointed to the absence of validation data of the Self-Harm Behavior Questionnaire (SHBQ; Gutierrez et al. 2001) for adolescent samples. We have attempted to address this issue by presenting a series of analyses to replicate as well as provide additional psychometric support for use of the SHBQ in adolescent clinical and nonclinical settings.

We used data that were collected as part of the Personal Adjustment Screening Survey (PASS) described previously. In particular, we randomly selected a sample of 420 protocols from the first two years of the project to conduct the exploratory factor analysis. In addition, we used data obtained from students during a two-year time period (n = 231) to conduct a series of validity analyses for scores on the SHBQ. The validation analyses included data from adolescent psychiatric inpatients (n = 130).

Method

PARTICIPANTS

High School Data Set I: Exploratory Factor Analyses   This sample (200 boys, 220 girls) was composed of 44.5% Caucasian, 32.1% African American, 9.3% Hispanic American, 2% other race/ethnicity; 12.1% did not identify race/ethnicity. Boys (M age = 15.71, SD = 1.95 years) and girls (M age = 15.55, SD = 1.37 years) did not differ significantly in age, $t(418)$ = .95, p = .34.

High School Data Set II: Validation Sample   This sample included 89 boys (M age = 15.72, SD = 1.45 years) and 142 girls (M age = 15.69, SD = 1.36 years). Boys and girls did not differ significantly in age, $t(229)$ = .12, p = .91. Of the sample, 44.2% were Caucasian, 33.8% were African American, 9.5% were Asian American, 1.3% were Hispanic American, and 0.4% were other ethnic groups; 10.8% did not provide information regarding ethnicity.

Adolescent Psychiatric Inpatient Sample: Validation Sample   Participants were consecutive admissions to two adolescent inpatient units. The sample (49 boys, 81 girls) was composed of 80.8% Caucasian, 13.1% African American, 1.5% Asian American, 2.3% Hispanic American, and 2.3% other race/ethnicity. Extensive review of the medical charts indicated that approximately 30.8% met diagnostic criteria for major depressive disorder, 18.5% for conduct disorder, 16.9% for oppositional defiant disorder, 10.0% for posttraumatic stress disorder, 7.7% for attention-deficit hyperactivity disorder, and 16.1% for other psychiatric diagnoses. Of these, 40.8% were admitted because of suicide attempts, 19.2% were due to severe suicidal ideation, and 40.0% were for other psychiatric problems. The high school youth and the adolescent inpatients were similar in age, $t(359)$ = 1.37, p = .17.

Adolescent Psychiatric Inpatient Sample: Test-Retest Subsample   We asked a subsample (n = 74; 26 boys, 48 girls) of the validation sample to complete the SHBQ at the time of admission (Time 1) and after a 2-week interval (Time 2) to assess estimates of test-retest reliability. This subsample included approximately 82.4% Caucasian, 14.9% African American, 1.4% Asian American, and 1.4% other ethnic groups. Boys (M age = 15.54, SD = 1.03 years) and girls (M age = 15.48, SD = 1.09 years) did not differ significantly in age, $t(72)$ = .23, p = .82.

These participants also completed the Adolescent Psychopathology Scale (APS; Reynolds, 1998). We used scores on the following APS subscales to estimate evidence of concurrent validity: self-concept, alienation-boredom, interpersonal problems, emotional lability, and suicide.

MEASURES AND PROCEDURES

All the study participants completed a brief background information questionnaire, the SHBQ, and a number of other self-report instruments. For the analyses prepared for this chapter, we included the following self-report data for the adolescent inpatient validation samples: (a) the four items contained in the Suicidal Behaviors Questionnaire-Revised (SBQ-R; Osman et al., 2001), the 20-item Beck Hopelessness Scale (BHS; Beck, Weissman, Lester, & Trexler, 1974), and the 30-item Reynolds Adolescent Depression Scale – Second edition (RADS-2; Reynolds, 2002). Recall that the test-retest sample completed the APS.

Results

FACTOR STRUCTURE OF THE SHBQ

The 22 items of the SHBQ subjected to a principal-axis factor analysis with promax rotation. Preliminary analyses that included parallel analysis and minimum average partial suggested a 4-factor solution. The Kaiser-Meyer-Olkin Measure of Sampling Adequacy (KMO) of .87 was adequate. Criteria for retention of an item on a factor was set at .40 or higher. We extracted four interpretable factors, similar to those reported for the adult normative samples. Factor 1 (Past Suicide Attempts) consisted of 6 items (variance = 41.35%) with loadings that ranged from .85 to .96. Factor 2 (Self-Harm) consisted of 5 items (variance = 14.52%) with loadings ranging from .80 to .96. Factor 3 (Suicide Threat) consisted of 6 items (variance = 10.46%) with loadings ranging from .54 to .95. Factor 4 (Suicide Ideation) consisted of 5 items (variance = 8.47%) with loadings that ranged from .45 to .98. Together, the four factors explained approximately 74.8% of the variance in the data. Intercorrelations among the factors ranged from .30 to .48. The factor loadings are presented in Table 5.2.

CONFIRMATORY FACTOR ANALYSIS

A multigroup Confirmatory Factor Analysis (CFA) procedure was implemented to assess invariance of the 4-factor oblique solution across the high school (n = 231) and the inpatient adolescent (n = 130) sample data. Because of the nonnormality of the responses on the SHBQ items, we used the robust estimation procedure in EQS for Windows (Bentler & Wu, 2005) for each analysis. Each item was specified to load freely on its respective factor, and the factors were allowed to correlate. The variance of each factor was set at 1.0. We used commonly specified descriptive fit indexes to evaluate the adequacy of each model: Relative robust χ^2 (SB-χ^2/df) value of 2 or less,

Table 5.2

Exploratory Factor Analysis—
Factor Pattern for the Self-Harm Behavior Questionnaire

Item		1. Past Suicide Ideation	2. Self-Harm	3. Suicide Threat	4. Suicide Attempts
1.	Risk	**.96**	.01	.05	-.02
2.	Intent	**.93**	.01	-.04	.03
3.	Medical treatment	**.91**	.02	-.07	-.01
4.	Method	**.88**	.03	.07	-.06
5.	Frequency	**.87**	.00	.05	-.03
6.	Related event	**.85**	-.06	-.03	.09
7.	Treatment	.03	**.96**	-.01	-.01
8.	Risk	-.00	**.94**	.05	-.01
9.	Disclosure	-.02	**.92**	-.04	.00
10.	History	.03	**.87**	.04	-.02
11.	Frequency	-.02	**.80**	-.06	.09
12.	Risk	.00	.06	**.95**	-.04
13.	History	.03	.01	**.93**	-.02
14.	Frequency	-.05	.06	**.81**	-.00
15.	Related event	-.10	-.04	**.79**	.09
16.	Method	.06	-.06	**.73**	.09
17.	Intent	.09	-.06	**.54**	-.02
18.	Plan	.06	-.02	-.04	**.98**
19.	Preparation	.06	-.01	-.01	**.94**
20.	Reaction of others	.01	.04	.05	**.83**
21.	Related event	-.14	.09	-.01	**.78**
22.	Method	.02	-.05	.13	**.45**

Factor columns labeled: FACTOR 1, FACTOR 2, FACTOR 3, FACTOR 4.

Note. Values in bold are salient loadings (values ≥ .40).

a robust-comparative fit index (R-CFI) of .90 or higher, and a root-mean-square error of approximation (RMSEA) value of .06 or less (see Browne & Cudeck, 1993; Hu & Bentler, 1999).

In the baseline analyses that included data from the high school sample, the 4-factor oblique model provided adequate fit to the sample data: SB-χ^2/df = 1.28, R-CFI = .950, and RMSEA = .035 (90% CI = .020, .047). Similarly, in the analyses that used the inpatient sample data, the model provided good fit to this sample data: SB-χ^2/df = 1.54, R-CFI = .965, and RMSEA = .065 (90% CI = .050, .078). Finally, when we imposed restraints on all the factor loadings and factor intercorrelations, evidence for invariance was strong: SB-χ^2/df = 1.48, R-CFI = .927, RMSEA = .052 (90% CI = .043, .060). Findings from these analyses indicate that the structure of the SHBQ is appropriate for use across high school and adolescent inpatient samples.

RELIABILITY ANALYSES

As in previous investigations with the SHBQ, we computed Cronbach alpha (α) estimates to evaluate the reliability of the SHBQ total and subscales scores for the high school and inpatient adolescent validation samples.

High School Validation Sample Among this sample, Cronbach α estimates for the SHBQ subscale scores were as follows: suicide attempts (α = .96, 95% CI = .95, .97; mean inter-item r = .80), self-harm (α = .93, 95% CI = .91, .94; mean inter-item r = .73), suicide threat (α = .88, 95% CI = .85, .90; mean inter-item r = .55), and suicide ideation (α = .90, 95% CI = .88, .92; mean inter-item r = .64). The coefficient α estimate for the total SHBQ was also high, .93 (95% CI = .92, .94; mean inter-item r = .38).

Adolescent Psychiatric Inpatient Validation Sample As in the high school sample, the Cronbach α estimates for the SHBQ subscales among the adolescent inpatient samples were high: suicide attempts (α = .94, 95% CI = .92, .95; mean inter-item r = .72), self-harm (α = .88, 95% CI = .84, .91; mean inter-item r = .59), suicide threat (α = .86, 95% CI = .82, .89; mean inter-item r = .51), and suicide ideation (α = .82, 95% CI = .77, .86; mean inter-item r = .48). The coefficient α estimate for the total SHBQ was also high, .95 (95% CI = .94, .96; mean inter-item r = .46).

Test-Retest Adolescent Inpatient Sample The test-retest reliability estimate over a two-week interval for the SHBQ total score was adequate, r_{tt} = .88, $p <$ .01. In addition, moderate and statistically significant concurrent links were observed between the SHBQ total score and scores on five of the Adolescent Psychopathology Scales at the time of post-test: low self-concept (r = .59) alienation-boredom (r = .54), interpersonal problems (r = .54), emotional lability (r = .54), and suicide (r = .64). The test-retest estimates for the subscales were as follows: suicide attempts (r_{tt} = .91), self-harm (r_{tt} = .84), suicide threat

$(r_{tt} = .82)$, and suicide ideation $(r_{tt} = .80)$. The results of these analyses suggest that scores on the SHBQ are internally consistent for the validation adolescent clinical and nonclinical samples.

NORMS AND GENDER DIFFERENCES

High School Validation Sample $(n = 231; 89$ boys, 142 girls)   Table 5.3 shows the descriptive statistics of the SHBQ (e.g., means and standard deviations) for the high school validation sample. Results of the multivariate analysis of variance (MANOVA), using gender as the independent variable and scores on the subscales as dependent measures, revealed that boys and girls did not differ significantly in their responses to the subscales, Hotelling's $T^2 = .005$, $p = .89$. It is noteworthy that, in the older undergraduate normative sample, Gutierrez et al. (2001) identified gender differences on three of the four subscale scores. Similarly, an independent samples t-test showed that boys $(M = 4.76, SD = 9.17)$ and girls $(M = 6.15, SD = 11.62)$ did not differ significantly in their responses to the total SHBQ, $t(229) = .96$, $p = .34$. The lack of a statistically significant difference here may be due to the relatively young sample. Gender differences in suicide-related behaviors are well documented in the adult literature, as are similar differences in rates of major depression and

Table 5.3

Means, Standard Deviations, Coefficient Alpha Estimates,

Zero-order Correlations Among the SHBQ Scale Scores—

High School Validation Sample $(n = 231)$.

						Descriptive Statistic	
Measure	*SA*	*SHB*	*S-Thrt*	*S-Idea*	*Coefficient Alpha*	*Mean*	*SD*
SHBQ					.93	5.62	10.75
SA	1.00				.960	.953	.82
SHB	.55*	1.00			.93	1.99	4.42
S-Thrt	.31*	.36*	1.00		.880	.92	3.00
S-Idea	.29*	.50*	.49*	1.00	.90	1.76	2.99

Note. SHBQ = Self-Harm Behavior Questionnaire; SA = Suicide Attempts; SHB = Self-Harm Behavior; S-Thrt = Suicide Threat; S-Idea = Suicide Ideation.

* $p < .01$.

Table 5.4

Means, Standard Deviations, Coefficient Alpha Estimates,

Zero-order Correlations Among the SHBQ Scale Scores—

Psychiatric Inpatient Validation Sample (n = 130)

Measure	SA	SHB	S-Thrt	S-Idea	Coefficient Alpha	Mean	SD
SHBQ					.95	29.95	22.44
SA	1.00				.94	9.82	9.40
SHB	.65*	1.00			.88	8.67	6.29
S-Thrt	.59*	.51*	1.00		.86	5.94	6.39
S-Idea	.71*	.64*	.57*	1.00	.82	4.83	4.42

Note. SHBQ = Self-Harm Behavior Questionnaire; SA = Suicide Attempts; SHB = Self-Harm Behavior; S-Thrt = Suicide Threat; S-Idea = Suicide Ideation.

* $p < .01$.

other correlates of suicide risk in adolescents; however, this divergence begins in middle adolescence and becomes more marked into early adulthood. Given that there was a difference in mean scores in the expected direction, we suspect that if this particular sample had been older, the gap would have been larger and hence attained significance.

Adolescent Psychiatric Inpatient Validation Sample Table 5.4 shows the descriptive statistics of the SHBQ for the adolescent psychiatric inpatient samples. Unlike the high school sample, the overall MANOVA was statistically significant, Hotelling's T^2 = .14, $F(4, 125)$ = 4.27, p <.003. Comparisons of mean differences on the four subscales showed that girls obtained statistically significant higher mean scores than did the boys on all the SHBQ subscales. Similarly, girls (M = 34.85, SD = 22.28) had a statistically significant higher SHBQ mean total score than did the boys (M = 20.00, SD = 19.62), $t(128)$ = 3.85, $p < .001$, Cohen's d = .70.

Known-Groups Validity A one-way between-groups MANOVA that included the high school and adolescent inpatient samples showed a significant main effect of group on all the SHBQ subscales, Hotelling's T^2 = .56, $F(4, 356)$ = 50.15, $p < .001$; partial η-squared = .36. Independent samples t-tests showed that the inpatient samples scored significantly higher than did the high school samples on all the SHBQ subscales: suicide attempts (Cohen's d = 1.38), self-harm (Cohen's d = 1.29), suicide threat (Cohen's d = 1.10), and suicide ideation (Cohen's d = 0.86). These group differences are large and clinically useful. Likewise, the inpatient samples had significantly higher SHBQ total scores than did the high school sample, Cohen's d = 1.48.

Concurrent-Convergent Validity   We used data from the adolescent psychiatric inpatient validation sample (n = 130) to evaluate evidence of convergent validity for the SHBQ scores. We found that the suicide attempts scale score correlated highly with the SBQ-R (r = .75) and moderately with both the BHS (r = .38), and the RADS-2 (r = .39) scale scores. The self-harm scale score correlated highly with the SBQ-R (r = .62) and moderately with the RADS-2 (r = .38) scale scores. The suicide threat scale score correlated moderately with the SBQ-R (r = .46) scale score, and the suicide ideation scale score correlated highly with the SBQ-R (r = .63) and moderately with the RADS-2 (r = .41) scale scores. The SHBQ total score correlated highly with the SBQ-R (r = .74) and moderately with both the BHS (r = .35) and the RADS-2 (r = .42) scale scores. All p values < .01.

Concurrent-Discriminant Validity   Data from the test-retest inpatient samples that included the five APS scale scores were used in this analysis as convergent measures. In addition, we included the APS psychosocial substance use difficulties, the introversion, and the social adaptation scales as the discriminant measures. Using dependent samples t-tests, we found strong evidence for discriminant validity. For example, the SHBQ total score was more moderately and significantly linked with the self-concept scale scores (convergent estimate) than with the (a) psychosocial substance use difficulties scale score, t = 3.19, p < .002, (b) the introversion scale score, t = 3.33, p < .001, and (c) the social adaptation scale score, t = 3.89, p < .002.

DIAGNOSTIC PERFORMANCE

We used data from the adolescent psychiatric validation samples (n = 130) to evaluate performance indicators for the SHBQ. We included the following in the comparative analyses: (a) suicide attempters versus psychiatric control groups (n = 53 and 52, respectively), and (b) suicide ideators versus psychiatric control groups (n = 25 and 52, respectively).

Results of the receiver operating characteristic (ROC) curve and related cut-off scores are presented in Table 5.5. A cut-off score of 22 was identified as most useful in differentiating the suicide attempters and ideators from the inpatient control groups. In particular, in the analysis involving the attempters and psychiatric controls, a cutoff score of 22 was linked with 96% sensitivity, 92% specificity, 92% positive predictive value, and 96% negative predictive value. The area under the curve (AUC) of .97 (95% CI = .923, .995) indicated high accuracy for the SHBQ total score.

Table 5.5

Cut-off Scores on the Self-Harm Questionnaire: Diagnostic Indicators

Cut-off Score	Sensitivity	Specificity	ppp	npp
Attempters v. Psychiatric Controls				
19	.96	.90	.91	.95
22*	.96	.92	.92	.96
24	.94	.92	.92	.94
26	.92	.92	.92	.92
28	.90	.92	.92	.90
Ideators v. Psychiatric Controls				
19	.84	.90	.80	.92
20	.76	.90	.79	.88
22*	.72	.92	.81	.87
26	.64	.92	.80	.84
28	.60	.92	.78	.81

Note. ppp = positive predictive power, npp = negative predictive power.

* derived cut-off scores

Evaluation of the SHBQ as a Screening Measure

We have presented a number of analyses to provide support for the invariance of the factor structure, reliability, and validity of scores on the SHBQ in clinical and nonclinical adolescent samples. Regarding the preestablished criteria, the SHBQ has a strong empirical foundation; it is also a multidimensional instrument. In particular, it is designed for use in both clinical and nonclinical settings to tap multiple dimensions of risk factors that are linked to suicidal behavior, such as suicide attempts and suicide ideation. In addition, we have offered clinical cut-off scores for screening purposes.

However, other psychometric limitations remain. For example, the SHBQ taps only risk factors that are linked to suicidal behavior; it does not tap protective factors. In addition, the performance of this new instrument has not been well established in diverse adolescent populations. Additional research is needed to replicate most of the findings presented in this chapter. Overall, the SHBQ should be considered a moderate screening measure of suicide-related behaviors.

Concluding Thoughts

The message from all of the psychometric data summarized and presented in this chapter is that both the SIQ and SHBQ are useful, easy to administer self-report measures that can be used for the purposes of risk screening in clinical and nonclinical settings. Neither measure can be said to be an adequate stand-alone screening tool, but when used in combination with other appropriate self-report measures, they form the basis of a solid screening packet. There are advantages and disadvantages to both measures.

The SIQ consists of a straightforward list of statements to which adolescents respond by darkening an oval corresponding to their rating. This is a format familiar to adolescents, who have taken numerous "bubble tests" during their formal education. Most nonclinical adolescents can easily complete the SIQ in 5–10 minutes and rarely experience any difficulty with the instructions. Another advantage is the hand-scoring template available from the publisher (i.e., Psychological Assessment Resources, Inc.), which makes quick work of checking critical items and overall scoring; however, this measure must be purchased, and the cost of record forms can add up quickly and substantially for large-scale projects.

The mixed-response format of the SHBQ may be less familiar to adolescents but has the advantage of allowing them to write specific responses in their own words in addition to circling answer choices. We have found that many adolescents like the opportunity to express themselves in this way and often provide important information that could not possibly be captured by forced-choice response options. It may take adolescents longer to complete the SHBQ, particularly in clinical settings, but it does not appear to require an unreasonable amount of effort. Scoring of the SHBQ is more complicated than the SIQ, but the detailed instructions in Chapter 8 and the score summary sheet provided in the Appendix facilitate the process. Finally, by purchasing this book you gain the right to reproduce and use the SHBQ at no additional charge.

Summary of Clinical Practice Implications

- Ideally screening tools should be able to be administered, scored, and interpreted in 15–30 minutes.

- The Suicidal Ideation Questionnaire (SIQ) is a 30-item measure appropriate for use with students in grades 10–12, while the SIQ-JR is suitable for those in grades 7–9; both assess a range of thoughts about suicide.

- Cut-off scores between 20 and 22 on the SIQ appear to have the most clinical utility for distinguishing between suicide attempters and controls.

- The SIQ is considered moderately useful as a screening instrument but is not recommended as the sole instrument used.

- The Self-Harm Behavior Questionnaire (SHBQ) assesses a full range of non-lethal suicide-related behaviors in individuals age 13 and older; it is appropriate for use in clinical and nonclinical settings.

- A total score of 22 on the SHBQ is the most useful cut-off in discriminating adolescent suicide attempters and ideators from psychiatric controls.

- The SHBQ is considered moderately useful as a screening instrument.

The Reasons for Living Inventory
for Adolescents and the
Suicide Resilience Inventory-25

In recent years, the comprehensive assessment and management of suicide-related behaviors in adolescents and young adults ages 15 to 25 years has focused on two broad areas: risk and protective factors. In Chapters 2 and 5, we identified risk factors (i.e., psychological and psychiatric) as those conditions that increase the probability of an individual engaging in self-harmful behaviors. Examples of risk factors for adolescent suicide-related behaviors include major depressive disorder, hopelessness, substance-related disorders, and past suicide attempts (e.g., Mazza & Reynolds, 1998; Sanchez, 2001; Smith, Buzi, & Weinman, 2001). In Chapter 3, we defined protective factors to include those resources that reduce the likelihood that the individual will engage in deliberate self-harmful behaviors. Examples of protective factors are effective problem-solving approaches, family cohesion, and positive friendship relationships (e.g., Dieserud, Roysamb, Braverman, Dalgard, & Ekeberg, 2003; Marion & Range, 2003). In addition, we expressed concerns about the limited attention that has been given to the development and validation of measures for assessing protective factors. Because protective factors make unique contributions to the assessment and management of suicide-related behaviors, we urged researchers to develop and validate adolescent-specific instruments for assessing a number of protective factors.

In this chapter, we describe two self-report instruments that we have developed for assessing protective factors against suicide-related behaviors: The Reasons for Living Inventory for Adolescents (RFL-A; Osman, Downs, et al., 1998) and the Suicide Resilience Inventory-25 (SRI-25; Osman et al., 2004). As we contended in Chapter 5, it is important for self-report screening instruments to meet some basic psychometric standards. Following the preestablished criteria presented in that chapter, we (1) discuss the conceptual and theoretical foundations that guided the development of each instrument, (2) provide normative information for the instrument development and validation samples, (3) review studies that have presented evidence for the reliability and validity of scores on the instrument, and (4) present current research data in further support of psychometric properties. Finally, we discuss the rationale for selecting each instrument as an evidence-based screening instrument for use in clinical and nonclinical settings.

The Reasons for Living Inventory for Adolescents

The Reasons for Living Inventory for Adolescents (RFL-A; Osman, Downs, et al., 1998) is a 32-item self-report instrument that was designed to assess five dimensions of the protective factor construct that serve as buffers against suicide-related behaviors. It was originally developed for use with adolescents ages 14 to 18 years. We have revised normative data to extend use of the RFL-A with adolescents ages 13 to 19 years (see below). It has a Flesch-Kincaid 6th-grade reading level index and an average of 10.8 words per sentence. Each item is rated on a 6-point scale that ranges from 1 (*not at all important*) to 6 (*extremely important*).

Theoretical Foundations of the RFL-A

Linehan, Goodstein, Nielsen, and Chiles (1983) developed the original adult version of the Reasons for Living (LRFL) inventory. Like the adult LRFL, development of the RFL-A was based on the cognitive-behavioral assumption that adaptive beliefs mediate the determination not to engage in suicide-related behaviors. In generating items for the adult LRFL, Linehan and colleagues followed the recommendations of Frankl (1959) by focusing on the "purpose or meaning" that people give for surviving a number of physically and emotionally challenging conditions. Thus, high scores on these protective instruments suggest strong adaptive reasons people give for not killing themselves when faced with life-threatening situations. We specified five dimensions to represent the domains or facets of the RFL-A as follows:

1. Future Optimism (FO): In adult and adolescent samples, hopelessness (negative expectations) about the future has been found to be a significant risk factor for suicide-related behaviors, such as suicide attempts (e.g., Beck, Weissman, Lester, & Trexler, 1974; Hunter & O'Connor, 2003). The FO scale is designed to assess positive expectations about future events; it is composed of 7 items. Sample FO scale items include, "I expect many good things to happen to me in the future" (Item 13), and "My future looks quite hopeful and promising" (Item 25).

2. **Suicide-Related Concerns (SRC):** Attitudes toward life and death have been identified as important variables in adolescent suicidality. Youngsters with strong attraction to death or repulsion by life attitudes or beliefs have been found to be at greater risk for various types of self-harmful behaviors (e.g., Orbach et al., 1991). The SRC is designed to assess those attitudes, anxieties, beliefs, and fears that adolescents hold regarding suicide-related behaviors. It is composed of 6 items. Sample SRC scale items include, "I am afraid to die, so I would not consider killing myself" (Item 8), and "The thought of killing myself scares me" (Item 20).

3. **Family Alliance (FA):** A range of familial factors including family violence, sexual abuse, and poor communication have been associated with severe forms of suicide ideation and suicide attempts in adolescents (Kosky, Silburn, & Zubrick, 1990; Mazza & Reynolds, 1998). Items on the FA scale are designed to assess those familial factors that serve as buffers in reducing the risk for suicide-related behaviors. It is composed of 7 items. Sample FA scale items include, "I feel emotionally close to my family" (Item 7), and "My family cares a lot about what happens to me" (Item 30).

4. **Peer Acceptance and Support (PAS):** Children and adolescents who lack the supportive resources of peers and friends are frequently at risk for various forms of psychopathology including major depressive disorder and substance-related problems (e.g., DiFilippo & Overholser, 2000; Sorenson & Rutter, 1991). Scores on the PAS scale evaluate the belief that peers and friends provide sources of support for "the wish to live"; it is composed of 6 items. Sample PAS scale items are, "My friends care a lot about me" (Item 10), and "My friends accept me for what I really am" (Item 27).

5. **Self-Acceptance (SA):** Research suggests that children and adolescents with low or unstable self-esteem are at higher risk for other forms of mental disorders. These may include major depressive disorder, negative attitudes, and self-harmful behaviors (Lewinsohn, Rohde, & Seeley, 1994; Overholser, Adams, Lehnert, & Brinkman, 1995; Overhosler, Freiheit, & DiFilippo, 1997). The SA scale is designed to assess perceived self-image that buffers against thoughts of suicide ideation and suicide attempts; it is composed of 6 items. Sample SA scale items are, "I accept myself for what I am" (Item 3), and "I feel good about myself" (Item 29).

Instrument Development and Related Normative Information

We generated the RFL-A items from multiple sources including high school and inpatient adolescents, high school teachers, clinical social workers, and psychologists. We asked participants to indicate specific reasons adolescents generally give for not committing suicide when the thought occurs to them. Following item refinement for grammatical structure and readability, we conducted exploratory factor analysis (EFA) and confirmatory factor analysis (CFA) to form the five factors. All of the factor loadings in the EFA and

Table 6.1

Demographic Characteristics for the Instrument Development and
Validation Samples: Reasons for Living Inventory for Adolescents

Variables	Study 1 ($n = 350$)[a]	Study 2 ($n = 654$)[b]	Study 3 ($n = 442$)[c]
Age (years)	14–18 years	14–18 years	14–18 years
Mean age (*SD*)	16.18 (1.18)	16.14 (1.25)	16.21 (1.14)
Gender—*n* (%)			
Boys	170 (48.6)	300 (45.9)	221 (50.0)
Girls	180 (51.4)	354 (54.1)	221 (50.0)
Ethnicity—*n* (%)			
Caucasian	326 (93.1)	585 (89.4)	397 (89.8)
African American	5 (1.4)	18 (2.8)	16 (3.6)
Latino / Hispanic	14 (4.0)	26 (4.0)	12 (2.7)
Other			
Ethnicities	5 (1.4)	25 (3.8)	17 (3.9)
Grade—*n* (%)			
9th grade	115 (32.9)	239 (36.5)	146 (33.0)
10th grade	87 (24.9)	154 (23.5)	150 (33.9)
11th grade	81 (23.1)	110 (16.8)	106 (24.0)
12th grade	67 (19.1)	151 (23.1)	40 (9.0)

[a] Exploratory Factor-Analytic Subsample.

[b] Confirmatory Factor-Analytic Subsample.

[c] Cross-Validation Subsample.

CFA procedures ranged from moderate to high (i.e., .50 to .92) and were statistically significant. Table 6.1 shows demographic information for the instrument development and initial validation samples. Table 6.2 shows normative data (i.e., means and standard deviations) for the instrument validation sample, the cross-validation sample, and a number of studies that have examined the psychometric properties of the RFL-A. Additional information on the development and validation of the RFL-A can be found in Osman et al. (1998).

As shown in Table 6.2, the mean RFL-A total score for the combined non-clinical instrument development sample ($M = 4.74$, $SD = 0.92$) was similar to the mean RFL-A score for the cross-validation nonclinical (M = 4.71, SD = 1.96) sample, $t(1,094)$ = .34, p = .73. As expected, the mean RFL-A score for the nonclinical cross-validation sample was significantly higher than the mean RFL-A score for the follow-up validation inpatient (M = 4.36, SD = 1.04) sample, $t(583)$ = 2.04, p < .04, Cohen's d = .20. Further examination of the descriptive statistics in Table 6.2 shows that the multiple suicide attempters who were recruited from the adolescent inpatient units had the lowest mean RFL-A (i.e., M = 3.64, SD = 1.17) score (see Gutierrez et al., 2000).

Reliability Analyses

Osman, Downs, et al. (1998) reported Cronbach α estimates for the RFL-A total and scales in the instrument development, initial validation, and cross-validation samples. In particular, results of the coefficient α estimates in Study 1 (n = 350), Study 2 (n = 654), and the cross-validation study (n = 442) demonstrated adequate estimates of internal consistency reliability for the RFL-A total and scale scores (all coefficient α estimates > .89). Similarly, Gutierrez et al. (2000) reported strong internal consistency reliability coefficients for the RFL-A scales (ranging from .92 to .94) and total (coefficient α = .97) scores in samples of adolescent psychiatric inpatients. Estimates regarding test-retest reliability for the RFL-A total and scale scores were not reported for the instrument development samples. We have addressed this limitation with data from our current adolescent inpatients (see below).

Validity Analyses

STRUCTURE OF THE RFL-A

Exploratory Factor Analysis (EFA) We conducted exploratory principal-axis factor analysis (PAF) with data from a random sample of 350 participants, drawn from the combined sample of 1,004 study participants (see Table 6.1, Study 1 and Study 2, for demographic information). The number of factors extracted was based on the eigenvalues equal to or greater than 1.0 and the scree plot criteria (Floyd & Widaman, 1995). To obtain a short and reliable measure, only items loading .40 or greater on a primary factor were retained for further analyses. Additionally, items loading on two or more factors were dropped. Using the PAF method with oblimin rotation, we retained five interpretable factors. All the factors met the preestablished criteria for meaningful retention and interpretation. The intercorrelations among the factors ranged from .42 to .62, suggesting moderate interrelationships. Together the five factors accounted for 64.8% of the variance in the RFL-A item scores.

Confirmatory Factor Analyses (CFA) In addition, Osman, Downs, et al. (1998) conducted confirmatory factor analytic (CFA) studies to evaluate the fit of the

Table 6.2

Normative Data for the Reasons for

Living Inventory–Adolescents (ages 14–18 years)

Sample Demographic	N	Mean	SD
Instrument Development Sample			
(Osman, Downs, et al., 1998)			
High School Combined Sample	654	4.74	0.92
High School, Girls	354	4.71	0.87
High School, Boys	300	4.77	0.98
Cross-Validation Sample			
(Osman, Downs, et al., 1998)			
High School Combined Sample	442	4.71	1.96
Follow-up Validation Sample			
(Osman, Downs, et al., 1998)			
Psychiatric Inpatients Combined Sample	143	4.36	1.04
Suicide Attempters	71	3.70	0.90
Psychiatric Control	72	5.00	0.71
High School Nonclinical Control	71	5.14	0.55

Other Investigations with the Reasons for Living Inventory-Adolescents

	N	Mean	SD
Adolescent Psychiatric Inpatients			
(Gutierrez et al., 2000)			
Nonsuicidal Inpatients	110	5.15	0.67
First-time Suicide Attempters	32	4.16	1.02
Multiple Suicide Attempters	64	3.64	1.17
Psychiatric Outpatients	100	4.70	0.90
(Schulein & Switaj, 2005)			
Medical Patients	12	5.00	1.00
(Schulein & Switaj, 2005)			
General Outpatients	99	4.90	0.80
(Schulein & Switaj, 2005)			

five-factor solution of the RFL-A data provided by (a) a subset of the study participants (Study 2; $n = 654$) and (b) a cross-validation sample (Study 3; $n = 442$). The five-factor oblique model was evaluated against the one-factor model for adequacy of fit. We used multiple fit estimates to evaluate the fit of each model to the sample data: the Robust relative χ^2 value of 2 or less, the normed fit index (NFI) and nonnormed fit index (NNFI) of .90 or higher, the Robust comparative fit index (Robust-CFI) of .90 or higher, and the root-mean-square error of approximation (RMSEA) value of .05 or less (see Hu, Bentler, & Kano, 1992). All estimates were obtained using the Robust confirmatory method in the EQS for Windows 6.1 program. Results from the estimated models in both studies showed that the five-factor oblique model fit the data better than the one-factor model. Using parcels as items for the RFL-A, Gutierrez et al. (2000) reported similar strong fit estimates for the five-factor oblique model for data obtained from adolescent inpatients: Robust-χ^2/df = 1.45, Robust comparative fit index (R-CFI) = .983.

Known-Groups Validity   Osman, Downs, et al. (1998) provided initial known-groups validity for scores on the RFL-A by showing that the high school nonclinical normative samples obtained significantly higher scores that did the (a) psychiatric suicidal and (b) psychiatric nonsuicidal youth on all the RFL-A total and scale scores (see Table 6.2). Planned comparisons also showed that the psychiatric nonsuicidal inpatients had significantly higher RFL-A total and scale scores than did the psychiatric suicidal inpatients (all p values < .05). In 2000, Gutierrez et al. reported that the nonsuicidal RFL-A total scores ($M = 5.15$, $SD = 0.67$) were substantially higher than were scores obtained for (a) the first-suicide attempter [$t(140) = 6.47$, $p < .001$, Cohen's $d = 1.30$], or the multiple suicide attempter [$t(172) = 10.84$, $p < .001$, Cohen's $d = 1.70$] groups. The means and standard deviations of the RFL-A for other adolescent samples, including psychiatric outpatients and medical patients, are presented in Table 6.2. Normative data have not been reported for adolescents with a range of psychiatric diagnoses including major depression and conduct disorders.

Concurrent-Convergent Validity   Pearson correlation analyses were conducted by Osman, Downs, et al. (1998) to examine evidence of concurrent validity for the RFL-A total and scale scores. Data from the high school cross-validation sample were used to conduct these analyses. Results of the analyses demonstrated good concurrent validity estimates. In particular, in the analyses that included 442 adolescents, moderately and negatively significant relations were found between the RFL-A total scores and scores on the following self-report measures: (a) the Suicide Probability Scale ($r = -.60$, SPS; Cull & Gill, 1982), (b) the Beck Hopelessness Scale ($r = -.65$, BHS; Beck, Weissman, Lester, & Trexler, 1974), and (c) the Depression subscale of the Brief Symptom Inventory ($r = -.48$, BSI; Derogatis, 1992).

In a study that examined further validity estimates for the RFL-A in adolescent psychiatric inpatients, Gutierrez et al. (2000) found moderate and significant correlations between scores on the RFL-A total scale and scores on selected content scales of the Minnesota Multiphasic Personality Inventory for Adolescents (MMPI-A; Butcher et al., 1992). Specifically, the RFL-A total scores were moderately and significantly correlated with the MMPI-A adolescent depression ($r = -.41$), MMPI-A adolescent alienation ($r = -.45$), and MMPI-A adolescent family problems ($r = -.44$) scales; all p values $< .05$. The RFL-A total scale score has been shown to be correlated moderately and significantly with total scores on the Inventory of Suicide Orientation-30 ($r = -.57$, $p < .01$; ISO-30, King & Kowalchuk, 1994) (see Osman et al., 2005).

Concurrent-Discriminant Validity In a path-analytic model, Osman, Downs, et al. (1998) demonstrated that the relation between scores on the RFL-A and a measure of suicide probability (coefficient $= -.60$) was substantially higher than the relation with a measure of general distress (coefficient $= -.42$). Additionally, in a multivariate logistic regression analysis, Osman, Downs, et al. found that the RFL-A score was more associated with the Suicide Probability (SPS; Cull & Gill, 1982) than with the Beck Hopelessness Scale (BHS; Beck et al., 1974) in differentiating between the responses of high school nonsuicidal and psychiatric suicidal groups. In combination, scores on these two scales correctly classified 88.7% of the nonsuicidal youth as nonsuicidal and 87.3% of the suicidal youth as suicidal.

Diagnostic Utility/Performance Gutierrez et al. (2000) used receiver operating characteristic (ROC) curve procedure to examine the diagnostic performance of the RFL-A in adolescent psychiatric inpatients. In particular, in the analyses that included scores on the RFL-A and the Beck Hopelessness Scale (BHS; Beck et al., 1974), these researchers found that the RFL-A cut-off score of 4.63 was most useful in maximizing sensitivity (76.6%), specificity (90.4%), positive predictive power (90.7%), and negative predictive power (75.8%) when differentiating between suicidal and nonsuicidal adolescents. These estimates have not been replicated with data from independent adolescent samples.

Predictive Validity It is also important to note that scores on the RFL-A total scale have well-established predictive validity in adolescent inpatient samples. In particular, in Chapter 11, we present data pointing to the ability of scores on the RFL-A to predict suicide reattempts (AUC $= .86$) and continuous suicide ideation (estimate $= -.30$, $p < .01$) two months following hospitalization to an inpatient psychiatric unit.

The Current Investigation—*Psychometric Properties of the Reasons for Living Inventory for Adolescents (RFL-A)*

Data Sets

Data for these analyses were drawn from our high school and adolescent inpatient data sets developed over three years. Detailed descriptions of the settings and procedures have been presented in Chapter 5.

Method

PARTICIPANTS

High School Nonclinical Sample Data from a randomly selected sample of 451 high school students (199 boys, 252 girls) who participated in the Personal Adjustment Screening Survey (PASS) within the last three years were used in this study. Participants ranged in age from 13 to 19 years (M age = 15.78, SD = 1.51). The sample was composed of 193 (42.8%) Caucasian, 146 (32.4%) African American, 47 (10.4%) Hispanic American, and 10 (2.2%) other ethnic groups; 12.2% did not volunteer ethnic/race information. Data from this sample were used to (a) examine gender differences in the RFL-A total and scale scores and (b) evaluate invariance of the five-factor solution of the RFL-A across nonclinical and clinical samples.

Adolescent Psychiatric Inpatient Validation Sample-I We included a total of 248 (129 boys, 119 girls) adolescent psychiatric inpatients in the current study. There was no significant difference between boys (M age = 15.72, SD = 0.94 years) and girls (M age = 15.56, SD = 1.00 years) in terms of age, $t(246)$ = 1.28, p = .20. The ethnic composition was as follows: 82.3% Caucasian, 6.5% African American, 4% Hispanic American, and 7.2% indicated other. Regarding diagnoses, 24.6% met the *Diagnostic and Statistical Manual of Mental Disorders* (DSM-IV-TR; American Psychiatric Association, 2000) criteria for mood disorders, 31.5% conduct disorder, 19.4% oppositional defiant disorder, 11.7% adjustment disorder, 3.2% anxiety disorder, and 9.7% other disorders.

Adolescent Psychiatric Inpatient Validation Sample-II This sample included 183 boys (M age = 15.66, SD = 0.96 years) and 205 girls (M age = 15.53, SD = 1.00 years). These participants were recruited to examine invariance of the five-factor structure of the RFL-A across the high school and adolescent inpatients. The sample was composed of 74.5% Caucasian, 18.8% African American, 3.4% Hispanic American, 2% Asian American, and 1.3% other. These participants completed a brief background information questionnaire and the RFL-A.

Adolescent Psychiatric Inpatient Sample: Test-Retest This sample included 24 boys (M age = 15.58, SD = 0.93 years) and 26 girls (M age = 16.00, SD = 0.94 years) from consecutive admissions to two inpatient units of a state psychiatric hospital. With regard to ethnicity, 80% were Caucasian, 6% African American, 4% Hispanic American, and 10% other. The majority of the participants met the DSM-IV-TR diagnostic criteria for mood disorders (44%), 24% conduct disorder, 10% oppositional defiant disorder, and 22% other psychiatric disorders. Boys and girls were similar in age, $t(48) = 1.58, p = .12$.

To assess estimates of test-retest reliability, all the participants completed the RFL-A at the time of admission to the unit (Time 1) and after a 2-week interval (Time 2).

MEASURES AND PROCEDURES

All the participants completed a brief demographic information questionnaire and the RFL-A following the informed consent or assent procedures. *The adolescent psychiatric inpatient validation sample-I* completed the 4-item Suicidal Behaviors Questionnaire-Revised (SBQ-R; Osman et al., 2001), the 21-item Beck Depression Inventory-II (BDI-II; Beck, Steer, & Brown, 1996), the 21-item Beck Anxiety Inventory (BAI; Beck & Steer, 1990), the 20-item Beck Hopelessness Scale (BHS; Beck et al., 1974), and the 36-item Suicide Probability Scale (SPS; Cull & Gill, 1982). Scores on these self-report instruments were used as validation measures to examine further psychometric properties for the RFL-A.

Results

GENDER DIFFERENCES – RFL-A TOTAL AND SCALE SCORES

A multivariate analysis of variance (MANOVA) was conducted with scores on the five RFL-A scales as dependent measures and gender as the independent variable. The overall MANOVA was statistically significant, $t(449) = 2.73, p < .007$, Cohen's $d = .26$ (small effect size). Follow-up one-way analysis of variance (ANOVA) showed significant gender differences on only one RFL-A scale. In particular, girls scored significantly higher than did boys on the RFL-A peer acceptance and support scale ($M = 5.18, SD = 1.13$ v. $M = 4.89, SD = 1.11$, respectively), $p < .007$. An independent samples t-test, using the RFL-A total score as the dependent variable, showed that boys and girls did not differ significantly on the total score of this inventory. Thus, we did not examine gender differences separately in the subsequent analyses.

CONFIRMATORY INVARIANCE ANALYSES

We conducted multi-sample confirmatory factor analysis (CFA) to examine whether the five-factor oblique solution would be invariant across the nonclinical high school ($N = 451$) and the psychiatric inpatient validation sample-II ($N = 388$) data. We used the EQS for Windows 6.1 (Bentler & Wu, 2005) program to carry out the analyses. We specified items to load on their respective factors and we set the variance of each factor at 1.0. The factors were allowed to correlate. The following contemporary fit estimates were used to evaluate the adequacy of each model to the sample data: Relative robust χ^2 (SB-χ^2/df) estimate of 2 or less, a robust comparative fit index (R-CFI) of .90 or higher, and a root-mean-square error of approximation (RMSEA) value of .06 or less. Results of the related fit estimates are presented in Table 6.3. The preliminary baseline analyses showed that the five-factor model was an adequate fit for each sample's data. Likewise, the five-factor model was invariant across the groups as indicated by strong goodness-of-fit estimates after all restraints were imposed on the factor loadings and factor intercorrelations. Overall, the structure of the RFL-A is similar for both the nonclinical and clinical samples.

TEST-RETEST RELIABILITY ESTIMATES

Results showed that the mean score for the test-retest sample at Time 1 on the RFL-A was 4.80 (SD = 0.92) and the mean Time 2 score was 5.01 (SD = 0.85). This change in mean scores was statistically significant, $t(49)$ = 2.17, p < .035, Cohen's d = -.31 (small effect size). Overall, the reliability estimate for this change over the two-week interval was statistically significant, r_{tt} = .70, p < .001. The test-retest estimates for the five scale scores were as follows: family alliance (r_{tt} = .73, p < .001), suicide-related concerns (r_{tt} = .69, p < .001), self-acceptance (r_{tt} = .45, p < .001), peer acceptance and support (r_{tt} = .76, p < .001), and future optimism (r_{tt} = .31, p < .03). As expected, increases were observed in the mean RFL-A total and scale scores because all the study participants were being successfully treated following admission to the respective units.

OTHER VALIDITY ESTIMATES: RFL-A AS CRITERION VARIABLE

In previous investigations, it has been established that the RFL-A has good evidence of internal consistency, convergent and discriminant validity, and structural validity. In the current study, we have shown invariance of the structure of the RFL-A as well as estimates of test-retest reliability. We used scores on the RFL-A to evaluate its performance as a criterion variable. Recall that Gutierrez et al. (2000) specified a cut-off score of 4.63 as most useful for differentiating the responses of subgroups of youth at risk for suicide-related behaviors. We used this cut-off score to develop two groups: *Protective group* composed of youth (n = 139; 77 boys, 62 girls) who obtained a mean RFL-A score of 4.63 or higher, and a *Risk group* that included youth (n = 109; 52 boys, 57 girls) who obtained a mean RFL-A score of 4.62 or less. It is important to note that we collected sample data from the same units as reported in Gutierrez et al.; we did not attempt to replicate the original cut-off scores that were established with data from these same units.

Using receiver operating characteristic (ROC) curves, we found that scores on the BDI-II (AUC = .78), BHS (AUC = .82), BAI (.72) and SPS (AUC = .82) were moderately accurate in differentiating between the

Table 6.3

Confirmatory Factor Analysis of the RFL-A: Multi-group Analysis

Fit Estimates	Clinic Sample	High School Sample	Invariance Model
SB χ^2	681.77	631.31	1,384.29
df	454	454	940
Relative Fit	1.50	1.39	1.47
R-NNFI	.971	.944	.954
R-CFI	.973	.949	.956
RMSEA	.036	.029	.034
(90%CI)	(.030, .041)	(.024, .035)	(.030, .037)

Note. SB = Satorra-Bentler, NNFI = Nonnormed fit index, CFI = comparative fit index, RMSEA = Root-mean-square error of approximation.

groups. Finally, use of the logistic regression analyses showed that the combined use of scores on the BHS (Odds Ratio = 1.17, 95% CI = 1.08, 1.28) and the SPS (Odds Ratio = 1.06, 95% CI = 1.02, 1.11) was most reliable in differentiating between the protective and risk groups.

Evaluation of the RFL-A as a Screening Measure

As noted above, scores on the RFL-A have met a number of psychometric standards. In particular, estimates of content validity were well established, the five-factor solution of this instrument has been shown to be similar across high school and inpatient samples, and estimates of test-retest reliability have been reported to be strong. In addition, we have provided normative data that support the use of the RFL-A with adolescents ages 13 to 19 years. Coefficient α estimates for the total and scale scores are high in nonclinical and clinical samples. Estimates of concurrent validity are strong, with scores showing moderate and significant links with related constructs. Scores on the RFL-A are useful in separating the responses of suicidal and non-suicidal adolescents. Estimates of predictive and criterion validity have been established. Given that these findings have not been replicated across various groups of clinical and nonclinical adolescent groups, we identify the RFL-A as a moderately useful instrument for screening purposes.

The Suicide Resilience Inventory-25

The Suicide Resilience Inventory–25 (SRI-25; Osman et al., 2004) is a 25-item self-report instrument constructed to tap three major resiliency factors that serve as buffers against suicide-related behaviors: Internal Protective, External Protective, and Emotional Stability. Each SRI-25 item is rated on a 6-point scale that ranges from 1 (*strongly disagree*) to 6 (*strongly agree*). This inventory was created to be used in clinical and nonclinical settings with adolescents and adults ages 14 and older. As a trait-like instrument, all the items evaluate responses in terms of personal attitudes, beliefs, or feelings.

Theoretical Foundations of the SRI-25

The SRI-25 was designed to evaluate a range of available adaptive responses of an individual when faced with suicide-related thoughts and situations. The dimensions of the SRI-25 reflect three global aspects of the resiliency construct (e.g., see Olsson, Bond, Burns, Vella-Brodricks, & Sawyer, 2003; Rutter, 1987; Seligman & Csikszentmihalyi, 2000; Smith, 1999). Following the recommendations of Olsson et al. (2003), Osman et al. (2004) conceptualized suicide resilience as "the perceived ability, resources, or competence to regulate suicide-related thoughts, feelings, and attitudes" (p. 1351). Content validity estimates were consistent with contemporary recommendations for developing psychometrically sound self-report instruments (e.g., Haynes, Richard, & Kubany, 1995). The three dimensions of this inventory were empirically derived. We describe these dimensions as follows: the Internal Protective facet is represented by 9 items, and it evaluates protective beliefs or feelings about the self and a number of life circumstances. Examples of items include being cheerful about the self as well as having the feeling of being emotionally strong (e.g., Item 2, "Most of the time, I see myself as a happy person"). The External Protective facet is composed of 8 items and evaluates the ability to recognize as well as use all the available external resources when faced with stress-laden situations. Examples of items include the ability to seek out familial others for support as well as the ease in talking about thoughts and feelings with others (e.g., Item 15, "I can ask for emotional support from people close to me if I were to think about killing myself"). The Emotional Stability dimension is defined by 8 items. The contents of these items relate to the ability to regulate suicide-related thoughts and behavior when confronted with distressing events (e.g., Item 8, "I can resist thoughts of killing myself when I feel emotionally hurt").

Instrument Development and Related Norms

We used data from clinical and nonclinical settings to develop and validate scores on the SRI-25. In particular, the normative sample included adolescents and adults in clinical and nonclinical settings. This instrument is new, and unlike the RFL-A (Osman, Downs, et al., 1998), it has not been used extensively with other clinical and nonclinical samples. Detailed information related to steps in the construction and development of the SRI-25 can be found in Osman et al. (2004).

As a brief overview, the SRI-25 items were generated from multiple sources including review of the extant protective factor literature and existing screening instruments. Items were generated to be relevant and representative of the prespecified dimensions of the instrument. The initial pool of 72 items was evaluated for item redundancy, wording, and grammatical structure. The 52 items that were retained following the item-screening procedure were administered to a sample of 168 psychiatric inpatients and high school adolescents and adults ranging in age from 14 to 32 years. Data were submitted to principal components analyses with oblimin rotation to retain the final 25-item version of the instrument. Formal content analyses were conducted, followed by the administration of the 25 items to the normative sample of 540 participants with a mean age of 18.7 years (SD = 2.8). The mean total SRI-25 score for the combined sample was 5.36 (SD = 0.70). The mean score for the subscales were as follows: Internal Protective, M = 5.22 (SD = 0.80); External Protective, M = 5.32 (SD = 0.84); and Emotional Stability, M = 5.56 (SD = 0.73). For adolescents ages 14 to 19 (n = 318), the mean total SRI-25 score was 5.27 (SD = 0.78). The mean score for the subscales were as follows: Internal Protective, M = 5.13 (SD = 0.88); External Protective, M = 5.22, (SD = 0.92); and Emotional Stability, M = 5.48 (SD = 0.83). Normative data were not reported separately for nonclinical and clinical adolescents ages 14 to 18 years. We address that concern in this chapter.

Overview of the Current Research

Because the initial normative and psychometric properties of the SRI-25 were not reported comprehensively for adolescents, we focus our attention in this chapter on addressing a number of psychometric concerns for this instrument. In particular, we present data in support of (a) factor structure, (b) estimates of internal consistency, (c) known-groups validity, and (d) criterion-related validity for the SRI-25 in adolescent clinical and nonclinical samples.

Study 1—*Confirmatory Factor Analysis*
Method

PARTICIPANTS, MEASURE, AND PROCEDURES

High School Sample: Confirmatory Factor Analysis Participants included 136 boys (Mean age = 15.79, SD = 1.40 years) and 164 girls (Mean age = 15.66, SD = 1.35 years) recruited from two high schools in the Midwest. The mean age of the participants was 15.72 years (SD = 1.37). Participants ranged in age from 14 to 19 years. Of these, 52% were Caucasian, 29.6% African American, 9% Hispanic American, 1.7% Asian American, and 7.7% other ethnic groups. All the participants completed informed consent following descriptions of the study procedures by the trained undergraduate research assistants.

Adolescent Psychiatric Inpatient Sample: Confirmatory Factor Analysis Participants were consecutive admissions to two adolescent units of a state psychiatric hospital. The sample included 107 boys (Mean age = 15.50, SD = 0.97 years) and 143 girls (Mean age = 15.51, SD = 0.96 years). Boys and girls were similar in age, $t(248)$ = .05, p = .96. The sample was composed of 51.6% Caucasian, 25.6% African American, 17.6% Hispanic American, 4.8% Asian American, and 0.4% other ethnic groups. Review of the medical charts showed that 30% met primary diagnostic criteria for major depressive disorder, 6% adjustment disorder, 24% oppositional defiant disorder, 24.4% conduct disorder, and 15.6% anxiety-related disorders. All diagnoses were based on the Diagnostic and Statistical Manual of Mental Disorders (DSM-IV-TR; American Psychiatric Association, 2000) criteria and were derived by the multidisciplinary treatment team. Participants also provided formal consent for participation in this project.

All participants completed a brief demographic information questionnaire and the 25-item Suicide Resilience Inventory-25. No participant declined invitation to participate in the project. The research assistants checked each completed questionnaire to ensure that the items were completed correctly; thus, there were no missing data.

Results

PRELIMINARY ANALYSES

Table 6.4 shows the means, standard deviations, and reliability estimates of the scores on the SRI-25 total and subscales for the high school and psychiatric inpatient study participants. We evaluated the internal consistency reliability estimates of the total and subscales of the SRI-25 for the separate high school and inpatient samples. All the Cronbach α estimates were high.

CONFIRMATORY FACTOR ANALYSIS: INVARIANCE ANALYSES

We conducted simultaneous confirmatory factor analysis (CFA) to evaluate the fit of the 3-factor oblique solution of the SRI-25 reported in Osman et al. (2004) for the instrument normative sample. We used the EQS for Windows 6.1 program (Bentler & Wu, 2005) to perform the robust maximum likelihood analysis. We used several goodness-of-fit estimates to judge the adequacy of the model to the sample data. As can be seen in Table 6.5, the 3-factor oblique model indicated adequate fit to each sample data. When the model was imposed simultaneously on the high school and inpatient sample data, strong evidence was obtained for the invariance of this model for both samples, Robust-comparative fit index = .927, root-mean-square error of approximation (RMSEA) value = .048 (90% CI = .042, .054). In the analyses involving the high

Table 6.4

Descriptive Statistics and Reliability Analyses of the SRI-25 for the Study Samples

Scale	Mean	SD	Range	Alpha Estimate	Mean Inter-Item Correlation
Combined Sample High School (n = 300)					
Internal Protective	4.94	1.01	1.00 – 6.00	.94	.64
Emotional Stability	5.18	1.07	0.88 – 6.00	.92	.59
External Protective	5.07	.96	1.13 – 6.00	.86	.43
Total Score	5.06	.88	1.16 – 6.00	.95	.43
High School Boys (n = 136)					
Internal Protective	4.92	1.05	1.00 – 6.00	.94	.64
Emotional Stability	5.23	.97	2.13 – 6.00	.89	.50
External Protective	5.05	.96	1.50 – 6.00	.84	.40
Total Score	5.06	.87	2.00 – 6.00	.94	.39
High School Girls (n = 164)					
Internal Protective	4.95	.97	1.11 – 6.00	.93	.60
Emotional Stability	5.13	1.14	0.88 – 6.00	.93	.62
External Protective	5.08	.97	1.13 – 6.00	.87	.46
Total Score	5.05	.89	1.16 – 6.00	.95	.43
Psychiatric Inpatient Boys (n = 107)					
Internal Protective	4.87	1.03	1.00 – 6.00	.93	.60
Emotional Stability	4.93	1.10	1.63 – 6.00	.93	.62
External Protective	4.96	.99	1.00 – 6.00	.90	.53
Total Score	4.92	.95	1.36 – 6.00	.96	.49
Psychiatric Inpatient Girls (n = 143)					
Internal Protective	4.42	1.14	1.33 – 6.00	.94	.64
Emotional Stability	4.52	1.19	1.25 – 6.00	.94	.66
External Protective	4.75	1.04	1.38 – 6.00	.89	.50
Total Score	4.56	1.01	1.60 – 6.00	.96	.49

school sample data, the coefficient RHO (a measure of reliability) was high, .958. Similarly, the RHO estimate for the model as assessed with the inpatient sample data was high, .970.

Study 2

The purpose of the analyses in this portion of the chapter is to present additional reliability and validity information for scores on the SRI-25 (Osman et al., 2004). As we noted previously, we have not presented extensive psychometric information for this newly developed instrument. Accordingly, we evaluated the reliability, factor structure, and criterion-related validity of scores on SRI-25 in independent cross-validation samples of high school and adolescent psychiatric inpatients. In particular, we reexamined evidence or estimates of internal consistency and invariance of the 3-factor structure (Internal Protective, Emotional Stability, and External Protective) across nonclinical and inpatient adolescents. In addition, we examined evidence of criterion-related validity.

Method

PARTICIPANTS, MEASURES, AND PROCEDURES

Participants were recruited from a Midwestern high school and two adolescent psychiatric inpatient units. All participants volunteered to complete the measures following the formal informed consent and assent procedures. The research packet included a brief background information questionnaire, the 25-item SRI-25 (Osman et al., 2004), the 4-item Suicidal Behaviors Questionnaire—Revised (SBQ-R; Osman et al., 2001), and the 20-item Beck Hopelessness Scale (BHS; Beck, Weissman, Lester, & Trexler, 1974).

High School Cross-Validation Sample This nonclinical comparison group was composed of 102 boys and 104 girls (age range = 14 to 18 years). Boys (Mean age = 16.43, SD = 1.38 years) were similar in age to girls (Mean age = 16.38, SD = 1.45 years), $t(204)$ = .29, p =.78. With regard to ethnicity, 81.6% were Caucasian, 7.8% African American, 2.4% Hispanic, 1% Asian American, and 7.2% other.

Psychiatric Adolescent Inpatient Cross-Validation Sample This sample (87 boys, 109 girls) included consecutive admissions to two adolescent psychiatric inpatient units of a Midwestern state hospital. Using chart reports and clinical consultation with caseworkers, we identified two subgroups: (1) Physical/Sexual Abuse plus Suicide Attempters (37 boys, 56 girls) and (2) Physical/Sexual Abuse plus Nonattempters (50 boys, 53 girls). All formal DSM-IV-TR diagnoses, including internalizing (e.g., major depressive disorder) and externalizing (e.g., conduct disorders) problems were assessed by the mul-

Table 6.5

Confirmatory Factor Analysis of the SRI-25: Multi-group Analysis

Fit Estimates	High School Sample ($n = 451$)	Clinic Sample ($n = 388$)	Invariance Model
SB χ^2	484.08	410.45	930.96
df	272	272	569
Relative Fit	1.78	1.51	1.64
R-NNFI	.890	.950	.922
R-CFI	.900	.955	.927
RMSEA	.051	.045	.048
(90%CI)	(.044, .058)	(.036, .054)	(.042, .054)

Note. SB = Satorra-Bentler, NNFI = Nonnormed fit index, CFI = comparative fit index, RMSEA = Root-mean-square error of approximation.

tidisciplinary assessment and treatment team members. The sample ranged in age from 14 to 17 years (*M* age = 15.41, *SD* = 0.99 years). Of these, the majority were Caucasian (77.6%), 14.3% were African American, 3.1% were Hispanic American, 2% were Asian American, and 3.1% were other.

Results

INTERNAL CONSISTENCY RELIABILITY ESTIMATES

Results of the coefficient α estimates were excellent within the high school sample (SRI-Internal Protective = .94; SRI-External Protective = .92, and SRI-Emotional Stability = .94) and the psychiatric inpatient sample (SRI-Internal Protective = .94, SRI-External Protective = .90, and SRI-Emotional Stability = .93). Estimates for the total SRI-25 scale scores were .96 and .95 in the high school and clinic samples, respectively.

CONFIRMATORY FACTOR ANALYSIS (CFA)

We conducted simultaneous CFA to evaluate invariance of the 3-factor solution in the high school and inpatient samples. Given the distributional properties of responses at the item levels (nonnormal), we developed parcels to serve as items (see Floyd & Widaman, 1995). We used exploratory factor analysis to assign two or three item scores to a parcel; then we computed the mean score to serve as items. There were 9 parcels for the 3-factor SRI-25 solution. We used the Robust estimation procedure in EQS for Windows 6.1 (Bentler & Wu, 2005) to conduct the analyses.

Results of the baseline models provided excellent fit estimates within each sample: clinical inpatient sample, SB-χ^2 = 28.45, df = 24, p = .24; normed fit index (NFI) = .969, comparative fit index (CFI) = .995, root-mean-square error of approximation (RMSEA) = .031 (90% CI = .000, .068); and the high school sample, SB-χ^2 = 19.17, df = 24, p = .74; NFI = .963, CFI = 1.00. The reliability estimates of the models were adequate, RHO = .953 for the clinical inpatient sample, and .964 for the high school sample.

Results of the invariance analyses showed that when no constraints were imposed on any aspect of the model, we found that the model could be replicated across the groups, SB-χ^2 = 45.36, df = 48, p = .58; NFI = .965, CFI = 1.00. The reliability of the model was also high, RHO = .964. The intercorrelations among the factors ranged from .779 to .822. The R-squared estimates ranged from .566 to .863. When equality constraints were imposed on the factor loadings and factor correlations, the model again attained excellent fit to the data, SB-χ^2 = 71.78, df = 54, p = .06 ns; NFI = .944, CFI = .981, and RMSEA = .029 (90% CI = .000, 0.45). The obtained RHO estimate was .939, and the R-squared values ranged from .685 to .849. Overall, these analyses show that the 3-factor solution is adequate for use with clinic and nonclinic adolescents.

CRITERION-RELATED VALIDITY ANALYSES

The initial one-way Multivariate Analysis of Variance (MANOVA) including the high school and inpatient sample data showed that scores on the SRI-25 scales were useful in differentiating between the groups, Pillai's Trace = 0.12, p <.001. Post hoc comparisons indicated that the high school sample obtained significantly higher scores than did the clinic samples on the Emotional Stability (M = 5.36, SD = 0.95 v. M = 4.87, SD = 0.99; Cohen's d = .62) and the Internal Protective (M = 5.07, SD = 0.96 v. M = 4.69, SD = 1.06; Cohen's d = .38) scale scores. In addition, the mean total SRI-25 score for the high school youth (M = 5.15, SD = 0.89) was significantly higher than those obtained from the adolescent inpatient samples (M = 4.76, SD = 0.94), Cohen's d = .43.

In the analyses involving the three groups (high school, abuse plus suicide attempts, and abuse without suicide attempts), the overall MANOVA was also significant, Wilks's λ = .736, p < .001. Pairwise comparisons showed that in each comparison, youth who were identified as abuse plus suicidal scored lower on the SRI-25 mean total and subscales when compared with the high school nonclinical samples, all p values < .001, as well as with the abuse without suicide attempts group, $t(194)$ = 8.52, p < .001.

LOGISTIC REGRESSION ANALYSES

We conducted logistic regression analyses to evaluate further the relative contributions of the mean SRI-25 total score to the differentiation of the clinic sample (coded as 1) and high school youth (coded as 0). The SRI-25 and the BHS total scores were used in this analysis. We found that scores on only the SRI-25 were statistically useful in differentiating between the groups, estimate = -.520, SD = .150, p < .001; odds-ratio = 0.60, 95% CI = 0.44, 0.798. Odds-ratio (OR) is a measure (of effect size) that is typically used to express the likelihood of a clinically relevant event occurring in one risk group (e.g., suicidal) relative to another (nonrisk) group. In logistic regression analyses, the confidence interval (i.e., range of scores around the OR) is frequently interpreted for clinically relevant effects because of problems with interpreting the magnitudes of ORs. In particular, intervals that include 1.0 are interpreted to make nonsubstantive contributions because the probability of the event occurring is simply multiplied by 1. In this case, a decrease in SRI-25 scores indicates that probability of being correctly classified in the clinical group is substantially increased because the OR is less than 1.0 and the CI does not contain 1.0. So, technically speaking, high scores on the SRI-25 should not be interpreted as "clinically useful" (i.e., correctly classified in the clinical group) because it is a measure of the protective factor of resiliency, and hence higher scores increase the probability of being classified in the nonclinical (i.e., low suicide risk) group.

Evaluation of the SRI-25 as a Screening Measure

We have extended work with the SRI-25 by examining its reliability and validity in independent adolescent samples. Estimates of internal consistency were adequate. Results of the CFAs showed that the 3-factor solution of the SRI-25 could be replicated across adolescent nonclinical and clinical samples. Results of the criterion-related validity analyses showed strong support for the construct validity of the SRI-25. The SRI-25 also contributes to the assessment literature because of its ability to differentiate between clinical and nonclinical samples when used with the BHS. Additional studies are being conducted to establish cut-off scores for the SRI-25. This instrument should be used with caution as it has limited reliability and validity estimates in the extant literature; however, we are encouraged by these preliminary results. Accordingly, we invite clinical researchers to evaluate the structure and psychometric properties of this instrument in clinical and nonclinical adolescent samples.

Concluding Thoughts

As in Chapter 5, we have presented an extensive amount of psychometric information about two self-report measures. In this case, both measures were developed by our research group, and we have conducted the vast majority of the evaluations of them. We have established extensive evidence in support of the RFL-A, and within the cautions already provided, are quite comfortable recommending its use as an addition to a screening protocol. The SRI-25 shows great promise as a screening instrument, but due to its recent development and relative lack of critical evaluation, we believe it is best considered a research (rather than clinical) instrument at this point. Unlike the measures reviewed in the previous chapter, the RFL-A and SRI-25 tap into a very different but equally important assessment domain—namely, protective factors. It is our belief, supported by research, that the best means to assess a given adolescent's likelihood of engaging in suicide-related behaviors is to view their risk profile in the context of their counterbalancing protective factors. Both of the measures presented in this chapter can be useful in elucidating protective elements in an adolescent's life.

For the individual engaged in clinical assessment or risk-screening activities, the RFL-A has several advantages. The brief set of items can generate responses in 5-10 minutes via circled answers. The instructions are clear, and we have observed very little confusion on the part of adolescents who have completed it over the years. Scoring and interpretation are also fast and easy. The details of both are provided in Chapter 8. The primary disadvantage is that independent evaluations of the psychometric properties of the measure are just now beginning to be conducted. We hope that the data presented in this chapter will motivate other clinical researchers to take on this task. Researchers wishing to work with the SRI-25 can also obtain detailed scoring and interpretation instructions in Chapter 8.

It is possible to gather information about protective factors against adolescent suicide through the use of the RFL-A and the SRI-25. It is our belief that gathering this information is an essential component of suicide assessment activities. In Chapter 7 we will introduce readers to two measures designed to simultaneously assess risk and protective factors, a process that yields a different sort of information than can be obtained from assessing the two domains independently.

Summary of Clinical Practice Implications

- The Reasons for Living Inventory for Adolescents (RFL-A) is a 32-item measure of five protective domains, appropriate for use with adolescents ages 13 to 19.

- The total score cutoff of 4.63 on the RFL-A is best at discriminating between suicidal and nonsuicidal adolescents.

- The RFL-A should be considered a moderately useful screening instrument.

- The Suicide Resilience Inventory-25 (SRI-25) is a 25-item measure of three resilience domains believed to buffer against suicide; it is meant for use in clinical and nonclinical settings with individuals 14 and older.

- Cut-off scores are not yet available for the SRI-25, but it was found to be useful in differentiating between clinical and nonclinical samples when used in conjunction with the Beck Hopelessness Scale.

- As of this writing, the SRI-25 should be considered most appropriate as a research rather than a clinical instrument.

Simultaneous Assessment of Risk and Protective Factors

The Positive and Negative Suicide Ideation Inventory
and the Multi-Attitude Suicide Tendency Scale

As we discussed in the two previous chapters, most assessment tools available today were designed to either assess risk factors or protective factors, not the two in combination. We have done work on the two combined, some of which has focused on measures for use with young adults (e.g., see Gutierrez, Osman, Kopper, Barrios, & Bagge, 2000; Osman, 1998). As far as we know, there is only one other existing measure specifically designed to assess risk and protective factors together. Therefore, in this chapter we will provide information about two measures—the Positive and Negative Suicide Ideation inventory (PANSI; Osman, Gutierrez, Kopper, Barrios, & Chiros, 1998) and the Multi-Attitude Suicide Tendency Scale (MAST; Orbach et al., 1991)—and to the extent possible provide information about their use with adolescents. We will also extrapolate from college student research conducted with these scales to make suggestions for applicability to adolescents. This is an approach we have criticized others for utilizing, but given the nature of these two measures, we believe it is justifiable, as we demonstrate below.

Before discussing the PANSI and MAST in detail, it is worth investigating why one would use these measures instead of administering separate risk and protective factor measures. The strongest argument is based on parsimony. Both measures are relatively brief and can typically be completed by adolescents in approximately five minutes. Neither of these measures needs to be purchased from a publisher, so once permission for use has been secured from the authors, the only costs associated with administration are those of reproducing the forms. We provide a copy of the PANSI in the Appendix and have always found Dr. Orbach (author of the MAST) willing to allow others to use his measure; however, for ethical reasons and professional courtesy, his permission should be sought before using the MAST. In research or applied settings with limited time and resources for gathering information, these two measures may be more practical than assembling a packet of measures consisting of those discussed in Chapters 5 and 6. Theoretically there may be advantages to assessing risk and protective factors with the same measure because of consistency in instructions, item type, and response format. It is possible that slight differences in reliability or validity of two separate measures used could lessen the value of the combined information. In other words, if the measure chosen to assess risk factors produces slightly more response error (due to the wording of items) than the protective measure, it will be difficult to determine how to differentially weight the data coming from the two scales.

Of course, one could also ask why we should bother to use anything *but* combined measures in light of these potential difficulties. Multimeasure assessments are always preferable because clinical decisions are then based on a broad range of information. In the final section of this book, we will demonstrate this point in our recommendations for tailoring the assessment protocol to different settings. At this time, let us accept that there is room for tools that assess risk and protective factors independently and in combination.

The Positive and Negative Suicide Ideation Inventory

We developed the PANSI (Osman, Gutierrez, et al., 1998) as a brief measure of risk and protective factors because of our interests in how these factors combine to influence overall level of risk and because of difficulties we continue to encounter with the MAST (Orbach et al., 1991), which will be discussed in this chapter. Initially we relied on contemporary scale construction techniques to generate potential items for the PANSI, narrow them down to a manageable number, and eventually ended up with the current 14-item scale (Osman, Gutierrez, et al., 1998).

Initial Development of the PANSI

The first studies developing and validating the PANSI used college student participants, typically less than 21 years old. In many ways, these individuals were similar to the older adolescents used to develop and validate the other measures presented in this book; therefore, we cautiously suggest applying our findings to true adolescent samples may be appropriate. We determined that the 14 PANSI items clustered nicely into 6 protective items (i.e., Positive Ideation) and 8 risk items (i.e., Negative Ideation) upon which males and females scored similarly. The modest correlations between the two factors ($n = 150$ men, 300 women; $r = -.41$) supported our belief that scores should be evaluated separately because a combined total scale score would be uninterpretable. Both factors (PANSI-positive, coefficient $\alpha = .80$; PANSI-negative, coefficient $\alpha =$

.91) were found to have acceptable reliability estimates, correlated in the expected direction with existing measures of related constructs, and were useful in predicting scores on measures of hopelessness, depressive symptoms, and psychological distress. It therefore was appropriate to conduct additional studies with the PANSI to further validate it.

Examination of PANSI for use with Adolescents

The first two studies with the PANSI were conducted with nonclinical college students for primarily practical reasons, but our real interest was in adolescents; we therefore undertook a study to validate the PANSI for use with younger individuals. This time the participants were drawn from consecutive admissions to a state psychiatric hospital and included young people with a broad range of suicidality. A total of 195 adolescents (107 boys, 88 girls, ranging in age from 14 to 17 years) completed the PANSI and a set of self-report measures that assessed history of suicide-related behavior, hopelessness, reasons for living, and current affective state (Osman et al., 2002). For all analyses, the participants were divided into one of three groups based on their current level of suicidality: suicide attempters (i.e., admitted following an attempt; $n = 55$), severely at risk (i.e., admitted due to serious suicidal ideation or threat; $n = 49$), and nonsuicidal controls (i.e., admitted for a range of psychiatric problems but no history of attempts; $n = 91$).

RELIABILITY AND VALIDITY

Reliability estimates for the Positive (coefficient $\alpha = .89$) and Negative (coefficient $\alpha = .96$) Suicide Ideation scale scores were acceptable and similar to those for the previous college student samples. Using confirmatory factor analysis (CFA), we also determined that the same items fit into the same factors as in the first two studies: Robust comparative fit index (R-CFI) = .980 and root-mean-square error of approximation (RMSEA) = .043 (90% CI = .02, .06). In other words, the PANSI validly assesses Positive and Negative Ideation in adolescents. There were again no gender differences in scores on the two factors. Scores across the three groups differed as expected, with the attempters reporting the most Negative Ideation ($M = 2.58$, $SD = 1.19$) and least Positive Ideation ($M = 2.91$, $SD = 0.95$), followed by the severely at-risk adolescents (PANSI-Negative, $M = 1.54$, $SD = 0.79$; PANSI-Positive, $M = 3.78$, $SD = 0.89$), and then the nonsuicidal controls (PANSI-Negative, $M = 1.23$, $SD = 0.38$; PANSI-Positive = 3.79, $SD = 0.88$). A subset of the participants ($n = 54$) completed the PANSI a second time, on average two weeks after the first administration, resulting in moderate correlations (PANSI-Negative, $r_{tt} = .79$; PANSI-Positive, $r_{tt} = .69$). This finding makes sense given the fluid nature of suicidality and is in keeping with other research on state measures of suicide-related behaviors and risk factors. Using logistic regression analyses, we determined that Negative Ideation scores were more useful in distinguishing between the three participant groups, but Positive Ideation scores did make a substantive contribution. For example, the scores on the combined use of the Beck Hopelessness Scale (BHS; Beck, Weissman, Lester, & Trexler, 1974— coefficient estimate = 0.21, p < .001) and the PANSI-Negative (coefficient estimate = 2.18, p < .001) were most useful in differentiating between the responses of the suicide attempters and the psychiatric inpatient controls.

Use of the PANSI with Minority Youth

These studies suggested that the PANSI is a promising research and screening tool for adolescent suicide risk and may provide more useful information than some existing measures that only assess risk factors, such as hopelessness; however, all of the samples were lacking in ethnic, cultural, and socioeconomic diversity and were drawn from similar geographic locations. We therefore had concerns about the generalizability of our findings, especially in relation to minority youth. To begin addressing these concerns, we conducted a study (Osman et al., 2003) that drew participants from two high schools in the Midwest—one urban and one in a midsized town—in addition to a small sample (n = 30) of adolescent inpatients from the same hospital used in the Osman et al. (2002) study just discussed.

Our efforts at recruiting a more diverse sample resulted in a group of 217 high school (i.e., nonclinical) participants who were approximately 78% Caucasian, 10% African American, and 12% other racial/ethnic backgrounds. The inpatient sample was a bit less diverse, as it was approximately 83% Caucasian. We again included self-report measures that assessed a range of risk and protective factors so we could further assess the validity of the PANSI. Subgroups of the sample were created based on suicide risk status. The 30 inpatients comprised the psychiatric suicide-risk subgroup (PSR), 29 of the students met criteria for inclusion in the high school suicide-risk subgroup (HSR), and the remaining 188 students were placed in the high school low-risk group (HSL).

RELIABILITY AND VALIDITY

As with the previous studies, the internal consistency reliability estimates for both Positive (coefficient α = .81) and Negative (coefficient α = .94) Ideation scales were acceptable in the high school sample. There were also no gender differences found for the two scale scores, nor were there any differences based on age or ethnicity. The three risk groups differed as expected on both scales. Specifically, the PSR group had the highest Negative Ideation (M = 2.73, SD = 0.99) and lowest Positive Ideation (M = 2.82, SD = 0.98) scores. The HSR group had lower Negative Ideation (M = 2.34, SD = 1.04) scores than the PSR group but higher scores than the HSL group (M = 1.16, SD = 0.39). The HSL group had the highest Positive Ideation (M = 3.93, SD = 0.73) scores, but the two risk groups did not differ from each other on this scale.

Diagnostic Utility/Performance To aid with interpretation of the PANSI, we utilized Receiver Operating Characteristic (ROC) analyses to determine cutoff scores. These analyses allowed us to determine specific scores on the two scales with the best sensitivity (i.e., the percentage of at-risk youth correctly identified as at-risk) and specificity (i.e., the percentage of nonsuicidal youth correctly identified as nonsuicidal). We concluded that in clinical samples, scores of 1.63 and above on the Negative Ideation scale indicate the need for further assessment. In nonclinical samples, the Negative Ideation scale score cutoff is 1.13. A score of 3.33 or lower on the Positive Ideation scale was found to have the highest sensitivity and specificity in both clinical and nonclinical samples but was determined not to be as useful in distinguishing between risk groups as Negative Ideation.

In the preceding two chapters we stressed the importance of replicating findings when evaluating the psychometric properties of new scales. Because the PANSI was not originally developed for use with adolescents and the study just summarized was the first of its kind, we determined that additional research is necessary. We describe below the results of analyses of more recent PANSI data gathered from adolescent samples.

Current Research with the PANSI Inventory

Data Sets

As with the other recent research we have presented, data for these analyses were drawn from our high school and adolescent inpatient data sets developed during a three-year period. Detailed descriptions of the settings and procedures have been presented in Chapter 5.

Method

PARTICIPANTS

High School Adolescent Sample Participants between the ages of 14 and 17 years provided written consent to participate in this project. The sample included 109 boys (M age = 16.06, SD = 1.29 years) and 95 girls (M age = 15.78, SD = 1.19 years) who were similar in age, $t(202) = 1.63$, $p = .10$. The sample was composed of 75% Caucasian, 14.2% African American, 5.9% Asian American, and 4.9% Hispanic American adolescents.

Adolescent Psychiatric Inpatient Sample Participants included 91 girls (M age = 15.35, SD = 1.12 years) and 112 boys (M age = 15.48, SD = 1.04 years). Both boys and girls were similar in age, $t(201) = .86$, $p = .39$. Of the participants, 83.3% were Caucasian, 10.8% were African American, 2% were Asian American, and 3.9% were Hispanic American. All the participants were consecutive admissions to two units of a state psychiatric institute.

MEASURES AND PROCEDURES

All the participants completed a brief demographic questionnaire and the PANSI (Osman, Gutierrez, et al., 1998) in small group sessions of approximately 30 to 35 students. In the high school setting, the questionnaire packets were administered by advanced undergraduates; each had completed at least a semester of a research experience course. In the psychiatric inpatient setting, all questionnaire packets were administered by the school teaching assistants, who had several years of training in a range of data collection procedures. The appropriate institutional research boards approved the project.

Results

RELIABILITY ANALYSES

Results of the descriptive statistics and reliability analyses are presented in Table 7.1. As shown in the table, the Cronbach α estimates were high for the PANSI-Positive and PANSI-Negative scales scores in the separate high school and inpatient samples (all the coefficient α values > .80). In addition, we have included the related 95% confidence intervals and mean inter-item correlations for potential comparisons with data from other samples.

CONFIRMATORY FACTOR ANALYSES

Baseline Models   Separate confirmatory factor analyses (CFAs) were conduced using the high school and the inpatient sample data. In estimating the fit of the 2-factor solution, Items 2, 6, 8, 12, 13, and 14 were constrained to load on the PANSI-Positive factor, and Items 1, 3, 4, 5, 7, 9, 10, and 11 were forced to load on the PANSI-Negative factor. The variance of each factor was set at 1.0, and the factors were allowed moderate correlations. Results of the fit estimates are presented in Table 7.2.

In the analyses involving data from the high school sample, all the fit estimates indicated strong fit to this sample data: Relative robust χ^2 = 1.30, robust comparative fit index = .952. The coefficient RHO of .79 indicated good estimates of internal consistency for the model. In the baseline model for the psychiatric inpatient sample data, the fit estimates showed excellent fit to the sample data, robust χ^2 = 96.35, p = .06. Similarly, the coefficient RHO estimate was high for this inpatient model, .84.

Multi-Sample Analyses   Results of the multigroup analyses are also presented in Table 7.2. Examination of the invariant result shows that when equality constraints were imposed on the factor loadings and factor intercorrelations, the model attained a good fit to the data for the high school and inpatient adolescents: robust relative χ^2 = 1.29, robust CFI = .967, and robust RMSEA = .039 (90% CI = .023, .053). Results provide strong support for the invariance of the 2-factor solution across the high school and psychiatric inpatient samples.

Table 7.1

Descriptive Statistics and Reliability Estimates of the PANSI Scales

	M	*SD*	Coefficient α	(95% CI)	Mean Inter-Item
1. High School Sample (*n* = 204)					
PANSI-P	3.76	0.83	.81	(.77, .85)	.42
PANSI-N	1.33	0.67	.94	(.93, .95)	.66
2. Psychiatric Inpatient Sample (*n* = 203)					
PANSI-P	3.55	0.98	.89	(.98, .98)	.57
PANSI-N	1.67	0.96	.96	(.95, .97)	.75

Note. PANSI-P = Positive and Negative Suicide Ideation—Positive; PANSI-N = Positive and Negative Suicide Ideation—Negative.

Table 7.2

Confirmatory Factor Analysis of PANSI items

Fit Estimates	Clinic Sample (*n* = 204)	High School Sample (*n* = 203)	Invariance Model
SB Chi-Square	96.35	98.97	215.23
df	76.0	76.0	164.0
Relative Fit	1.27	1.30	1.29
R-NNFI	.982	.942	.963
R-CFI	.985	.952	.967
RMSEA	.036	.039	.039
(90%CI)	(.000, .057)	(.009, .058)	(.023, .053)

Note. SB = Satorra-Bentler; NNFI = Nonnormed Fit Index; CFI = Comparative Fit Index; RMSEA = Root-mean-square error of approximation.

Evaluation of the PANSI as a Screening Measure

In the evaluation of scores on the PANSI, we found that this instrument has met most of the preestablished criteria specified in Chapter 5. In particular, in previous investigations, we have presented data regarding excellent estimates of internal consistency and test-retest reliability for scores on the PANSI. In addition, estimates regarding criterion-related validity (e.g., known-groups) have been satisfactory. Cut-off scores are available for using the PANSI in clinical and nonclinical settings. There does not appear to be a need for separate gender norms, and preliminary evidence suggests that age and race/ethnicity also do not affect responding. In this chapter, we have provided additional evidence for the adequacy of internal consistency. In addition, we have evaluated invariance of scores on the PANSI across high school and psychiatric inpatients. Thus, comparisons in mean PANSI scale scores should be considered appropriate; however, as with most screening self-report instruments, the PANSI should be administered concurrently with other clinically relevant measures when used in clinical and nonclinical settings.

Development and Validation of the Multi-Attitude Suicide Tendency Scale (MAST)

The MAST was originally developed by Orbach and colleagues (1991) in Israel and is based on the theory that all individuals experience differing levels of attraction to and repulsion from life and death. The authors proposed that suicidal youth could be distinguished from nonsuicidal youngsters based on the pattern of these four attitudes (Gutierrez et al., 2004). Specifically, repulsion by life (MAST-RL) is an indication of experiences of pain and stress, attraction to death (MAST-AD) is a reflection of traditional religious beliefs in a positive afterlife, attraction to life (MAST-AL) reflects high satisfaction with life and an overall sense of well-being, and repulsion by death (MAST-RD) is primarily an indication of death fears. Although significant support exists for the reliability and validity of the MAST when used with Israeli youth (e.g., Orbach, Lotem-Peleg, & Kedem, 1995; Orbach et al., 1996), psychometric support is less clear when it has been used in the U.S. (e.g., Osman, Barrios, Grittman, & Osman, 1993; Payne & Range, 1995). In several studies we have noted problems with MAST-RD in particular (Hagstrom & Gutierrez, 1998; Osman et al., 1993; Osman et al., 1994; Osman et al., 2000).

Theoretical Considerations Regarding the MAST

Despite the psychometric problems noted with the MAST, we remained interested in it because it assesses both risk and protective factors and is based on a coherent theory of youth suicide risk. The more we thought about the MAST, the more we came to believe that the difficulties we were experiencing might be due less to problems with the measure per se and more with cultural differences between Israeli youth—for whom it was originally developed—and young people in the U. S. In discussing this possibility with Orbach, he agreed that differences in religious beliefs and life experiences could well influence how youth respond to items on the MAST. To attempt to better understand cultural differences in MAST scoring, we conducted a study (Gutierrez, Osman, et al., 2004) comparing the responses of African American and Caucasian young adults. We also had data from other racial/ethnic groups but not of sufficient numbers to allow for all the planned comparisons. A number of interesting differences were found.

Racial/Ethnic Differences in MAST Scores

Although we (Gutierrez, Osman, et al., 2004) did not recruit adolescents for our study, the college student volunteers who participated were a fairly young group: 480 undergraduate students with a mean age of approximately 19. We found that the MAST-AL discriminated best between the two groups, with Caucasians scoring significantly higher than did African Americans. By contrast, African American students scored higher than Caucasians on the other three subscales. We conducted item-level analyses to better understand what might be driving these differences and concluded that the most meaningful differences were on items about family relations. In addition, results of confirmatory factor analyses conducted with the data from the two racial groups separately indicated good model fit for the Caucasian data but poor fit for the African American, i.e., Caucasian students in our sample responded to the MAST items in similar ways as youth from Israel and the U. S. included in previous research, but African American students did not. We believe this provides indirect evidence for culture explaining the psychometric differences found in previous research. We argued that for MAST-RL, the different roles of family in the two cultures likely contribute to how participants responded, whereas for MAST-AL more global factors are at play. It should be noted that the largest item-level differences were found on these two subscales.

We concluded that the MAST is not equally valid across racial and ethnic groups—at least not in this particular sample of young adults. It may be either that the relationship between the attitudes assessed by the MAST and suicide risk differ across groups or that items on the MAST are not equally culturally relevant. We strongly recommend confirmation of our results with future research and consideration of either different MAST norms based on race/ethnicity or a revision of the MAST to make it more universally culturally relevant. Readers interested in undertaking this task—or understanding the complexities of this type of research better—are directed to Chapter 10.

Current Research with the
Multi-Attitude Suicide Tendency (MAST) Scale

As noted above, we continue to experience problems with establishing strong psychometric evidence for the MAST as a brief screening self-report instrument in a number of U.S. samples. As a result, we have sought and received permission from Orbach to revise the MAST for use with clinical and nonclinical samples in the U.S. Because this project is currently in progress, in this chapter we report problems with the structural dimensions of the MAST in high school and clinical samples. In particular, we examined the adequacy of fit of the 4-factor oblique solution of the MAST in samples of high school and adolescent psychiatric inpatients.

Method

PARTICIPANTS

High School Adolescent Sample We recruited participants between the ages of 14 and 17 years for evaluating the fit of the 4-factor MAST solution. The sample was composed of 85 boys (M age = 15.73, SD = 1.49 years) and 136 girls (M age = 15.68, SD = 1.37 years); they did not differ significantly in age, $t(219)$ = .27, p = .79. This sample included approximately 71.5% Caucasian, 18.6% African American, 8.6% Hispanic American, and 1.4% Asian American students.

Adolescent Psychiatric Inpatient Sample Participants included in this analysis were 84 girls (M age = 15.49, SD = 1.00 years) and 50 boys (M age = 15.58, SD = 1.01 years). Boys and girls did not differ significantly in age, $t(132)$ = .51, p = .61. Of the participants, 85.1% were Caucasian, 9% were African American, 1.5% were Asian American, and 1.4% were Hispanic American. Participants were also consecutive admissions to two units of a state psychiatric institute.

MEASURES AND PROCEDURES

Participants completed a brief demographic questionnaire and the MAST (Orbach et al., 1991) following the informed consent procedure. In the high school setting, the questionnaire packets were administered by advanced undergraduates. These students were also trained in data collection and management procedures. In the psychiatric inpatient setting, the questionnaire packets were again administered by the school teaching assistants. We obtained institutional research board approvals from each setting before initiating data collection.

Results

CONFIRMATORY FACTOR ANALYSIS (CFA)

We conducted CFA to assess fit of the 4-factor oblique solution with the separate high school (n = 221) and the inpatient adolescent (n = 134) sample data. Because of the nonnormality of the responses on the MAST items, we used the robust estimation procedure in EQS for Windows (Bentler & Wu, 2005). As in the previous analyses, we constrained items to load on their respective factors and we allowed the factors to correlate. We set the variance of each factor at 1.0. We used commonly specified descriptive fit indexes to evaluate the adequacy of each model: Relative robust χ^2 (SB χ^2/df) value of 2 or less, a robust-comparative fit index (R-CFI) of .90 or higher, and a root-mean-square error of approximation (RMSEA) value of .06 or less (see Browne & Cudeck, 1993; Hu & Bentler, 1999). Results of the CFA are presented in Table 7.3.

Table 7.3

Confirmatory Factor Analysis of MAST Items

Fit Estimates	Clinic Sample ($n = 134$)	High School Sample ($n = 221$)	Combined Model ($n = 355$)
SB χ^2	610.68	638.26	773.78
df	399	399	399
Relative Fit	1.53	1.60	1.94
R-NNFI	.853	.881	.886
R-CFI	.865	.891	.895
RMSEA	.063	.052	.052
(90%CI)	(.053, .073)	(.044, .059)	(.046, .057)

Note. SB = Satorra-Bentler, NNFI = Nonnormed Fit Index, CFI = Comparative Fit Index, RMSEA = Root-mean-square error of approximation.

In the analyses that included data from the high school sample, the 4-factor oblique model did not provide an excellent fit to the sample data: SB χ^2/df = 1.60, R-CFI = .891, and RMSEA = . 052 (90% CI = .044, .059). Similarly, in the analyses that used the inpatient sample data, the model provided poor fit to the sample data: SB χ^2/df = 1.53, R-CFI = .865, and RMSEA = .063 (90% CI = .053, 073). Finally, as in Osman et al. (1994), the analysis was conducted with the combined high school and inpatient sample data. Again, the model provided poor fit to the sample data: SB-χ^2/df = 1.94, R-CFI = .895, RMSEA = .052 (90% CI = .046, .057). These findings provide support for our plan to continue to explore the content, structure, and psychometric properties of the MAST in U.S. adolescent samples.

Evaluation of the MAST as a Screening Measure

At this time we cannot recommend using the MAST in screening efforts in the U.S., as too many problems with the measure have yet to be resolved; however, as previously discussed, the theoretical foundation of the MAST is solid, and it has been used quite successfully for many years in Israel. We hope one day to be able to address the problems experienced when using the MAST in the U.S. and provide an update of this chapter in a subsequent edition.

Concluding Thoughts

Two self-report measures designed to concurrently assess risk and protective factors for adolescent suicide were reviewed in this chapter. Evidence in support of the PANSI and caution against use of the MAST was provided. For those who see value in this approach to assessment, the PANSI offers a valid, reliable, and easy to administer (see Chapter 8) option. In addition, one of the concerns about most existing self-report measures, lack of information about measurement equivalence (see Chapter 10), has been preliminarily addressed. Specifically, the PANSI appears to be appropriate for use with both Caucasian and African American adolescents. These findings will need to be replicated by independent researchers, but they appear promising. We believe the PANSI is a useful tool for both research and clinical settings in which brief risk assessments are being conducted.

Summary of Clinical Practice Implications

- The Positive and Negative Suicide Ideation inventory (PANSI) is a simple to administer and score 14-item measure yielding separate positive (i.e., protective) and negative (i.e., risk) scores.

- Scores on the PANSI do not differ as a function of gender, age, or race.

- The Negative Ideation cut-off score in clinical settings is 1.63 and in nonclinical settings is 1.13; adolescents at or above those scores should be further assessed.

- In both settings, a Positive Ideation cut-off score of 3.33 (i.e., scores lower than that are problematic) has been determined to indicate the need for further assessment but is of less use than the Negative Ideation cut-off.

- PANSI scores could be used to help determine which protective factors to strengthen and which risk factors to target.

- The PANSI could be used as a simple way to track treatment progress over time.

- PANSI scores should be interpreted as a reflection of the balance between the risk and protective factors present in an adolescent's life.

- The Multi-Attitude Suicide Tendency Scale (MAST), while promising as a screening instrument, should only be used in the U.S. for research purposes at this time.

Part III

Guides to the Assessment of Suicide

Administration, Scoring, and Interpretation of Questionnaires

In this chapter, we provide brief steps in the administration, scoring, and interpretation of scores on four of our self-report instruments: the Self-Harm Behavior Questionnaire (SHBQ; Gutierrez, 1998), the Positive and Negative Suicide Ideation inventory (PANSI; Gutierrez, Kopper, Barrios, & Chiros, 1998), the Reasons for Living Inventory for Adolescents (RFL-A; Osman, Downs, et al., 1998), and the Suicide Resilience Inventory-25 (SRI-25; Osman et al., 2004).

Basic Considerations for Questionnaire Administration, Scoring, and Interpretation

We consider the following guidelines to be relevant for the administration, scoring, and interpretation of scores on all our self-report instruments discussed in this chapter:

1. The instrument (e.g., the SHBQ) can be administered in a number of settings including clinical settings, such as psychiatric inpatient and correctional institutions, as well as nonclinical settings, such as high school and community outpatient settings.

2. The questionnaire can be administered by professionals or nonprofessionals who are familiar with the American Psychological Association (APA; 2002) or National Council on Measurement in Education (1999) standards for test administration and interpretation.

3. The questionnaire can be administered in small groups or individually. It is important for the person administering the questionnaire to make sure that items are completed correctly by the youth. Whenever possible, individuals who are very familiar with the respondent (e.g., friends or family members) should not administer the questionnaire.

4. The scoring and interpretation of scale scores on an instrument require formal training in mental health, psychological assessment, or basic psychometrics. In most settings, the appropriate professional to engage in this task will be a school, counseling, or clinical psychologist. When such a professional is not available, consultation should be sought from an outside individual who is qualified to interpret test data.

5. As with any screening instrument, data from other methods of assessment (e.g., psychosocial history documentation, unstructured interviews, and other self-report instruments with established psychometric properties) should be implemented concurrently when using the questionnaire for screening purposes. For example, we have found that scores on the Suicidal Behaviors Questionnaire-Revised (SBQ-R; Osman et al., 2001) provide useful demographic and convergent validity information. In Chapter 6, we have shown empirically that the RFL-A is most clinically useful as a screening instrument when it is administered concurrently with either the Beck Hopelessness Scale (Beck, Weissman, Lester, & Trexler, 1974) or the Suicide Probability Scale (SPS; Cull & Gill, 1982).

6. In most research settings, it is important to obtain informed consent (ages 14 and older) as well as assent (13-year-old youngsters) before administering the instrument.

7. It is important for the person administering the questionnaire to be familiar with the materials needed as well as the *content* of the questionnaire. Regardless of the setting, the individual respondent should have a pencil or a pen when completing a questionnaire packet.

8. Responses to the items are to be entered directly on each questionnaire by the respondent. We are not aware of any clinical or research data that suggest that exposure to these questionnaire items increases the chance for engaging in self-harmful behaviors. In fact, a recent study (Gould et al., 2005) found that asking adolescents about suicide actually decreased their scores on risk measures; however, it is important to observe the responses of the respondent when she/he is completing an instrument and take steps to make the appropriate referral if such a need is identified.

9. Each of the questionnaires contains specific instructions for completing the relevant items. Practice or sample items are not included. Questionnaires should not be administered to individuals who show difficulties understanding the instructions and related items. We have not evaluated the clinical or research effects of administering these instruments orally or to individuals with specific disabilities.

10. Because of the sensitive contents of some of the risk items, it is important to protect the privacy and confidentiality of the respondent when administering the questionnaire.

11. Because we have not developed specific procedures for handling missing items, it is important to review the completed questionnaire with the respondent to double-check that all items have been completed to allow for normative comparisons.

Measure and Administration

The Self-Harm Behavior Questionnaire (SHBQ)

The SHBQ takes approximately 15 to 20 minutes to administer and score. Exploratory principal-axis factor analysis with promax rotation identified four correlated factors (range = .30 to .48): Past Suicide Attempts (6 items), Intentional Self-Harm (5 items), Suicide Threat (6 items), and Suicide Ideation (5 items). (See Chapter 5.)

TARGET POPULATION

The Self-Harm Behavior Questionnaire was designed for use with adolescents and adults ages 13 and older to identify a number of risk factors that are associated with suicidal behavior.

SCORING PROCEDURE AND INTERPRETATION

Listed below are the individual items on the SHBQ along with instructions for how to score each. Also included are the subscale identifiers for each part of the measure. Note that there is no place on the form for respondents to indicate their current age, but this information is necessary to compute certain scores. We typically have access to other forms that contain age data (e.g., the Suicidal Behaviors Questionnaire that we have included in the Appendix). If you will be using the SHBQ in a setting where you will not be able to determine participants' ages through some other means, then it is acceptable to ask them to write their current age on the top of the form. Also, note that not all items are assigned a numeric score. Those items are intended to provide clinical information useful when interpreting participants' responses to the SHBQ. Each part of the SHBQ generates a subscale score, representing a distinct domain of suicide risk. It is also possible to calculate a total SHBQ score by adding up the individual subscales, thus generating a global risk value; however, relying solely on a total score on a multidimensional measure such as the SHBQ diminishes the advantage of examining the contribution of distinct components of suicide risk.

Cut-off Scores In interpreting the total SHBQ scores, it is important to note that in Chapter 5, the SHBQ total score of 22 was found to yield strong estimates of sensitivity (96%) and negative predictive values (96%).

SHBQ Subscales Each subscale taps a range of clinically relevant suicide-related responses:

Part A: Self-Harm Behavior (SHB)

Examples of issues assessed by this subscale include the frequency of self-harmful behavior, recent history of self-harmful behavior, and history of treatment for self-harmful behaviors.

Part B: Suicide Attempts (SA)

Examples of facets assessed by this subscale include past intentional suicide attempts, specific methods of suicide attempts, and time of most recent suicide attempt.

Part C: Suicide Threat (ST)

Examples of issues evaluated by this subscale include threats of committing suicide, potential methods for suicide-related attempts, and expectations of the responses of others to the threat.

Part D: Suicide Ideation (SI)

Examples of areas assessed by this subscale include thoughts of severe suicide-related behaviors, plans for attempting suicide, and steps taken previously to prepare to end one's life.

The specific scoring procedures are as follows:

PART A: SHB

Things you may have actually done to yourself on purpose

1. Have you ever hurt yourself on purpose?   YES   NO
(e.g., scratched yourself with finger nails or sharp object.)

(If YES, code 1 for SHB-Status; Code 0 for Control).

If **no**, go on to question #2 (Score 0 for each, Items 1 – 5.)

If **yes**, what did you do?_____

Item #1 — *Self-Harm Behavior Frequency (SHB-Freq)*

a. Approximately how many times did you do this?_____

(Blank = 0; once = 1; twice = 2; 3 times = 3; 4 or more times = 4.)

Item #2 — *Self-Harm Behavior History (SHB-Hx)*

b. Approximately when did you first do this to yourself? (*write your age*) _____

c. When was the last time you did this to yourself? (*write your age*) _____

(If a range of ages or fractional age is listed [e.g., 12½], then use the younger age or lower full number age.)

Compute <u>difference score</u>: age at last attempt (c) minus age at first attempt (b):
(Blank = 0; 0-1 year = 1; 2-3 years = 2; 4-5 years = 3; 6 or more years = 4.)

Item #3 — *Self-Harm Behavior Risk (SHB-Risk)*

> Compute <u>difference score</u>: Stated chronological-age given in background information minus age at last attempt (c):
> (Blank = 0; 1 year or less = 4; >1 year but < 2 years = 3; $\geq$2 years = 2.)

Item #4 — *Self-Harm Behavior–Disclosure (SHB-Dis) (Enter Response Circled.)*

d. Have you ever told any one that you had done these things?   YES   NO

              (1)   (2)

Item #5 — *Self-Harm Behavior–Treatment (SHB-Rx) (Enter Response Circled.)*

If **yes**, who did you tell?_____

e. Have you ever needed to see a doctor after doing these things?   YES   NO

              (3)   (2)

> **Total SHB** (sum Items 1 to 5) **Score:** _____

PART B: SA

Times you hurt yourself badly on purpose or tried to kill yourself

2. Have you ever attempted suicide?   YES   NO

If **no**, go on to question # 4. (Score 0 for each, Items 1 – 6).

If **yes**, how?_____

> (If YES, Code 1 for SA-Status; Code 0 for Control. If NO, but they report an attempt behavior, then Code 1 for SA-Status. If YES, but behavior reported was clearly not an attempt, Code 0 for Control.)

(Note: if you took pills, what kind?_____ ; how many?_____ ;
over how long a period of time did you take them? _____)

Item #1 — *Suicide Attempt Method (SA-Mth) (For multiple methods, enter highest score.)*

> (Blank = 0; Overdose (OD) on one substance, small (e.g., 10 pills or less) amount = 1; OD on the same substance, large (e.g., 10 pills or more) amount = 2; OD on 2 or more of mixed/odd substances = 3; Harm/Injury to any part of body = 3; Traumatic/lethal – hanging, suffocating, jumping from height, use of firearms = 4.)

Item #2 — *Suicide Attempt Frequency (SA-Freq)*

a. How many times have you attempted suicide? _____

> (Blank = 0; once = 1; twice = 2; 3 times = 3; 4 or more times = 4.)

Item #3 — *Suicide Attempt Risk (SA-Rsk)*

b. When was the most recent attempt? (*write your age*) _____

Compute <u>difference score</u>: Stated chronological-age given in background information minus age at most recent attempt (3b):
(Blank = 0; 1 year or less = 4; >1 year but <2 years = 3; ≥ 2 years = 2.)

c. Did you tell anyone about the attempt?   YES   NO

Who? _____

Item #4—*Suicide Attempt—Medical Treatment (SA-MRx) (Enter Response Circled.)*

d. Did you require medical attention after the attempt?   YES   NO

(4)   (2)

If yes, were you hospitalized overnight or longer?   YES   NO

How long were you hospitalized? _____

e. Did you talk to a counselor or some other person like that after your attempt?

YES   NO   Who? _____

3. If you attempted suicide, please answer the following:

Item #5—*Past Suicide Attempt Event (SA-Evn)*

a. What other things were going on in your life around the time that you tried to kill yourself? _____

(If specific things/events listed, count each separately; if response is vague [e.g. "lots of things"] or general, then only count as 1 event.)
(Blank = 0; 1 event = 1; 2 events = 2; 3 or more events = 4.)

Item #6—*Suicide Attempt-Intent (SA-Int)*

b. Did you actually want to die?   YES   NO

(3)   (1)

c. Were you hoping for a specific reaction to your attempt?   YES   NO
If **yes**, what was the reaction you were looking for? _____

d. Did you get the reaction you wanted?   YES   NO
If you *didn't*, what type of reaction was there to your attempt? _____

e. Who knew about your attempt? _____

Total SA (sum Items 1 to 6) **Score:** _____

PART C: ST

Times you threatened to hurt yourself badly or try to kill yourself

4. Have you ever threatened to commit suicide?   YES   NO

(If YES, Code 1 for ST-Status; Code 0 for Control).

If **no**, go on to question # 5.

If **yes**, what did you threaten to do? _____

Item #1—*Suicide Threat Method (ST-Mth)(For multiple methods, enter highest score.)*

(Blank = 0; Overdose (OD) on one substance, small (e.g., 10 pills or less) amount = 1; OD on the same substance, large (e.g., 10 pills or more) amount = 2; OD on two or more of mixed/odd substances = 3; Harm/Injury to any part of body = 3; Traumatic/lethal— hanging, suffocating, jumping from height, use firearms = 4.)

Item #2—*Suicide Threat Frequency (ST-Freq)*

a. Approximately how many times did you do this? _____

(Blank = 0; 1-2 times = 1; 3-4 times = 2; 4 or more times = 3)

Item #3—*Suicide Threat History (ST-Hx)*

b. Approximately when did you first do this? (*write your age*) _____

c. When was the last time you did this? (*write your age*) _____

Compute <u>difference score</u>: age of last threat (c) minus age of first threat (b):
(Blank = 0; 0-1 year = 1; 2-3 years = 2; 4-5 years = 3; 6 or more years = 4.)

Item #4—*Suicide Threat—Risk (ST-Rsk)*

Compute <u>difference score</u>: Stated chronological-age given in background minus age information of last threat (c):
(Blank = 0; 1 year or less = 4; >1 year but <2 years = 3; ≥ 2 years = 2.)

Item #5—*Suicide Threat Event (ST-Evn)*

d. Who did you make the threats to? (e.g., mom, dad) _____

e. What other things were going on in your life during the time that you were threatening to kill yourself? _____

If specific things/events are listed, count each separately; if response is vague (e.g. "lots of things") or general, then only count as 1 event.
(Blank = 0; 1 event = 1; 2 events = 2; 3 or more events = 3.)

Item #6—*Suicide Threat Intent (ST-Int)*

f. Did you actually want to die?   YES   NO
                                                                         (2)   (0)

g. Were you hoping for a specific reaction to your threat?   YES   NO
If **yes**, what was the reaction you were looking for?_____

h. Did you get the reaction you wanted?   YES   NO
If you didn't, what type of reaction was there to your attempt?_____

Total ST (sum Items 1 to 6) **Score:** _____

PART D: SI

Times you talked or thought seriously about attempting suicide

5. Have you ever talked or thought about:

	YES	NO
–wanting to die	YES (1)	NO (0)
–committing suicide	YES (1)	NO (0)

> If NO, Score 0 for each Item Below, Items 1-5
> (If YES, Code 1 for SI-Status; Code 0 for Control, and continue, using the scoring below).

Item #1—*Suicide Ideation Method (SI-Mth) (For multiple methods, enter highest score.)*

    a. What did you talk about doing? _____

> (Blank = 0; Overdose (OD) on one substance, small (e.g., 10 pills or less) amount = 1;
> OD on the same substance, large (e.g., 10 pills or more) amount = 2; OD on two or more
> of mixed/odd substances = 3; Harm/Injury to any part of body = 3; Traumatic/lethal –
> hanging, suffocating, jumping from height, use of firearms = 4.)

    b. With whom did you discuss this? _____

Item #2—*Suicide Ideation Event (SI-Evn)*

    c. What made you feel like doing that? _____

> (If specific things/events listed, count each separately; if response is vague [e.g. "lots of
> things"] or general, then only count as 1 event.)
> (Blank = 0; 1 event = 1; 2 events = 2; 3 or more events = 3.)

Item #3—*Suicide Ideation Plan (SI-Pln)*

    d. Did you have a specific plan for how you would try to kill yourself?   YES (2)   NO (1)

    If yes, what plan did you have? _____

    f. In looking back, how did you imagine people would react to your attempt?

    _____

Item #4—*Suicide Ideation Reaction (SI-Reac)*

    g. Did you think about how people would react if you did succeed in killing yourself?   YES (1)   NO (2)

    If **yes**, how did you think they would react? _____

Item #5—*Suicide Ideation Preparation (SI-Pre)*

    h. Did you ever take steps to prepare for this plan?   YES (2)   NO (0)

> If **yes**, what did you do to prepare? _____

Total SI (sum Items 1 to 5) **Score:** _____

> To facilitate scoring of the SHBQ, a score summary sheet we developed for our research
> projects is included in the Appendix.

Measure and Administration

The Positive and Negative Suicide Ideation (PANSI) Inventory

Most individuals can complete this 14-item inventory in 5 to 10 minutes. Exploratory principal axis-factor analyses resulted in the retention of two moderately correlated factors: PANSI-Positive and PANSI-Negative (see Osman, Gutierrez, et al., 1998).

TARGET POPULATION

The PANSI was designed for use with adolescents and adults ages 14 and older to identify risk and protective factors that are associated with suicidal behavior.

SCORING PROCEDURE AND INTERPRETATION

1. The PANSI is a 14-item self-report instrument designed to assess the *frequency* of positive and negative thoughts that are associated with suicide-related behavior (e.g., suicide attempts). It is used as a screening—*not* a diagnostic—instrument.

2. Items on the PANSI are rated on a 5-point scale: 1 (*none of the time*) to 5 (*most of the time*).

3. The PANSI is composed of two moderately correlated ($r = -.45$; $N = 450$) scale scores.
   PANSI-Positive (6 items: Items 2, 6, 8, 12, 13, & 14).
   PANSI-Negative (8 items: Items 1, 3, 4, 5, 7, 9, 10, & 11).

4. Each PANSI scale score is obtained by computing the MEAN of the ratings for all items in the scale. A TOTAL PANSI scale score is NOT computed.

5. Higher scores on the PANSI-Positive suggest higher frequency of protective thoughts that buffer against suicidal behavior. Some of the PANSI-Positive items tap perception of control, confidence about plans for the future, feelings of accomplishment, and perceived ability to cope with problematic situations.

6. Higher scores on the PANSI-Negative suggest higher frequency of suicide-related thoughts and ideation. Some of the items on the PANSI-Negative address issues related to helplessness about the future, feelings of being unhappy about interpersonal relationships, inability to deal with failure, and doubts about living up to the expectations of other people.

Measure and Administration

The Reasons for Living Inventory for Adolescents (RFL-A)

The RFL-A is composed of 32 items and takes approximately 15 to 20 minutes to administer and score. Results of the multi-sample confirmatory factor analyses provided adequate support for invariance of the RFL-A scores across high school and psychiatric adolescent inpatients. (See Chapter 6.)

TARGET POPULATION

The RFL-A was developed and normed using data from adolescents ages 14 to 18 years. We presented data in Chapter 6 to justify use of the RFL-A with adolescents ages 13 to 19 years. The instrument taps the adaptive resources of an individual when faced with reasons for killing herself/himself.

SCORING AND INTERPRETATION

1. The RFL-A has a Flesch-Kincaid 6th-grade reading level index and an average of 10.8 words per sentence. Normative data of the RFL-A has been developed for interpreting the responses of adolescents ages 13 and older. It is designed as a screening instrument.

2. Each RFL-A item is rated on a 6-point scale ranging from 1 (*not at all important*) to 6 (*extremely important*).

3. The RFL-A is composed of five scales with moderate correlations among the factors that are empirically derived.

4. Scoring the RFL-A is completed by determining the MEAN score for each scale as follows:

   Future Optimism (FO) contains 7 items. Compute mean rating for scores on Items 4, 11, 13, 15, 19, 25, 28.

   Suicide-Related Concerns (SRC) contains 6 items. Calculate mean rating for scores on Items 2, 8, 20, 21, 26, 32.

   Family Alliance (FA) contains 7 items. Calculate mean rating for scores on Items 1, 7, 12, 17, 23, 24, 30.

   Peer Acceptance and Support (PAS) contains 6 items. Calculate mean rating for scores on Items 5, 6, 10, 16, 22, 27.

   Self-Acceptance (SA) contains 6 items. Calculate mean rating for scores on Items 3, 9, 14, 18, 29, 31.

   RFL-A Total Score: Calculate mean rating for scores on Items 1 to 32.

Higher scores on the RFL-A total and scale scores suggest stronger reasons that adolescents give for living.

The RFL-A total score can range from 1.0 to 6.0. Cut-off scores for the RFL-A continue to be developed for different clinical and nonclinical populations. We note, however, that a preliminary cut-off score has recently been constructed by Gutierrez, Osman, Kopper, and Barrios (2000) using the receiver operating characteristic (ROC) curve analyses.

Cut-off Scores: In particular, in samples of psychiatric adolescent inpatients admitted to a state psychiatric institute because of suicide-related behaviors ($n = 64$) and other psychiatric problems ($n = 52$), a *total RFL-A cut-off score of 4.63* had maximum sensitivity (76.6%), specificity (90.4%), positive predictive value (90.7%), and negative predictive value (75.8%). Gutierrez, Osman, Kopper, and Barrios (2000) cautiously noted that, "this cut-off score may vary in other investigations . . . sample" (p. 185). We have used this cut-off score of 4.63 to establish scores on the RFL-A as a criterion validity measure. (See Chapter 6.)

The RFL-A subscale items tap a range of protective aspects for living:

Future Optimism: Some of the items on this subscale tap the ability to look forward to the future as one grows older, the desire to accomplish specific plans for the future, and the expectation of being successful in the future.

Suicide-Related Concerns Some of the items on this subscale evaluate fears of taking one's life, fear of dying, fear of using any method to harm oneself, and fear of making any plan to end one's own life.

Family Alliance: Several items on this subscale evaluate issues related to the ability to turn to family members for support or advice, feelings of being emotionally close to one's family, and feelings of being cared about by family members.

Peer Acceptance and Support: Items included in this subscale tap issues related to feelings of being accepted by close friends, feelings of being valued and appreciated by friends, and the ability to count on friends in times of need.

Self-Acceptance: Items included in this subscale address issues regarding feelings about the self, feelings of being happy with oneself, and feelings of accepting oneself unconditionally.

Measure and Administration

The Suicide Resilience Inventory–25 (SRI-25)

The Suicide Resilience Inventory-25 (Osman, Gutierrez, et al., 2004) takes approximately 15 to 20 minutes to administer and score. Multi-sample confirmatory factor analysis of the SRI-25 items showed that the scores on the three factor scales of this instrument are invariant across clinical and nonclinical adolescent samples (see Chapter 6).

TARGET POPULATION

The Suicide Resilience Inventory-25 was designed for use with adolescents and adults ages 14 and older to identify a number of protective factors that serve as internal, external, and environmental factors. These factors are designed to serve as buffers against suicide-related behaviors.

SCORING AND INTERPRETATION

1. The SRI-25 is a 25-item self-report instrument designed to tap three global dimensions of the protective construct. In general, the factors identified above frequently help defend against suicidal thoughts and behaviors.

2. Items on the SRI-25 are rated on a 6-point scale ranging from 1 (*slightly disagree*) to 6 (*strongly agree*).

3. The SRI-25 is composed of three moderately correlated factors (25 items) with varying numbers of items in each scale.

   Factor 1: Internal Protective (9 items: Items 1, 2, 5, 9, 11, 13, 19, 20, & 25)

   Factor 2: Emotional Stability (8 items: Items 4, 8, 10, 12, 14, 18, 23, & 24)

   Factor 3: External Protective (8 items: Items 3, 6, 7, 15, 16, 17, 21, & 22)

4. The SRI-25 scale scores are derived by *averaging* the items in each scale. A total inventory scale score is derived by averaging all 25 items.

5. The higher the score on the SRI-25, the more resilient that person is to committing suicide.

The SRI-25 subscale items are designed to tap a number of protective issues and considerations.

Internal Protective: Items included in this subscale evaluate satisfaction with self, ability to set reasonable goals, feelings of being proud of oneself, and feelings of being happy when faced with a number of challenging life events.

Emotional Stability: Items in this subscale tap the ability to resist thoughts of engaging in self-harmful behaviors, ability to handle thoughts of suicide, and the ability to handle a range of emotions in response to several enviromental stressors.

External Protective: Items included in this subscale tap beliefs that relatives and friends will offer supportive care, the ability to talk openly about feelings or thoughts of suicide, the ability to seek out the supportive resources of other people, and the ability to seek out the emotional support of significant others.

Summary of Clinical Practice Implications

- Following the 11 guidelines at the beginning of the chapter assures proper use of the SHBQ, PANSI, RFL-A, and SRI-25 in clinical and nonclinical settings.

- Asking young people questions about suicide will **not** elevate their level of risk and may actually **lower** it.

- The SHBQ can be administered to individuals 13 and older in 15-20 minutes. The respondent's age must be known in order to properly score. Not all items are scored, but some provide clinical context.

- SHBQ subscale scores (i.e., Self-Harm Behavior, Suicide Attempts, Suicide Threat, Suicide Ideation) provide a broader range of information than just relying on the total score. A score summary sheet is provided in the Appendix.

- The PANSI can be administered to individuals 14 and older in 5-10 minutes.

- There are PANSI-Positive and PANSI-Negative scores but no total score.

- Higher PANSI-Positive scores indicate more frequent protective thoughts that buffer against suicide; higher PANSI-Negative scores indicate more frequent suicide-related thoughts.

- The RFL-A can be administered to adolescents ages 13 to 19 in 15-20 minutes.

- Mean scores on Future Optimism, Suicide-Related Concerns, Family Alliance, Peer Acceptance and Support, and Self-Acceptance are calculated to determine specific reasons endorsed for not engaging in suicide-related behaviors (higher scores indicate more reasons); a total score can also be calculated.

- The SRI-25 can be administered to those 14 and older in 15-20 minutes.

- Average scores on the SRI-25 are calculated for Internal Protective, Emotional Stability, and External Protective subscales; the total score is the average of all 25 items.

- For the three SRI-25 subscales and total score, higher scores indicate greater resilience.

Assessment in High Schools and Other Nonclinical Settings

Basic Screening Considerations

The importance of adequately assessing for suicide risk when working with adolescents in clinical settings is obvious. We know that these individuals are at greater risk than the general population by virtue of having one or more diagnosed mental illnesses. This reason alone justifies the time and effort of targeted assessment. Determining which teens warrant assessment in nonclinical settings is less straightforward. The resources generally do not exist to have every youth in a school complete a battery of assessment tools on a regular basis. Therefore, concerned schools typically rely on relatively brief screenings to identify those students most likely to be at heightened risk for suicide and hence in need of more comprehensive assessment. For our purposes, screening will refer to the use of any tools designed to detect presence of symptoms, thoughts, and behaviors associated with elevated risk of suicide. The length and complexity of a screening can vary widely depending on the goals and resources.

A logical venue for adolescent suicide risk screening is within the school system. Not only do schools have access to most youth within a given geographic area, but educators may also have a legal obligation to intervene (Leenaars & Wenckstern, 1990; Sandoval, London, & Rey, 1994). A widely accepted approach to the prevention of suicide was described by Caplan in 1964 (cited in Leenaars & Wenckstern, 1990). This approach distinguishes between primary, secondary, and tertiary prevention. Primary prevention consists of efforts to remedy the conditions that may lead to suicide before it occurs. Secondary prevention involves dealing directly with a suicidal crisis or problem. Its goal is to prevent a condition that already exists from progressing to a more serious problem (Miller & DuPaul, 1996). Tertiary prevention involves the provision of services to suicide survivors after the suicide has occurred.

We will focus on secondary prevention efforts that require speaking directly with students about suicide. It has been suggested (e.g., Garland, Shaffer, & Whittle, 1989; Miller & DuPaul, 1996; Shaffer, Garland, Vieland, Underwood, & Busner, 1991; Shaffer et al., 2004) that systematic screening to identify adolescents at risk is an important component of secondary prevention efforts. Although identification of at-risk adolescents is inherently difficult, given the relatively low base rate of completed suicide (CDC, 1999), screenings for depression and more frequently occurring suicide-related behaviors, such as suicidal ideation, are a logical way to identify at-risk individuals. These efforts may result in the over-identification of at-risk youth, but the cost of false positives is low. That is to say, the cost is low in terms of potential loss of life but may be much higher in terms of additional resources (e.g., qualified staff to conduct screenings and subsequent interventions). In addition, adolescent suicide risk is a fluid construct that may fluctuate dramatically within brief periods of time. As a result, the issue of how often to conduct screenings must be given careful consideration. Adolescents who screen negative on one day might screen positive only a few days later, not because of any measurement issues, but simply because of natural fluctuations in risk status. With these issues in mind, we will conclude this chapter with an example of a cost-effective approach to screening.

Different Goals of Screening

Before discussing the necessary components of effective risk screening, we want to briefly address the differences between risk screening for research purposes and prevention efforts. Because suicide-related behaviors are rare, statistically speaking, researchers face the constant challenge of identifying and recruiting large enough samples of suicidal youth for their studies. Many researchers do not have easy access to clinical populations in which the percentage of teens exhibiting elevated levels of suicidality are high. Randomly sampling from a general high school population might result in 5% showing signs of risk outside the normal range. For most research designs, that type of sample will be too small to yield adequate statistical power for all but the most basic of comparisons.

This is where risk screening becomes a useful research tool as well. Rather than conducting a single random sample of high school students, the savvy researcher will first screen as many of the students in a school as possible for markers of elevated risk. Quickly screening several hundred—or even thousand—students in this way leads to good sized samples of high-risk adolescents in a reasonable amount of time. While their level of suicidality may not be as high as one would find in a psychiatric inpatient unit, they will all be exhibiting levels that warrant concern. It now becomes possible to test hypotheses regarding adolescent suicide and produce findings that should generalize to both the overall adolescent population and to clinical populations as well. The types of studies that rely on this method of participant recruitment include epidemiology, exploration of novel risk factors, model testing, and exploration of a variety of group differences. For example, it is possible to recruit samples that are racially and ethnically diverse, hence increasing the generalizability of the findings (Gutierrez, Muehlenkamp, Konick, & Osman, 2005).

Risk screening as a research tool is an approach that is well supported in the empirical literature for studying a wide variety of problems in addition to suicide risk. In the areas of depression and suicide risk screening, the work of Bill Reynolds is particularly noteworthy. He and his colleagues have been using this technique for over 20 years, in the process producing a wealth of valuable information and providing an exemplary role model for all of us following in his footsteps. A brief list of his publications appears in this book's references.

Makeup of Screening Protocols

Most risk screening efforts rely primarily on self-report measures. A common concern raised about simply asking teens to admit if they are depressed or suicidal is the difficulty of validating their self-reports; however, as we discussed in Chapter 1, there is ample empirical evidence to support the use of self-report measures. This assertion holds whether the purpose of the screening is to identify potential participants for a research study or when screening is the primary purpose of the project. The composition of the screening protocol depends on what is an acceptable ratio of false positives to false negatives, time constraints, and resources to support the project. Specifically, the costs associated with purchasing or reproducing the screening measures, providing staff to administer, score, and interpret them, and providing appropriate follow-up for those identified to be at highest risk must all be taken into consideration during the planning phase.

The most basic approach is a large scale cross-sectional risk screening. Schools wishing to quickly gauge the level of risk of their students may conduct this type of screening either as a stand-alone event or as an integrated component of a more comprehensive health/mental health evaluation. The most successful programs will screen every student present at school on the designated day. We recommend a minimum of one measure of depressive symptoms and one measure of suicidal ideation. For junior and senior high schools (i.e., students 12 to 18 years old), the measures with the best empirical support are the Reynolds Adolescent Depression Scale (RADS; Reynolds, 1987, 2002) and the Suicidal Ideation Questionnaire (SIQ; Reynolds, 1988). The SIQ was discussed in detail in Chapter 5. We did not present data on the RADS because it is not a measure specifically of a suicide-related construct, although depressive symptoms are clearly associated with elevated suicide risk and other life problems. Although this issue has not been empirically tested (see Chapter 5), based on discussions with several colleagues familiar with the 30-item SIQ and the 15-item SIQ-JR, as well as our use of both for many years, we believe that the shorter version is adequate for the entire adolescent age range.

A significant advantage of this protocol is the minimal amount of time required for administration. On the other hand, the cost of purchasing enough measures to screen even a moderately sized school adds up quickly. Additional challenges of conducting a broad-based screening relate to administration and scoring of the measures. Classroom teachers can appropriately supervise students while they complete the RADS and SIQ. A scoring template is available for the SIQ, and the second edition of the RADS (RADS-2; Reynolds, 2002) now comes as a self-scoring form; however, all of the scored measures need to be reviewed in a timely fashion (ideally within 24 hours) to identify those students scoring above the clinical cutoff and those meeting criteria for further assessment based on their responses to the critical items. Both the cut-off scores and critical items are discussed in detail in the respective manuals. It is at this point that the other challenges of large scale screenings become apparent. Consider the following scenario: you have just administered the RADS and SIQ-JR to all 1,000 students at your school during their homeroom period and managed to score them all by the end of the next school day. You are feeling pretty good about what you've accomplished but are now faced with 50 students (a fairly conservative estimate of 5%) who met one or both criteria for follow-up. What do you do with them now?

Proper Infrastructure for Screening Support

Large scale screenings are only practical if the resources exist to provide every identified high-risk youth with adequate follow-up services within a few days of identification. Minimally this means having each one assessed by a qualified school psychologist, social worker, counselor, or other mental health professional. We recommend that the follow-up assessment consist of a face-to-face interview between the identified adolescent and someone trained in suicide and depression risk assessment. The following questions should be useful in determining the adolescent's risk status, but should not be considered comprehensive, and must be guided by your best clinical judgment.

1. Have you been feeling more sad or down lately?

2. Are you having trouble sleeping? Has your appetite changed recently? Do you feel like you have less energy than you used to?

3. Does life seem like less fun?

4. How long have you been feeling this way?

5. Have you had any thoughts about killing yourself lately? How about in the last month? The last 6 months?

6. How often have you had these thoughts? (Daily, couple times a week, couple times a month?)

7. What have you thought about doing to yourself?

8. Have you shared these thoughts with anyone else?

9. Have you actually tried to kill yourself or hurt yourself on purpose in the last month? In the last 6 months?

10. Does anyone know about what you've done to yourself?

The answers to these questions should help you determine the appropriate course of action to meet each student's mental health needs. Fortunately you will find that the majority of these high-risk adolescents' needs can be met by resources already in your school (e.g., meeting with their guidance counselor, additional one-on-one work with a teacher), but some will require more intensive interventions. Some schools employ various mental health professionals who can offer treatment for those who need it, but there must be contingencies in place should the number of at-risk students exceed a school's resources. Therefore, it is essential that schools are able to make referrals: that child and adolescent psychological and psychiatric treatment options be known and available before undertaking a screening such as the one described above. We know that asking kids if they are suicidal will not cause them to become suicidal (Gould et al., 2005). But asking them and not providing them with the help they obviously need might be seen by them as the final bit of evidence that their situation really is hopeless and that they should just quit trying.

Risk Screening as Suicide Postvention

So far we have been focusing on screening as a general means of secondary suicide prevention. However, many schools first face the issue of risk assessment in the aftermath of a completed suicide. This situation is painful and difficult for every member of the school community and understandably raises concerns about other deaths following in the wake of the first. But, when handled appropriately, there is little evidence that knowing someone who has died by suicide is a specific risk factor for adolescent suicide (Watkins & Gutierrez, 2003). It is therefore not necessary or appropriate to conduct emergency risk screenings of the entire student body. We recommend instead that all school personnel be alert for signs of extreme reactions to the death (i.e., more than normal grief) in students for several months. When concerns arise about individual students, these individuals should be asked about their feelings about and reactions to the death and should be assessed for suicide risk only if their responses to initial questions indicate it may be necessary.

Making Risk Screening More Manageable

We have discussed the costs and benefits of several approaches to risk screening that may have left readers believing that screening is a great idea but not practical given their circumstances. Therefore, we conclude this chapter with an overview of a project that combines a research and a general risk screening component in a cost-effective and fairly manageable way. Some of the information provided below originally appeared as a journal article (Gutierrez, Watkins, & Collura, 2004), which we have supplemented with additional details.

The Adolescent Risk Project

The Adolescent Risk Project (ARP) was initially launched in 1998 as a study of risk and protective factors for adolescent suicide. A relationship was formed with an urban high school based on multiple contacts with their school psychologist to discuss the possibility of conducting research at the school. After almost a year of meetings, submission of written proposals, and leaping over other hurdles, the school district granted administrative approval to begin the study. At first the goal was to recruit a representative sample of students from the school, regardless of level of risk; however, one of the requirements for gaining Institutional Review Board (IRB) approval was to have a mechanism for identifying and following up with the highest risk participants. Since the protocol already contained the RADS and SIQ, we decided to use the critical items on each as our screening tool and refer all students meeting criteria to the school psychologist for follow-up. As will be discussed below, this approach proved so effective that the screening component took on a life of its own. The exact composition of the protocol changes periodically based on the research needs of the team. However, in addition to the RADS and SIQ, it always contains the Reasons for Living Inventory for Adolescents (Osman et al., 1998; see Chapter 6), Self-Harm Behavior Questionnaire (Gutierrez et al., 2001; see Chapter 5), and a background questionnaire that asks about age, gender, race/ethnicity, and the respondents' degree of exposure to suicide-related behaviors in others.

RECRUITMENT ISSUES

Because we never accomplished our goal of using ARP to conduct school-wide screenings, we have had to rely on a variety of methods to recruit participants. One of the less successful efforts was attending parent/teacher conference nights to speak directly to parents passing through the main hallway at the school on their way to pick up their son/daughter's report card. Another effort has attained legendary status amongst our students concerning how much can go wrong with a research project. Plans were in place to send letters about ARP to the parents of all in-coming freshman prior to the first ever new student orientation at the school. We developed an elaborate system involving different colored stickers placed on name badges to identify students whose parents had returned the letters either granting or denying consent, distinguishing them from students whose parents had not returned the letter. A large crew of graduate and undergraduate research assistants was assembled, along with enough protocols for 500 participants, in anticipation of what was to be our largest data collection effort. Things started to go badly when the two-day event was reduced to one day. Next, we learned that the procedure for collecting consent letters from parents prior to orientation had not been implemented as planned. When the administration decided that orientation was no longer mandatory, we began to hear the bell tolling. But we remained optimistic. By the end of the day we managed to collect approximately 25 consent forms (for participation at a later point) and data from one student.

Having learned from our failed efforts, participant recruitment now relies on making presentations to individual classes and distributing information / consent letters to the students. The teachers who allow us to recruit from their classes have also graciously agreed to give their students extra credit for taking the letters home and bringing them back with a parent's signature. We now average 70% return rates, with a 30 to 40% consent rate.

SCREENING PROCEDURES

When feasible, all students in a given classroom are administered the measures by graduate and undergraduate research assistants. Those without parental consent are given work to do at their seats by their teacher. When this approach is not feasible (i.e., low classroom consent rate), groups of no more than 12 students at a time are given passes out of one class period to complete the packet in a small conference room, again supervised by research assistants.

After students complete the questionnaires, they are asked to wait while a research assistant looks over their packets. The questionnaires are examined for completeness, and the critical items on the SIQ and RADS are checked. Students who meet criteria on any of these measures then participate in a brief suicide risk assessment conducted by one of the graduate students in a private setting. As part of the assessment, students are questioned regarding current depressive symptomatology, suicidal ideation, and recent engagement in suicide-related behavior, using the follow-up questions outlined above.

After the critical item review and an individual risk assessment as necessary, students are placed in one of four risk categories based on the information obtained during the brief assessment. Specifically, clinical judgments are made regarding students' intent to harm themselves, level of distress in the form of depressive and/or suicidal thoughts, and current availability of support resources (e.g., whether the student is already in treatment or in contact with the school psychologist), based on the information students provide.

REFERRAL MECHANISM

Those individuals identified in the most serious category, *at-risk / in crisis,* require immediate intervention. An individual would be placed in this category if the brief assessment suggested that individual is currently depressed (endorsed at least 4 symptoms of depression) and thinking seriously about suicide. We define serious suicidality as thoughts of suicide within the past month, with a clear plan, occurring either daily or a couple of times a week or having made a suicide attempt within the past month about which no one knew. Students placed in this group are assumed to pose a large enough threat to their own safety that they should not be allowed to leave school without additional follow-up. Furthermore, parents or guardians of these students are contacted as soon as possible by the school psychologist. The next level is labeled *notable concern,* which warrants further contact with the student and exploration of possible intervention. Students are placed in this category if they endorse 2-3 symptoms of depression, have been feeling bad for at least a month, have had any thoughts about suicide within the last month, or have made a suicide attempt within the past 6 months. These students are not seen as posing an imminent threat to themselves, but their level of distress might lead to more serious problems in the absence of intervention. Those considered to be in *apparent need* are seen as requiring some degree of follow-up but are not assumed to be immediately at risk. Students qualify for this category if they endorse fewer than two symptoms of depression, have been feeling bad for less than a month, have had thoughts about suicide (without a plan) within the last 6 months (but more than one month ago), and have never actually attempted suicide. It is assumed that students in this group will continue to function adequately until further contact (within several days of participation) can occur. The remaining participants are placed in the *no indicators* category because of no apparent need for follow-up. The guidelines for risk categorization are based on a combination of our experiences as clinical researchers, those of the school psychologist, and a review of the relevant literature (e.g., Goldman & Beardslee, 1999).

Each year we have recruited larger numbers of participants for ARP and are currently able to gather data from approximately 20% of the student population. We consistently find that around 10% of students who complete the protocol meet criteria for some level of follow-up. Roughly equal numbers of students (3 to 4%) are identified into one of the risk categories each year. None of the identified at-risk students has ever refused the offered referral, and all had subsequent contact with a member of the student support services staff.

FOLLOW-UP

While the focus of this book is assessment, a few details about the intervention component of ARP may be useful to those considering starting a similar program. It should be noted that care for the student rests solely in the hands of the appropriate school staff (i.e., school psychologist, social worker, or guidance counselor), not the research team. All efforts are made to involve the student in the decision making process, but their safety is the primary concern, and sometimes decisions have to be made with which adolescents are unhappy.

Interventions are tied to students' assessed level of initial risk. An immediate response and comprehensive follow through is required for those in the most serious risk category (i.e., *at-risk/in crisis*). Once identified, these students are promptly introduced to the school psychologist for an in-depth interview. The parents are also quickly contacted to apprise them of the situation. With assent of the student (ideally), information from both the protocol and interview is shared with the individual's parent(s), along with recommendations for a comprehensive mental health assessment. In some cases this recommendation specifies a psychiatric or hospital emergency room evaluation or referral to the crisis resources of the local mental health center. Parental consent is also sought to share information with the targeted community resource. Students undergo additional psychiatric evaluation and begin treatment, which often includes psychopharmacology. When students return to school, supportive counseling and ongoing monitoring are established and maintained. Some students continue outpatient therapy in the community.

Students in the intermediate risk group (i.e., *notable concern*) are given support to address their issues of concern. Options for problem solving or treatment are explored, and efforts are made to reduce their overall level of distress. Specifically, these students are introduced to the school psychologist and offered several times for an appointment in the next couple of days. They are also given a list of more immediate alternatives (e.g., crisis line number), should issues escalate for them. The main goal of this level of intervention is to ensure that the student is not at immediate risk for suicide-related behaviors and to investigate the student's need for counseling. Available interventions include counseling or therapy at various community agencies, counseling contacts at school, or short-term, problem-focused sessions with the school psychologist or social worker. Issues in addition to suicidal ideation and depressive symptoms are often discovered through continued contact with these students. For example, previously undiagnosed ADHD and learning disabilities are fairly common problems contributing to the difficulties they are experiencing.

Interventions for students in the lowest risk category (i.e., *apparent need*) involve monitoring by student support services personnel with follow-up contacts as deemed necessary. During the risk assessment conducted by the research assistant, these students are encouraged to pay a visit to the school psychologist and asked if their names may be given to him. Mechanisms for monitoring include attendance records, grades, and behavioral discipline reports that are seen as indicating poor adjustment or escalating problems. Parents of these students are typically not contacted unless a significant change in risk status is noted through one of the monitoring mechanisms.

This three-tiered model for intervention is organized so that the ascending steps of services to students include those services offered to students at the lower levels. For example, the services implemented for an intermediate intervention also include monitoring of student adjustment and progress. The components provided for an intensive intervention likewise include both counseling resources to some degree and monitoring, in addition to the parent contact and mental health referral. Students subsequently showing greater risk for self-harm receive additional and more intensive services.

EVIDENCE SUPPORTING SCREENING EFFORTS

Of course all of this information begs the question, "But does it do any good?" Tracking of students with whom we have had follow-up contact by the school psychologist led us to the impression that ARP is having a very real and positive impact on the mental health of the students identified as potentially at-risk. In addition, analyses of qualitative data reinforced the research team's original impressions of the impact of the project. Risk screening, identification of high-risk students, referral for appropriate services, and supportive follow-up are all possible within the confines of a high school environment. Those identified as potentially at-risk seem to be fairly representative of the larger sample of adolescents who have participated in ARP.

A variety of unexpected positive outcomes have also occurred. First, significant amounts of distress have been noted in students who otherwise appeared to be functioning well and who would go undetected by the standard procedures in most high schools. These students are usually identified only by chance—for example, when a teacher discovers notebooks, other notes, or drawings communicating distress. Participation by the school in this project has changed the atmosphere among faculty and staff regarding the appropriateness of talking about issues of suicide and other mental health concerns. Teachers and guidance counselors now regularly refer students about whom they are concerned to participate in ARP. Parents who call with questions about available screening services at school are also told about us. With the student's assent (unless the risk is deemed high enough to override assent) we can then discuss the results of screening directly with their parents. Some students have sought out the school psychologist for services after initial participation. Others have referred friends to participate in ARP after being told about thoughts or feelings that worried them.

COSTS OF SCREENING

Implementing a project like ARP involves certain costs, which would be prohibitive without the active collaboration between the research team and school staff members. Most obvious is the cost of buying the RADS and SIQ and photocopying the other materials. These costs are solely borne by the researchers through the support of their academic department. It is a time-consuming process for us to recruit participants, administer the study materials, and utilize the screening process appropriately. Without the commitment of the school psychologist, other staff, and faculty members at the school, the burden would be much larger. The school's principal also has been very supportive of our efforts over the years, and we cannot emphasize enough what a huge benefit that has been. We fully appreciate that during specific points in the research process, the workload of the school staff is increased because of their participation. It should also be noted that the school is struggling, as are many other schools around the country, to provide an increasing level of student services without additional funding or personnel. What we have been able to accomplish has largely been due to the willingness of school staff members to voluntarily increase their workload. Because they are dedicated professionals, they recognize the direct benefits to the students and the related indirect benefits to the entire school community. Collaborating on this project makes resources available to the school that would not otherwise exist without access to a research university.

We have weighed the costs and benefits of running ARP and concluded that we will keep it up and running as long as the school wants us there. It may not be the best model for every school, but we encourage school administrators to make contact with a local college or university and explore the possibility of launching a similar project. We suggest researchers approach schools in their areas and offer to collaborate with them. We have found that the mutually beneficial aspects of ARP make it one of the most rewarding professional experiences in which we regularly engage.

A CONCLUDING THOUGHT

Few feelings are better than knowing your research may have helped save a life. One additional story illustrates this point nicely. Several years ago a small group of us were at the school running subjects. One of our undergraduate students noted that a young lady had met criteria on the critical items and referred her to a graduate student for follow-up. This girl was visibly upset, exhibited numerous symptoms of depression, admitted to active thoughts of suicide, and briefly noted several things that were going poorly in her life. When she was asked if she had any specific plans to kill herself, she said yes. She said that everything had gotten so bad that she did not think she could try any more. Her parents were not going to be home after school, and she planned to go home and kill herself. She had access to the means to carry out her plan. The graduate student expressed concerns about her safety and told her that she needed to speak with the school psychologist right away. She consented to the referral and said she was glad that someone finally knew how bad things were. This young lady did not go home and kill herself, but instead was admitted to a local hospital directly from school. She is alive and well today. There is no guarantee that she would have carried out her plan had we not been lucky enough to have been running an ARP data collection that day, but we like to think we were there for a reason and that we played a part in getting her back on the path to wanting to live.

Summary of Clinical Practice Implications

- Most school-based risk screening efforts rely solely on self-report measures.

- The makeup of a screening battery is based on an acceptable ratio of false positives to false negatives, time constraints, and support resources.

- Minimally, large scale screenings should contain one depression measure and one measure of suicidal ideation (e.g., RADS-2, SIQ-JR).

- The appropriate infrastructure to score measures, identify those meeting criteria, and following up with identified youth must be in place **before** starting any screening project.

- Wide scale screening at a school in the aftermath of a suicide death of a student, teacher, or staff member is **not** indicated.

- The Adolescent Risk Project (ARP) provides one successful model for cost-effective screening when collaborations between schools and researchers exist.

Suggested reading

Reynolds, W. M. (1991). A school-based procedure for the identification of adolescents at risk for suicidal behaviors. *Family Community Health, 14,* 64-75.

Reynolds, W. M. (1994). Assessment of depression in children and adolescents by self-report questionnaires. In W. M. Reynolds & H. F. Johnston (Eds.), *Handbook of depression in children and adolescents.* (pp. 209-234). New York: Plenum Press.

Reynolds, W. M., & Mazza, J. J. (1994). Suicide and suicidal behaviors in children and adolescents. In W. M. Reynolds & H. F. Johnston (Eds.), *Handbook of depression in children and adolescents.* (pp. 525-580). New York: Plenum Press.

Reynolds, W. M., & Mazza, J. J. (1999). Assessment of suicidal ideation in inner-city children and young adolescents: Reliability and validity of the Suicidal Ideation Questionnaire-JR. *School Psychology Review, 28,* 17-30.

Reynolds, W. M., & Mazza, J. J. (1998). Reliability and validity of the Reynolds Adolescent Depression Scale with young adolescents. *Journal of School Psychology, 36,* 295-312.

Assessment of Minority Youth

It seems the most common thing written about minority youth in the psychological literature is that more research needs to be done in order to determine if the findings from research with predominantly Caucasian samples apply. Our goal for this chapter is to go beyond that basic recommendation, to the extent that it is possible. We will begin with a nontechnical overview of the statistical issues involved in determining measurement equivalence across racial/ethnic groups. Next, we will review the emerging findings on suicidality in minority youth populations, including some of our work. We will conclude with a discussion of issues to be considered when assessing minority youth and what we see as the most pressing gaps in the existing literature.

Understanding the literature on racial, ethnic, and cultural differences in adolescent suicidality is complicated by the way in which terminology is used as well as a concern about using politically correct labels. Therefore let us define the terms we will use throughout the chapter. Race and ethnicity are often used interchangeably, although they represent different concepts (Muehlenkamp, Gutierrez, Osman, & Barrios, 2005). Race typically refers to the common physical characteristics of a particular group of people, but it can also represent sociopolitical aspects of a group (Sue & Sue, 1990). Ethnicity is a multidimensional construct referring to characteristics, practices, and beliefs that are shared among a particular group of people (Sue & Sue). Members of different ethnic groups share a common culture, but ethnicity does not necessarily define cultural group membership. For example, members of a religious denomination could be said to make up a cultural group, but they would not all necessarily be of the same race or ethnicity. For the sake of clarity, we decided to use the term *race/ethnicity* when broadly describing existing research findings. *Culture* will refer to commonalities of a social group independent of race and ethnicity. We recognize that there are numerous subgroups within each ethnic group distinction and that within-group differences may be even more important than between-group differences.

Measurement Equivalence

Knight and Hill (1998) provide a fine introduction to the concept of measurement equivalence, how it relates to racial/ethnic adolescent research, and statistical techniques to test for it. They define cultural bias in measurement of psychological constructs as systematic error that is unknowingly caused by cultural factors that differ across groups or subgroups. Furthermore, they identify three specific types of cultural bias: the mean difference fallacy, subjective judgment, and the standardization fallacy. Researchers commit the mean difference fallacy when the assumption is made that group differences do not exist, and therefore observed differences are attributed to cultural bias in the scale, rather than accepting that the groups naturally differ on the construct of interest. When one assumes that the content of a measure is culturally bound, and therefore the measure must be biased if it was not specifically created for a particular group, the subjective judgment bias is committed. The standardization fallacy is a related concept as it assumes that because a measure was developed and normed in one group, it will be culturally biased when administered to members of another group unless it is renormed. However, if the items are truly biased, renorming or rescaling accomplishes next to nothing, because the meaning of the items has not been changed. A similar problem can arise when measures are translated from one language into another unless the translation is cultural as well (e.g., accounting for dialectical differences).

To address the problem of culturally biased measures, it is necessary to achieve measurement equivalence (Knight & Hill, 1998). We often do not know, but assume, that operational definitions are valid across racial and ethnic groups and/or different language translations of the same measure. But group differences may not be the result of differences in how members of the comparison groups think. It is therefore necessary to assess the extent to which reliability and validity coefficients in minority samples are comparable to those generated by majority samples. There are three forms of measurement equivalence to assess: item, functional, and scalar. A measure has item equivalence if the individual items on it have the same meaning to members of different groups. Functional equivalence occurs when scores on a measure are the result of similar antecedents, outcomes, and correlates across groups. Finally, scalar equivalence, which is the most important and hardest form to demonstrate, means that the same score on a measure reflects the same degree of the construct being assessed, regardless of group membership.

Knight and Hill (1998) argue that it is unlikely for underlying constructs being measured to differ across groups if comparisons are being made between individuals in fairly similar environments (e.g., the same country). Therefore it may be possible to adjust for random error variance in scores across groups with statistical transformations, rendering group comparisons meaningful. A simple test of equivalence is to compare validity coefficients between and within racial/ethnic groups or to compare individuals' responses across different language translations of the same measure. Presumably if these coefficients are similar, then measurement equivalence has been achieved. These comparisons can be made by examining correlation coefficients (i.e., evidence of empirical or construct validity; see Chapter 4), constrained structural modeling, or regression coefficients and intercepts. We won't go into the technical details here, but interested readers should consult Knight and Hill (1998). Since there is no single statistical test for measurement equivalence, it is necessary to examine several levels of evidence based on multiple analysis strategies. For example, one could begin by holding focus groups with members of different racial/ethnic groups (e.g., parents of suicidal teens) to assess whether individual items and the related operational definitions make sense within each group. This approach can also help identify if there are key elements of the construct not being adequately assessed by the measure. When conducting focus groups, look for important themes and issues arising on a consistent basis. Following up with individual interviews can help you examine and clarify your observations. Next, reliability coefficients should be compared across two or more racial/ethnic groups, looking for both item- and scale-level equivalence. Comparing item-total correlations across groups helps identify nonidentical specific items that may need to be revised before use in a different racial/ethnic group. Knight and Hill (1998) recommend conducting confirmatory factor analyses in multiple groups as the preferred method for the final test of equivalence. If data from the comparison groups fit the model well, then the items must be relatively equivalent. Comparing constrained to less constrained models will then help identify individual nonequivalent items in need of revision or deletion.

Before moving on to our review of the current racial/ethnic differences literature, a few cautionary notes must be made regarding measurement equivalence. It is possible for scores on a measure to be equivalent across the majority group and a subsegment of a minority population but not the entire minority group. Alternatively, measurement equivalence may not hold across members of the same group if individuals differ in their level of ethnic identity or acculturation (Knight & Hill, 1998). Most of the studies reviewed here suffer from some problems related to measurement equivalence issues and should therefore be considered tentative findings until these issues are addressed and the results verified.

Current Findings Regarding Minority Adolescent Suicide

Suicide Completion Rates

A review of prevalence data for specific racial/ethnic groups in the U.S. reveals an alarming lack of information about adolescent suicide and suicide-related behaviors. Hovey and King (1997) stated that completed suicide appears to be a larger problem for Hispanic youth than elderly in that culture, although the rates are lower in all age groups compared to the total population. They also observed that rates are lower in those born in Mexico compared with those born in the U.S. Similarly, suicide rates for Puerto Rican youth living in the U.S. are higher than for those living in Puerto Rico, and risk appears to increase the longer they live in this country (Committee on Cultural Psychiatry, 1989b). Among Latinas, completed suicide occurs at roughly half the rate as for Caucasian females, but Latino(a)s tend to be younger when they die than Caucasians (Roberts, 2000). Finally, suicide rates among American Indians are dramatically higher than in the overall population, but there is significant variation by tribe (Garroutte et al., 2003).

It is also possible that minority suicide is underreported, at least in the African American community. For example, African American males die at much higher rates than females due to various types of violent accidents that may be veiled suicides (Gibbs & Hines, 1989). Molock, Kimbrough, Lacy, McClure, and Williams (1994) stated that the methods chosen by African Americans tend to be more ambiguous and therefore are more likely to be classified as accidents. Misclassified overdoses may also be suicide-related (Gibbs & Hines, 1989).

None of this information comes from nationally representative epidemiological data, making these observations tentative and hindering our true understanding of minority suicide. While still limited relative to the amount of research conducted on majority youth, more is known about suicide-related behaviors among minority adolescents than previously.

Nonlethal Suicide-Related Behaviors

The majority of the existing research looking at racial/ethnic differences in adolescent suicidality has been conducted with Hispanic and African American youth, as compared with European American young people. Hovey and King (1997) found that Hispanic adolescents have higher rates of suicidal ideation compared to European American peers, and Kann et al. (2000) reported that young Hispanic females' suicide attempt rates are almost twice that of European Americans (see also Canino & Roberts, 2001; Rew, Thomas, Horner, Resnick, & Beuhring, 2001; Tortolero & Roberts, 2001). Hispanic youth also have been found to have higher levels of suicidal ideation and a greater number of suicide attempts relative to their African American and Asian American peers (Canino & Roberts, 2001; CDC, 1998; Rew et al., 2001; Shiang, 1998). Hispanic youth are more likely than African American youth to have thought about attempting, more likely than Caucasian or African American youth to have made a suicide plan, and more likely than Caucasian youth to have made a suicide attempt (Tortolero & Roberts, 2001).

Studies find that African American youth tend to report lower levels of suicidal ideation and attempts (Gutierrez, Osman, Kopper, Barrios, & Bagge 2000; Kann et al., 2000; Morrison & Downey, 2000) although completion rates are on the rise (CDC, 2001). A secondary analysis of a large, nationally representative sample of African American and Caucasian adolescents determined that Caucasian females had the highest suicide attempt rates and African American males the lowest (Watt & Sharp, 2002). However there were no racial differences between males and females for any of the suicide-related variables examined.

A small number of studies have compared rates of suicide-related behavior across multiple racial/ethnic groups. Roberts, Chen, and Roberts (1997) conducted a school-based survey of Metro Houston students in grades 6-8. The final sample of over 5000 youth was approximately 29% African American, 18% Caucasian, 18% Mexican American, 8.2% mixed, 7.3% Vietnamese American, 6% Central American, 4.5% Asian Indian, 4.2% Chinese American, and 3.7% Pakistani American. They found that the Pakistani American youth were almost twice as likely to report suicidal ideation and that the Mexican American and Vietnamese American risk was close to 1½ times the other groups. Pakistani American youth were over three times more likely to report making a suicide plan within the prior two weeks or a recent attempt. Those of mixed race/ethnicity had almost twice the risk of having made a plan within the prior two weeks. A recent meta-analysis (Evans, Hawton, Rodham, & Deeks, 2005) compiled data from a large number of international studies on adolescent suicide-related behavior to attempt to discern global patterns. Significant variation across studies was found, which was attributed primarily to methodological differences. In general, studies conducted in North America find higher rates of suicidality than those done in Europe. Females are consistently found to have higher rates of all forms of nonlethal suicide-related behaviors. Lifetime attempts and suicidal ideation is significantly higher for Caucasian adolescents than Asians, but Asians report higher levels of recent ideation.

Risk Factors

A consistent theme in the literature we have reviewed so far is that various racial/ethnic groups may be affected by risk factors for suicide that European Americans may not face, such as acculturative stress, racial discrimination and oppression, a fatalistic philosophy, and passive coping (Canino & Roberts, 2001; Shiang, 1998). As we noted in the introduction to this chapter, the ways in which constructs are defined in these studies may affect the ability to detect meaningful differences. Ethnicity has been assessed in a variety of ways, ranging from superficial self-identification, birthplace, or generational level to more complex elements of acculturation level and ethnic identity (Roberts, 2000). Acculturation measures often focus on language use, ethnic affiliation, knowledge of country of origin, and relation between one's own group and another. Ethnic identity looks at pride in one's ethnicity, sense of belonging to the group, importance of the group's way of doing things, and loyalty to the group. Finally, many subjective components, such as importance of ethnicity to the individual and perceptions of prejudice and discrimination, can be, but rarely are, assessed (Roberts, 2000). The vast majority of the work done in this area has focused on African American and Hispanic youth. We will review the literature for these groups separately.

African American Youth

The early work attempting to explain factors placing African American individuals at risk for suicide focused on the role of social status and the strain caused by being members of a minority group (Davis & Short, 1977). In attempting to explain why suicide rates among young African Americans began to dramatically increase two decades ago, it was suggested that acculturation may be important (Committee on Cultural Psychiatry, 1989a). It was proposed that the degree to which these youth feel power to exert change in their lives—in order to overcome the negative effects of institutional racism—determines whether they feel a strong will to live or profound hopelessness. Applying this idea to acculturation theory, the Committee suggested that marginalized African Americans (i.e., those who reject both their own and the dominant culture) are at the highest risk for suicide. At the other end of the spectrum, those seeking integration (i.e., value their own culture and want a positive relationship with the dominant culture) would be the most psychologically healthy and hence at the lowest risk. It was also believed that younger generations of African Americans had a weaker connection to the church and its protective influence. Heacock (1990) argued that young African American males struggle more with identity issues related to occupational choice, gender, and social roles. Confronting racism, which keeps them from fulfilling their desired roles, may trigger suicide (Gibbs & Hines, 1989). In addition, Gibbs and Hines suggested that boys' self-concept and impulse control is affected more strongly by absent fathers and that they are taught to repress their aggression for fear of retribution from Caucasian society. When not given healthy alternative outlets, they may become suicidal. African American females, on the other hand, tend to have stronger family ties and support, are more often affiliated with the church, and are more willing to seek help for their problems. As a result, their risk for suicide is much lower (Heacock). Watt and Sharp (2002) theorized that the history of significant struggles for African Americans has led to a cultural resilience. In other words, a higher value is placed on life and striving to overcome adversity, and therefore suicide is viewed as weak and unacceptable.

The limited empirical data that does exist have produced mixed findings regarding African American adolescent suicide risk. For example, family problems and a lack of social cohesion have been associated with increased suicide risk in African American adolescents (Chance, Kaslow, Summerville, & Wood, 1998; Harris & Molock, 2000; Kaslow, Thompson, Brooks, & Twomey, 2000; King, Raskin, Gdowski, Butkus, & Opipari, 1990). In addition, high levels of life stress have been found to interact with family dysfunction to elevate risk (Chance et al., 1998; Kaslow et al., 2000). Having depression or a history of other psychological problems also has been associated with increased risk for suicide among African American adolescents (Chance et al., 1998). For example, in a prospective study of 1,242 African American adolescents, Juon and

Ensminger (1997) found that current depression or a history of depression was significantly related to suicidal behaviors. It must be noted that similar results are found in studies of European American adolescents, and only research specifically comparing multiple groups can determine if the risk factors function differently across racial/ethnic groups. Gould, Fisher, Parides, Flory, and Shaffer (1996) conducted a psychological autopsy of 120 completed suicides of individuals under the age of 20. These deaths occurred over a two-year period in New York and 28 surrounding counties. Although accounting for fewer of the suicide deaths, African American youth who died by suicide had higher socioeconomic status than the comparison group. As a result, the authors concluded that closer affiliation with Caucasian culture for more affluent African American families may be weakening traditional protective factors. An alternative explanation was offered by Molock and colleagues (1994), who hypothesized that measurement issues with assessing nonlethal suicide-related behaviors may skew true estimates. As we discussed above, if the items on commonly used assessment tools are not culturally relevant for African Americans, then the data produced by them will not be valid.

Hispanic Youth

We now turn to the other minority group that has been studied in some detail: Hispanic adolescents. In addition to the limited number of studies conducted, another challenge of drawing conclusions about this group is the incredible subgroup diversity. Terms such as Hispanic and Latino are imposed on individuals from widely diverse cultures by outsiders who have little grasp of the differences between, for example, Mexican and Puerto Rican culture. The assumption seems to be that speaking Spanish is the most important defining characteristic of the group as a whole and that country of origin or region within a country are minor determinants of cultural differences. As a result, fine-grained classifications of cultural origin are rarely made, and potentially important differences are masked by the heterogeneity of the samples.

In reality, individuals from these different areas living in the United States differ significantly on education level, family size and composition, employment status, and economic profile (Committee on Cultural Psychiatry, 1989b). The Committee also notes that Mexicans and Puerto Ricans differ in racial background due to various combinations of American Indian, African, and Caucasian ancestry. For the sake of consistency, we will refer to youth from Mexico, Central America, South America, and the various island nations (e.g., Puerto Rico, Cuba) of Spanish descent as Hispanic. When specific subgroups of Hispanic youth are participants in a study, their country/culture of origin will be identified.

Hovey and King's (1997) study of suicide risk among Mexican American high school students yielded a key finding. Adolescents living or born in the United States reported higher rates of depressive symptoms and suicidal ideation than those living or born in Mexico. The authors proposed that suicide risk may be moderated by level of acculturative stress. A study comparing junior high aged youth in New Mexico and Texas (Tortolero & Roberts, 2001) found that Mexican American females reported levels of suicidal ideation almost twice as high as European American girls. A similar pattern existed for Mexican American males relative to European American males. After controlling for gender, age, family structure, depression, and perceived discrimination, risk of suicidal ideation remained higher for Mexican American youth. These findings, although limited in generalizability due to sampling issues, seem to suggest a cultural difference in suicide risk.

There also has been debate about the role of fatalism—the belief that one's life is controlled by outside forces—in Mexican American youth suicide risk (Hovey & King, 1997) and whether it is a cultural factor or a social class factor (i.e., poverty causes fatalism). A study examining normative data for a commonly used depression self-report measure found Mexican American fourth and fifth grade students reporting disproportionately high levels of suicidal ideation (Cowell, Gross, McNaughton, Ailey, & Fogg, 2005). The authors saw this as potential evidence of more pessimistic and fatalistic thoughts among Mexican American children; however, they qualified that interpretation by noting that the differences could be due to bias in the measure or participation rates in their particular study. Tortolero and Roberts' (2001) observation that a stronger belief in external control (i.e., fatalism) among Mexican American youth is a risk factor for suicidal ideation has yet to be empirically tested. They did find that those Mexican American youth who reported personally experiencing discrimination were 3.7 times more likely to report suicidal ideation than youth not experiencing discrimination. And even perceiving discrimination against their ethnic group elevated risk of suicidal ideation by a factor of almost two. These two findings led Tortolero and Roberts to conclude that family conflict resulting from discrimination and limited opportunities may elevate stress levels of Mexican American youth and increase their risk of mental health problems.

Another important issue in studies of Hispanic youth is the interaction between gender, ethnicity, and suicide risk. Zayas and colleagues (2000; 2005) have developed—and are beginning to test—a complex model to explain Hispanic female adolescent suicide-related behaviors. They propose an interaction between cultural, family (primarily mother-daughter relations), developmental, and psychological factors. Suicide attempts are believed to be triggered by conflict between the teen and her family, often around issues of autonomy and dating. Differences in level of acculturation between teens and their parents, particularly in lower socioeconomic status families, frequently contribute to the problem. Specifically, less acculturated parents tend to have much more controlling parenting styles and to believe that their daughters should be deferential to parental control. When girls in such families are more closely aligned with the dominant culture, it can create great strain between these girls and their parents. Traditional (i.e., patriarchal and authoritarian) parents may be less flexible in handling acculturating girls.

Zayas, Kaplan, Turner, Romano, and Gonzales-Ramos (2000) focused on mother-daughter conflicts because fathers were underrepresented in the existing research. They suggested that traditional values of Hispanic women—with their husbands being the first source of help—caution against seeking help from outside the family. For immigrant families, perceived sources of help may be quite limited, leading to potentially enmeshed relationships between mothers and daughters. In addition, foreign-born mothers will have a harder time modeling gender roles for their acculturating daughters. Hispanic females are taught not to express anger, so teens' poor coping skills may result in suicide attempts because they do not know how to handle their intense anger and frustration with their mothers. A similar theory was proposed by Heacock (1990), who argued that conflict between traditional gender roles, passivity and dependence, and the dominant culture produce distress, which Hispanic females do not know how to handle. Low lethality suicide attempts may serve as a way to communicate distress for these teens, which then mobilizes (albeit in an unhealthy way) helping resources. Recently Zayas, Fortuna, Lester, and Cabassa (2005) have stated that there is insufficient empirical data on which to build models of Hispanic female suicide; however, the dramatically higher rates of suicide attempts across Hispanic subgroups in nationally representative risk surveys supports their belief in the importance of learning more about cultural differences. Findings from Evans et al.'s (2005) international study also support these theories. They found that when Hispanic adolescents are a minority group in their community, their risk of engaging in nonlethal suicide-related behaviors is elevated.

Protective Factors

African American Adolescents

Researchers have speculated that African Americans are protected from suicide as a result of close social ties, family cohesion, and connections to the church (Early, 1992; Stack & Wasserman, 1995). Religion may function as a protective factor because involvement in the church encourages social connection, fosters self-esteem, and may actually provide meaning to one's life, thus creating a greater attraction to life (Early & Akers, 1993; Neeleman, Wessely, & Lewis, 1998). Morrison and Downey (2000) found that African American college students reported significantly more reasons for living than their Caucasian peers. In addition, the African American participants scored significantly higher on moral objections to suicide and survival and coping beliefs, suggesting that religious values may lessen suicidal behaviors. This hypothesis is supported by findings that African Americans were less accepting of suicide than Caucasians as a result of their religious beliefs (Neeleman et al., 1998). However, if social ties or religious connections are broken or absent, African Americans may be at a greater risk for suicide-related behaviors. Most of this research was not conducted with adolescents, and therefore caution should be taken in applying the findings to younger individuals. For example, a more recent study (Watt & Sharp, 2002) utilizing a large nationally representative sample of Caucasian and African American youth found no protective influence of religion. These findings suggest that revising our theories regarding protective factors for African American adolescents may be in order.

Hispanic Adolescents

In most Hispanic cultures the Catholic church plays a strong role, and church affiliation may be an important protective factor. The church's teaching that suicide is a sin and suffering in this life is rewarded in the afterlife may also be protective (Hovey & King, 1997). In addition, Hovey and King stated that religious ceremonies are important social events that strengthen family and community bonds as well as social obligations. They also suggested that positive family functioning and orientation toward the future may serve as protective factors that combine to increase the safety net for at-risk Mexican American teens. The Committee on Cultural Psychiatry (1989b) offered additional insights regarding Mexican American youth suicide rates. They hypothesized that larger extended family support networks and more two-parent households may decrease risk. Oquendo and colleagues (2005) conducted a study of 460 psychiatric patients with major affective disorders or schizophrenia. They found that Hispanic participants reported lower levels of suicidal ideation but did not differ on likelihood, intent, or lethality of attempts. Being Catholic and regularly attending services was associated with lower risk among Hispanics. It was found that Catholicism was associated with greater moral objections to suicide. Hispanic participants also reported a stronger sense of responsibility to their families as a reason for not acting on suicidal thoughts. The authors concluded that cultural beliefs, more than ethnicity, are the true protective factors.

Comparative Risk Models

Although scarce, some studies have made the necessary comparisons to begin testing hypotheses about different patterns of risk and protective factors across racial/ethnic groups. We sought to replicate previous findings based on college student data in a study of high school students participating in a risk-screening project (Gutierrez, Muehlenkamp, Konick, & Osman, 2005). Our model looked at the effects of exposure to suicide on current suicide ideation, as mediated by depression and reasons for living. It was hypothesized that adolescents exposed to suicide-related behaviors in others, and who reported high levels of depressive symptoms and few reasons for living, would endorse the highest levels of current suicidal ideation. The first step was to determine how well the model functioned in the overall sample and then to make comparisons between European American and African American youth. We had originally hoped to include Hispanic and Asian Americans, but there were not enough adolescents of those two races/ethnicities to conduct the necessary statistical tests.

Our findings not only supported the hypothesized relationships between the risk and protective factors but indicated that these relationships held up in both racial/ethnic groups. In other words, at least in this preliminary study, the variables included in this model provide an accurate gauge of risk for suicide ideation in European and African American adolescents. While to the best of our knowledge this was the first study to test a specific model of suicide risk (i.e., suicidal ideation) across racial/ethnic groups, other researchers have examined individual risk factors and, to a lesser extent, protective factors for different groups.

Molock et al. (1994) tested the reliability of two commonly used self-report measures in a comparison of African American and Caucasian college students. Overall, the two groups were similar in terms of rates of nonlethal suicide-related behaviors, impulsivity, reported problems contributing to suicidality, and gender differences. African American students reported slightly lower levels of suicidal ideation and were less likely to have used alcohol or other drugs when making an attempt. The authors speculated this finding could be related to lower suicide completion rates of African Americans but cautioned against generalizing beyond the fairly affluent (i.e., middle class) students attending a predominantly African American university, where there is strong social support and insulation against racism and discrimination. More directly related to our interests, Guiao and Thompson (2004) analyzed data from a nationally representative adolescent health survey to determine that Hispanics were at greater risk of depression than Caucasian, African American, or Asian youth. Caucasian and Hispanic teens reported drinking more than African Americans or Asian Americans. But no differences in suicidality based on race or ethnicity were found.

Implications for Future Research

Given the diversity of findings regarding the influence of race, ethnicity, and culture on risk and protective factors for adolescent suicide and similarities/differences in suicidality across racial/ethnic groups, what conclusions can be drawn regarding minority youth assessment? Most obviously, we have much still to learn—starting with valid and reliable measures of the constructs of interest, for each racial/ethnic group being studied must be the starting point. This necessitates rigorously and systematically evaluating existing self-report measures, diagnostic interviews, and other tools for measurement equivalence. Poor performing measures should be revised and reevaluated, and new measures will need to be developed. Researchers and clinicians interested in scale construction are advised to pay heed to issues of racial/ethnic measurement equivalence discussed earlier in this chapter. Once a set of appropriate, well validated assessment tools exist, we can set about truly testing different models of adolescent suicide in the diverse culture of the United States. We also need to determine the true differences (or lack thereof) in rates of nonlethal suicide-related behavior and completed suicide by racial/ethnic group, which can only come from carefully conducted epidemiological research. Categorization of race/ethnicity should go beyond group membership and include language preference, generational status, ethnic identity, and perceived discrimination (Roberts et al., 1997). Hovey and King (1997) suggested that mixed qualitative and quantitative designs, which provide a sense of the individual experience, may aid in the identification of specific aspects of culture that increase risk as well as serve a protective function. As Roberts (2000) noted, significant differences in social class across ethnic groups suggest some observed differences may be less a function of race/ethnicity than of socioeconomic status. Therefore future research should include careful assessment of social class. The data generated by these types of studies will inform decision making regarding which groups are at the highest risk and the factors to target within those groups in order to lower risk levels and prevent adolescent suicide.

Assessment Implications

Until the goals we just laid out have been accomplished, the existing literature we have reviewed and our own research suggests that assessing the traditional risk factors of hopelessness, depression, and suicidal ideation makes sense regardless of the race/ethnicity of the adolescent. Assessing protective factors with the RFL-A also appears to be warranted, although interpreting the findings based on the adolescent's race/ethnicity may be somewhat more complicated due to a poorer understanding of how these factors operate across cultures. Also unclear is the importance of religion in the lives of African American and Hispanic youth. It appears that a meaningful relationship with a faith community can be protective for both groups of adolescents, which necessitates care when assessing religion-related constructs. Specifically, simply knowing if an adolescent considers him/herself to be religious does not appear to be enough. The meaning of religion in their lives, the extent to which they affiliate with a faith community, the extent and nature of social support derived from that affiliation, and their beliefs about the consequences of suicide (e.g., it's a sin and you'll go to hell if you kill yourself) must all be assessed. These recommendations are embarrassingly light, given the number of studies we reviewed. Unfortunately, due to the diversity of findings, potential problems with data related to measurement and design issues, and scarcity of large-scale multigroup comparison studies, this appears to be the current state of our understanding.

We hope the information provided in this chapter will allow readers to more critically examine existing studies and carefully consider the potential impact of race, ethnicity, and culture when assessing youth for suicide risk. In addition, we hope we have inspired researchers to begin facing the challenges of multicultural research so that the field can finally get to the point at which we no longer have to conclude every article and book chapter with admonitions that these results are tentative and more research is needed.

The Importance of Predictive Validity

As we have been saying throughout this book, adolescent completed suicide is a statistically low probability occurrence. Because of serious ethical considerations, it is not possible to design prospective studies specifically to test predictors of completed suicide. Prediction of nonlethal suicide-related behaviors is somewhat easier to study but still fraught with numerous ethical and methodological challenges. However, the whole point of adolescent suicide assessment is to attempt to gain a good handle on the likelihood of any given adolescent engaging in suicide-related behaviors so that these outcomes can be prevented. As a result, determining the predictive validity of existing measures is critical. Briefly, predictive validity refers to the extent to which scores on a measure correlate with a criterion behavior in the future. The stronger the association, the better the predictive validity of the measure. For example, if you determine that 70% of adolescents who achieve above a certain score on a measure of depressive symptoms are subsequently diagnosed with major depressive disorder, then you would conclude that measure had good predictive validity. In this chapter, we have used data from adolescent clinical samples to illustrate strategies for establishing predictive validity for scores on self-report instruments. The data were obtained from a study designed to evaluate the usefulness of responses on risk and protective self-report measures as potential predictors of adolescent suicide re-attempts and physical aggressive behavior.

Previous Work Examining Predictors of Adolescent Suicide Attempts

Several studies have linked psychological and psychosocial risk factors, such as hopelessness, depression, and problem solving deficits to suicide attempts in children and adolescents (e.g., Maris, Berman, Maltsberger, & Yufit, 1991; Rotheram-Borus, Trautman, Dopkins, & Shrout, 1990; Sadowski & Kelley, 1993). However only a few have evaluated the impact of risk and protective factors that are related to *ongoing* adolescent suicidal behavior in the course of treatment. We will describe a study designed to evaluate the predictive utility of scores on selected Minnesota Multiphasic Personality Inventory—Adolescents (MMPI-A) content scales (Butcher et al., 1992), the Beck Hopelessness Scale (BHS; Beck & Steer, 1993), and the Reasons for Living Inventory for Adolescents (RFL-A; Osman, Downs, et al., 1998) in a sample of adolescent psychiatric inpatients. Although we will be using some fairly technical statistics terminology in this chapter, nonresearchers should not be frightened away as the information gleaned from studies like this is directly applicable to clinical work. Readers may wish to refer to Chapter 4, where we discuss in more detail the types of statistics used in analyzing the data from this study.

Spirito, Valeri, Boergers, and Donaldson (2003) confirmed the positive relationships between baseline measures of (a) family functioning, as assessed with the McMaster Family Assessment Device (FAD; Epstein, Baldwin, & Bishop, 1983), (b) feelings of hopelessness, as assessed with the Hopelessness Scale for Children (Kazdin, French, Unis, Esveldt-Dawson, & Sherick, 1983), (c) abilities to regulate affect, as assessed with the Regulation of Affect and Impulses scale (RAI; Pelcovitz, van der Kolk, Roth, Mandel, & Kaplan, 1997), (d) depressed mood, as assessed with the Center for Epidemiologic Studies Depression scale (CES-D; Radloff, 1991), and (e) continued suicidal ideation and re-attempts by comparing baseline and 3-month follow-up assessment.

Participants in Spirito et al.'s (2003) study were a small mixed sample of children and adolescents (N = 58) ages 12 to 18 years who were receiving medical interventions for suicide-related behaviors in either an emergency department or a pediatrics ward of a children's hospital. Following the admission evaluations, the authors randomly assigned the study participants to either a standard disposition planning or a compliance enhancement intervention group. All participants were administered packets of self-report instruments, noted previously, to establish baseline levels of functioning. Doctoral-level researchers conducted brief telephone interviews with the participants 3 months following the baseline assessments.

The 3-month follow-up interviews were conducted to collect information on (a) the occurrences or nonoccurrences of suicide ideation or self-harm and (b) suicide re-attempts or nonattempt. The authors defined suicide attempt as recommended in O'Carroll et al. (1996) to include self-harmful behavior with the indication or intent of ending one's life. They conducted several independent samples *t*-tests to examine differences between the (a) suicide ideators and nonideators and (b) suicide reattempters and nonreattempters on the baseline measures.

Results regarding the suicide ideation outcome at 3 months showed that youth with suicidal ideation reported higher depressive symptoms, hopelessness, poorer regulation of affect, and poorer family problem-solving skills than the nonideators (all *p* values < .05). In the analyses involving suicide re-attempts, adolescents who reattempted suicide scored significantly higher on the baseline measures of depression, family general functioning, and family communication than those who did not reattempt. Finally, to evaluate the relative impact of depressive mood on the other baseline measures, the authors conducted partial correlational analyses using scores on the CES-D as covariate. They found that depressive mood at baseline was uniquely associated with both continued suicidal ideation and re-attempts.

Methodological Considerations

Gray et al. (2003) identified several methodological problems that may be related not only to Spirito et al.'s (2003) investigation but also to the practice of collecting longitudinal outcome data in outpatient settings. Specifically, the authors drew attention to the potential for obtaining inaccurate accounts of predictive validity study outcomes because of *differences in the contexts* in which interventions are implemented for at-risk behaviors and follow-up data are collected. In addition to Gray et al.'s (2003) concerns, we will address four major considerations for clinical researchers in designing predictive validity studies in adolescent suicidality. The first concern is the difficulty in monitoring in an outpatient setting dimensions including the frequency and severity of most relevant internalizing dependent variables, such as suicide ideation and suicide re-attempts. With this in mind, it might be useful to conduct predictive validity studies of suicide and suicide-related constructs only at inpatient institutions. The second concern is that follow-up data collection intervals exceeding 1 to 2 months may pose clinical and ethical problems for clinical researchers. The data suggest that youngsters who have attempted suicide are at greater risk of making subsequent re-attempts; these individuals should be monitored over shorter time intervals. The third concern is that most suicide and suicide-related assessment instruments, including self-report, are designed for use as state-based measures. Thus the use of these instruments to recall information such as the frequency of suicidal thoughts over long intervals may result in substantially biased estimates. Indeed, long time-interval data is only useful when the construct we attempt to evaluate is stable. Our fourth concern is that the high rate of participant attrition in existing studies could be addressed in part if follow-up data are collected within shorter time intervals. As indicated in Chapter 4, we conducted the study described in this chapter to illustrate some of these methodological concerns.

The Current Study—*Prediction of Suicide Attempts*

Purpose

The study we discuss here attempted to modify and extend several of the methodological strategies implemented by Gray et al. (2003) in a forensic psychiatric inpatient population. For example, following Gray et al., the criterion (e.g., suicide reattempt) and predictor variables (e.g., MMPI-A, Beck Hopelessness Scale) in this study were collected objectively within an inpatient setting. In addition, we used structured procedures to collect data on our dependent measures;

however, in contrast to the commonly used 3-month follow-up interview periods, we conducted follow-up assessment interviews after 2 months of admission to the inpatient unit in order to (a) minimize participant attrition and (b) control for the substantially differing follow-up assessment periods previously noted.

We believe this study is an important improvement over previous attempts to identify a clinically useful set of risk or protective factors, such as depression, hopelessness, anger, satisfaction with life, and fewer reasons for living in adolescent suicidality (Gutierrez, Osman, Kopper, & Barrios, 2000; Heisel & Flett, 2004; Osman et al., 2002). It is our hope that this study and others like it, designed to identify factors that *continue to increase risk* for suicide re-attempts, will contribute to the development of effective prevention strategies for suicide completion as well as inform clinical decisions regarding discharge of the patient.

Method
Participants

Participants were consecutive admissions to two inpatient units of a state psychiatric hospital. The sample included 55 boys (Mean age = 15.56 years, SD = .94) and 48 girls (Mean age = 15.71 years, SD = 0.87) with an overall mean age of 15.62 years (SD = 0.91; range = 14 to 17 years). Participants who were admitted to the units because of severe suicide-related behaviors (i.e., suicide attempt or re-attempts) were recruited for study participation. The majority (87.4%) of the participants were Caucasian, 3.9% were African American, 2.9% were Hispanic, and 5.8% were other ethnic groups.

The primary diagnoses, as assigned by the multidisciplinary assessment teams, were as follows: 47.6% major depressive disorder, 31.1% conduct disorder, 14.6% oppositional defiant disorder, and 6.7% other primary diagnoses. All diagnoses were based on the *Diagnostic and Statistical Manual of Mental Disorders* (4th ed. [DSM-IV]; American Psychiatric Association, 1994). The assessment and treatment teams used multiple assessment procedures including semi-structured psychiatric interviews, standardized intellectual functioning, academic achievement, personality testing, and psychosocial history information in deriving consensus diagnoses.

Measures and Procedures

All participants were recruited within 2 weeks of admission to the units. The study protocol was approved by the relevant institutional review boards. Participants individually provided informed consent or assent, depending on age, before the initial data collection.

Baseline Evaluations

The study participants completed the following self-report instruments: (a) the 478-item MMPI-A (Butcher et al., 1992) to identify a range of risk factors on the content scales, such as depression, low self-esteem, and family problems; (b) the 4-item Suicidal Behaviors Questionnaire–Revised (SBQ-R; Osman et al., 2001) to assess self-reported suicide-related behaviors; (c) the 20-item Beck Hopelessness Scale (BHS; Beck & Steer, 1993) to assess symptoms of hopelessness about future events; and (d) the 32-item Reasons for Living Inventory for Adolescents (RFL-A; Osman et al., 1998; see Chapter 6) to assess reasons adolescents give for not taking their own lives. Scores on selected MMPI-A content scales (see the Preliminary Analysis section below), the BHS, and the RFL-A served as the predictor variables. The measures were administered by a teacher's assistant who was trained in the questionnaire administration. In our study, the internal consistency estimates of the SBQ-R (α = .87; mean inter-item r = .69), the BHS (KR-20 = .93, mean inter-item r = .39), and the RFL-A (α = .97, mean inter-item r = .49) were acceptable.

FOLLOW-UP EVALUATIONS (2 MONTHS)

The following assessments were conducted two months following the initial self-report administration.

The (Modified) Overt Aggression Scale (OAS; Yudofsky, Silvaer, Jackson, Endicott, & Williams, 1986) We modified items on the OAS to record observed incidents of physically aggressive behavior and suicide re-attempts. We defined *physically aggressive* behavior as any overt behavior (e.g., kicking, hitting, and spitting) that is directed at staff, another patient, or property (Part A). All instances of physical aggression against the self (self-harm) that resulted in medical or staff interventions were recorded, as were incidents of suicide attempts (OAS, Part B; *Suicide Re-attempts*). The modified OAS was adopted by both units as an incident report form for recording the aggressive behaviors of all patients.

All direct care staff on the units were trained by Dr. Osman, who is the hospital's psychology consultant, in using the OAS. We did not assess inter-rater reliability estimates; however, staff members were informed that reliability in completing the OAS would be monitored occasionally by the psychology consultant, the unit psychologists, or the director of nursing. Staff members were not informed that, for the purposes of this study, the OAS data would be used for only youths who were admitted because of suicide-related behaviors. At the end of each week, copies of the completed forms were placed in the mailbox of the psychology consultant by a staff nurse.

The Suicidal Behaviors Interview (SBI; Reynolds, 1990) The SBI is a semi-structured interview designed to assess suicidal behaviors in adolescents. Items on the SBI were generated from the suicide literature and clinical interviews with suicidal adolescents. Professionals, including school and mental health personnel, participated in evaluating the item content and scoring procedures of the SBI. This instrument is composed of two sections, each with a set of items that are rated on global scales of either 0 – 2 or 0 – 4. Estimates of inter-rater reliability have been found to be high for advanced student raters (r_{icc} = .99). Scores on the SBI have also been found to correlate positively and significantly with scores on measures of suicidal ideation (r = .62), suicide attempt (r = .69), and adolescent depression (r = .47), suggesting good evidence for convergent validity (Reynolds, 1990).

We trained advanced undergraduate and graduate students with at least one month of experience working as psychologist trainees on these units to conduct individual interviews using the SBI. The training procedures were similar to those implemented by Reynolds (1990) in the development of the instrument. Raters initiated data collection only after (a) attaining 80% or higher estimates of intra-rater reliability and (b) conducting a comprehensive review of the assigned medical records. For our study, we scored 3 items from Part II of the SBI that are specific to suicidal ideation: (a) recent suicidal thoughts (Item 6) rated 0 = *absent*, to 4 = *most of the time*, (b) suicidal intent (Item 8) rated 0 = *absent*, to 4 = *extremely serious, 100% sure*, and (c) current suicidal ideation (Item 20) rated 0 = *absent*, to 4 = *very serious*. We summed these ratings to derive a continuous suicide ideation index. The reliability estimate of the continuous suicide ideation index was adequate, .89 (mean inter-item r = .96).

Results

Preliminary Analysis

(At this point readers should be familiar with the types of statistics used in this study, based on discussions in previous chapters. But a quick review of Chapter 4 might be useful if you find yourself confused by any of these analyses.)

We first conducted a simultaneous regression analysis to identify a set of MMPI-A content scales to include in the subsequent analyses. The MMPI-A content scale scores served as predictor variables, and the SBQ-R admission suicide status score served as the criterion variable.

Table 11.1 shows the results of this analysis. We selected the MMPI-A Adol-dep (depression), Adol-con (conduct problems), Adol-alse (low self-esteem), and Adol-fam (family problems) scales as potentially useful predictors in the subsequent analyses.

Overview of the data analytic plan

Predictor Variables The following baseline measures were used as predictor variables: scores on (a) the four selected MMPI-A content scales (depression, conduct, low self-esteem, and family problems), (b) the BHS, and (c) the RFL-A.

Criterion Variables We used the following variables as dependent measures: (a) *Suicide Reattempt* status. Analyses of the OAS Part II data showed that 11.7% (n = 12) made one suicide attempt, 28.2% (n = 29) made two or more attempts, and 60.2% (n = 62) did not make any subsequent attempt. We combined data of all the

Table 11.1

MMPI-A Content Scales as Predictors of Suicide Attempt Status

Variable	r^a	sr^2	Estimate	p
Adol-Anxiety	.47**	.02	.04	ns
Adol-Obsessiveness	.41**	-.09	-.21	ns
Adol-Depression	.60**	.21	.46	< .01
Adol-Health Concerns	.34**	.00	.00	ns
Adol-Alienation	.48**	-.04	-.09	ns
Adol-Bizarre Mentation	.41**	.03	.05	ns
Adol-Anger	.30**	.04	.06	ns
Adol-Cynicism	.26	-.11	-.15	ns
Adol-Conduct Problems	.42**	.15	.23	< .05
Adol-Low Self-Esteem	.52**	.15	.31	< .05
Adol-Low Aspirations	.14-	.09	-.14	ns
Adol-Social Discomfort	.35**	.03	.06	ns
Adol-Family Problems	.48**	.16	.21	< .05
Adol-School Problems	.24	-.13	-.20	ns
Adol-Negative Treatment Ind.	.49**	.00	.01	ns

Note. MMPI-A = Minnesota Multiphasic Personality Inventory-Adolescent
[a]Bonferroni's alpha; ** $p < .003$.

suicide reattempters to create dichotomous groups of reattempters (coded as 1; $n = 41$) and nonattempters (coded as 0; $n = 62$); (b) we recoded the number of incidents of physically aggressive behaviors on the OAS to create dichotomous groups of physically aggressive ($n = 34$) and nonaggressive ($n = 69$) participants; and (c) we summed the three SBI suicide ideation items to obtain a continuous index of suicide ideation.

First, we conducted Pearson correlational analyses to examine intercorrelations among the predictor variables. We expected moderate correlations among scores on these predictor measures. Additional analyses were carried out to evaluate relations between scores on each predictor measure and scores on the separate criterion measures.

Second, we conducted receiver operating characteristic (ROC) curve analyses, using scores on the separate predictor variables and the reattempt (coded = 1) and nonreattempt (coded = 0) groups. These scores were used to evaluate the predictive validity of each predictor during hospitalization.

Third, we conducted binary logistic regression analyses to evaluate the clinical utility of each predictor during hospitalization. The Odds Ratios and the 95% confidence intervals (CIs) were used to guide interpretation in identifying each predictor as clinically useful in the assessment of suicide reattempt and physically aggressive behavior.

Fourth, as recommended by Gray et al. (2003), we computed median (midpoint of a distribution) scores for each of the predictor variables. Participants who scored above the median value (cut-off score) on each measure during baseline were assigned to the risk group (coded as 1), and participants who scored below the median value were assigned to the low-risk group (coded as 0). Predictive or discriminative validity is established for an instrument (e.g., the BHS) when those who score above the median value obtain significantly higher scores on a follow-up measure (in this study, the suicide reattempt and physical aggression behavior scores) than those who score below the median value. As in Gray et al., the subsequent analyses did not include scores that fell at the exact median of the score range to more clearly include only extreme and stable subgroups in the analyses. Separate nonparametric independent samples *t*-tests (for small sample sizes) were conducted for each predictor variable using the StatXact program.

Finally, simultaneous regression analyses were conducted to examine the relative predictive validity of the predictor variables to the prediction of continuous suicide ideation during 2 months of hospitalization.

INTERCORRELATIONS AMONG THE PREDICTOR MEASURES

Table 11.2 shows the intercorrelations among the study measures. These correlations ranged from -.24 to .79, indicating low to moderate significant relationships among scores on the instruments. The correlations between the RFL-A scale scores and scores on the risk measures suggest that youth with moderate distress conditions including depression and low self-esteem reported fewer reasons for living.

PREDICTING SUICIDE REATTEMPT AND PHYSICAL AGGRESSION

Results of the analyses involving the suicide reattempt variable as criterion measure are reported in Table 11.3. Table 11.4 contains the analyses for physical aggression as a criterion measure.

Adol-Depression Scale The Depression scale score correlated moderately and significantly with the suicide reattempt (*r* = .62) and slightly with the physical aggression (*r* = .34) variable scores (*p* values < .05). In addition, the Depression scale score discriminated between the suicide reattempter and nonattempter

Table 11.2

Intercorrelations Among the Predictor Measure Scales

Variable	1	2	3	4	5	6
1. Adol-Depression	1.00					
2. Adol-Conduct Problems	.48**	1.00				
3. Adol-Low Self-Esteem	.79**	.47**	1.00			
4. Adol-Family Problems	.58**	.44**	.50**	1.00		
5. Beck Hopelessness Scale	.72**	.33**	.62**	.47**	1.00	
6. Reasons for Living-Adolescents	-.52**	-.24*	-.45**	-.53**	-.61**	1.00

*$p < .05$. **$p < .01$.

Table 11.3

Correlations, AUCs, ORs (95% CIs), Mann-Whitney Exact p Values, Cohen's Effect Size d for the Suicide Reattempt Behavior

Variable	r	AUC	OR[a] (95% CI)	Mann-Whitney Exact p	Effect Size d
MMPI-A Adol-Depression	.62**	.87	1.14 (1.09 –1.21)	< .01	1.55
Adol-Conduct Problems	.48**	.78	1.09 (1.05 –1.13)	< .01	0.79
Adol-Low Self-Esteem	.56**	.84	1.12 (1.07 –1.17)	< .01	1.52
Adol-Family Problems	.49**	.81	1.08 (1.04 –1.11)	< .01	1.26
Hopelessness Scale BHS	.63**	.88	1.46 (1.26 –1.70)	< .01	1.82
Reasons for Living RFL-A	-.58**	.86	0.24 (0.13 –0.43)	< .01	1.21

Note. MMPI-A = Minnesota Multiphasic Personality Inventory-Adolescent; AUC = Area Under the receiver operating characteristic curve; OR = Odds Ratio; BHS = Beck Hopelessness Scale; RFL-A = Reasons for Living Inventory for Adolescents.
[a] All p values < .01. **$p < .01$.

groups and between the physically aggressive and nonaggressive youth. The score attained medium accuracy in predicting suicide reattempt (AUC = .87) and medium accuracy in predicting physically aggressive behavior (AUC = .71). This scale score was also identified as useful in the assessment of suicide re-attempts (OR = 1.14, $p < .01$) and physically aggressive behavior (OR = 1.07, $p < .01$).

Adol-Conduct Problems Scores on the Conduct Problems scale correlated moderately with the suicide re-attempts ($r = .48$) and low with the physical aggression ($r = .21$) variable scores (p values $< .05$). The scale score discriminated between the responses of the suicide reattempter and nonattempter groups. In addition, it had medium accuracy in predicting suicide reattempt (AUC = .78); it had low accuracy in predicting physically aggressive behavior (AUC = .65) during hospitalization. The scale was identified as useful in assessing the responses of the suicide reattempters and nonattempters; however, the scale was not useful in distinguishing between the responses of the aggressive and nonaggressive youth during admission to these inpatient units.

Table 11.4

Correlations, AUCs, ORs (95% CIs), Mann-Whitney Exact p Values, Cohen's Effect Size d for Physical Aggression

Variable	r	AUC	OR[a] (95% CI)	Mann-Whitney Exact p	Effect Size d
MMPI-A Adol-Depression	.34**	.71	1.07 (1.03 –1.11)	< .01	0.67
Adol-Conduct Problems	.21**	.65	1.04 (1.00 –1.07)	ns	0.32
Adol-Low Self-Esteem	.31**	.69	1.06 (1.02 –1.10)	< .01	0.59
Adol-Family Problems	.23**	.65	1.04 (1.00 –1.07)	< .01	0.58
Hopelessness Scale BHS	.36**	.71	1.27 (1.10 –1.47)	< .01	0.75
Reasons for Living RFL-A	-.30**	.69	0.48 (0.29 –0.79)	< .02	0.51

Note. MMPI-A = Minnesota Multiphasic Personality Inventory-Adolescent; AUC = Area Under the Receiver operating characteristic curve; OR = Odds Ratio; BHS = Beck Hopelessness Scale; RFL-A = Reasons for Living Inventory for Adolescents.

[a]All p values $< .01$.   ** $p < .01$.

Adol-Low Self-Esteem   The Low Self-Esteem scale score correlated moderately with the suicide reattempt ($r = .56$) and low with the physical aggression behavior ($r = .31$) variable scores (p values $< .05$). The scale score was useful in discriminating between the suicide reattempter and nonattempter groups and between the physically aggressive and nonaggressive groups. The scale had medium accuracy in predicting suicide attempts (AUC = .84) and low accuracy in predicting physically aggressive behavior (AUC = .69). Scores on this scale were useful in the assessment of suicide re-attempts and physically aggressive behaviors.

Adol-Family Problems   Scores on the Family Problems scale correlated moderately with the suicide re-attempts ($r = .49$) and low with the physical aggression behavior ($r = .23$) variable scores (all p values $< .05$). The scale score differentiated between the suicide reattempter and nonattempter groups and between the physically aggressive and nonaggressive youth. In addition, the scale score had medium accuracy in predicting suicide re-attempts (AUC = .81) and low accuracy in predicting physically aggressive behavior (AUC = .65). The scale score was also identified as useful in the assessment of suicide reattempt and physically aggressive behavior.

Beck Hopelessness Scale (BHS)   In the analyses involving the BHS total score, we found moderate and significant correlations between the total score and the suicide reattempt ($r = .63$) variable score and a low but statistically significant correlation with the physical aggression ($r = .36$) variable score. The total BHS score also differentiated between the suicide reattempter and nonattempter groups and between the physically aggressive and nonaggressive youth. The total score had medium accuracy in predicting suicide reattempt (AUC = .88); it also attained medium accuracy in predicting physically aggressive behavior (AUC = .71). Furthermore, the BHS total score was identified as useful in the assessment of suicide reattempt and physically aggressive behaviors.

Reasons for Living Inventory for Adolescents (RFL-A)   The RFL-A total inventory score correlated negatively and moderately with the suicide reattempt ($r = -.58$) variable score, and it correlated negatively and weakly with the physical aggression ($r = -.30$) variable score (p values $< .05$). The total inventory score discriminated between the suicide reattempter and nonattempter groups and between the physically aggressive and nonaggressive participants. The total RFL-A score had medium accuracy in predicting suicide reattempt (AUC = .86) and low accuracy in predicting physically aggressive behavior (AUC = .69). This inventory was significant in the assessment of suicide re-attempts and physically aggressive behavior.

SIMULTANEOUS REGRESSION ANALYSES: PREDICTING SCORES ON THE INDEX OF SUICIDE IDEATION

Finally, we conducted simultaneous regression analyses to evaluate the relative predictive ability of each scale score in predicting continuous suicide ideation, as assessed with the SBI. Results of these analyses are presented in Table 11.5. We found that only scores on the MMPI-A conduct problems scale, the BHS, and the RFL-A were useful in predicting continuous suicidal thoughts during hospitalization.

Discussion

In this chapter, we have attempted to address several methodological issues with previous studies evaluating the predictive validity of scores on well-designed self-report instruments. We will now look at each of these issues in some detail and discuss how our study attempted to address each.

Table 11.5

Correlations, AUCs, ORs (95% CIs), Mann-Whitney Exact p Values, Cohen's Effect Size d for Continuous Suicide Ideation

Variable	r^a	sr^2	Estimate	p
MMPI-A Adol-Depression	.53**	.023	.04	ns
Adol-Conduct Problems	.42**	.184	.22	<.02
Adol-Low Self-Esteem	.48**	.019	.03	ns
Adol-Family Problems	.43**	.003	.00	ns
Hopelessness Scale BHS	.58**	.173	.27	<.02
Reasons for Living RFL-A	-.56**	-.220	-.30	<.01

Note. MMPI-A = Minnesota Multiphasic Personality Inventory-Adolescent; AUC = Area Under the Receiver operating characteristic curve; OR = Odds Ratio; BHS = Beck Hopelessness Scale; RFL-A = Reasons for Living Inventory for Adolescents.
[a]All p values < .01.   ** $p < .01$.

First, we identified a shorter time interval (i.e., 2 months rather than 3) that might be useful in evaluating the predictive validity of scores on self-report measures of adolescent suicidality. As expected, the participant attrition rate was highly controlled; all participants at baseline provided data at the 2-month follow-up assessment. Most longitudinal studies do not come close to achieving zero attrition. In addition, we found that at a 2-month follow-up assessment approximately 11.7% of our study participants had reattempted suicide within the hospital setting, which is consistent with rates found in similar studies. For example, Spirito et al. (2003) reported 12% reattempts for their mixed sample of inpatient and outpatient adolescents; however, because of the setting in which the study was conducted, none of those attempts were fatal. Subsequent risk of the reattempters was closely monitored to ensure their continued safety. This level of monitoring is not possible in outpatient or community settings and is a major ethical concern when conducting adolescent suicide research.

Second, the results of our study provide strong support for the predictive validity and clinical utility of a combined set of self-report measures of risk (i.e., selected MMPI-A content scales and BHS) and protective factors. Specifically, scores on the 4 MMPI-A content scales, the BHS, and the RFL-A scale were identified as good predictors of suicide re-attempts during hospitalization. Scores on the MMPI-A Depression, Low Self-Esteem, Family Problems, BHS, and RFL-A measures were effective predictors of physically aggressive behavior during psychiatric hospitalization. While it would be premature to recommend wide scale adoption of this protocol for use in psychiatric hospitals and other clinical settings, we hope that our study will serve as a model for other researchers working in this area. When sufficient evidence, based on replication of our work, exists to support the use of self-report measures for prediction of future suicide-related behavior, we will have made a significant step forward in our efforts to prevent adolescent suicide.

Third, because of the low base rate of completed suicide, we identified continuous suicide ideation as a clinically useful criterion measure. Results of the simultaneous regression analyses suggest that combining scores on the MMPI-A conduct problems, hopelessness, and low reasons for living measures produced the best set of predictors for continuous suicide ideation within this inpatient setting. Minimal empirical evidence exists in the suicide literature in support of the predictive validity of most of the commonly used self-report instruments. Once again, our study needs to be replicated by other researchers in order to produce additional information about the predictive validity of scores on these scales but demonstrates that such research can be conducted safely.

We should also mention several limitations of our study. For example, we did not include nonclinical adolescents in any of the analyses. Because these results may not generalize beyond the current inpatient samples, the results need to be confirmed through replication with other clinical and nonclinical samples. In addition, we sampled only a small proportion of potential risk and protective factors that are associated with adolescent suicide-related behaviors to serve as predictor variables (see Chapters 2 and 3). Future analyses involving other risk and protective factors might yield different results. Regardless of these limitations, we hope we have illustrated some clinically useful research strategies for conducting predictive validity investigations in the area of adolescent suicide-related behaviors.

Concluding Remarks

We have highlighted the issues one must consider when reading the assessment literature, conducting research on adolescent suicide, or engaging in various types of prevention efforts. The chapters critically reviewing specific measures should aid researchers, clinicians, and other professionals in making sound decisions about the most appropriate tools for the intended purpose. Based on the empirical evidence presented in this book, we believe that several of the measures we have developed over the years are among the best options for assessing risk and protective factors; therefore, copies of our scales are provided in the appendix to this book. Readers are welcome to use these measures—and the corresponding scoring and interpretation information provided in Chapter 8—for their clinical work and research projects. This book is the culmination of over a decade of our work. None of it would have happened were it not for the assistance of dozens of dedicated undergraduate and graduate student research assistants, professional staff members at numerous data collection sites, and the volunteer participants in our many studies. We would like to thank each and every one of them for their help in our efforts to better understand and prevent adolescent suicide.

Summary of Clinical Practice Implications

- The Adolescent Depression scale of the MMPI-A fairly accurately predicts suicide re-attempts and acts of physical aggression.

- The MMPI-A Adolescent Conduct Problems scale fairly accurately predicts re-attempts but not physical aggression.

- Both the MMPI-A Low Self-Esteem and Adolescent Family Problems scales are better predictors of re-attempts than physical aggression.

- The BHS and RFL-A total score (i.e., low RFL-A scores) are useful in predicting re-attempts and aggression.

- The MMPI-A Conduct Problems Scale, BHS, and RFL-A total score are all useful in predicting ongoing suicidal ideation.

- Before recommending wide scale adoption of a protocol comprised of these measures, our results should be confirmed by independent researchers.

- This protocol (i.e., selected MMPI-A scales, BHS, and RFL-A) has promise for ongoing clinical investigations and research.

Appendix

Assessment Tools and

Score Sheets

A

Positive and Negative Suicide Ideation

(PANSI) Inventory

Name / Code Number _____ Gender: M / F   Age _____   **PANSI**

Marital Status _____ Education _____ Date ___/___/___

Below is a list of statements that may or may not apply to you. Please read each statement carefully and circle the appropriate number in the space to the right of each statement.

During the <u>past two weeks</u>, including today, how often <u>have you</u>:

		1 = **None of the time**	2 = Very rarely	3 = Some of the time	4 = A good part of the time	5 = Most of the time
1.	Seriously considered killing yourself because you could not live up to the expectations of other people?	1	2	3	4	5
2.	Felt that you were in control of most situations in your life?	1	2	3	4	5
3.	Felt hopeless about the future and you wondered if you should kill yourself?	1	2	3	4	5
4.	Felt so unhappy about your relationship with someone you wished you were dead?	1	2	3	4	5
5.	Thought about killing yourself because you could not accomplish something important in your life?	1	2	3	4	5
6.	Felt hopeful about the future because things were working out well for you?	1	2	3	4	5
7.	Thought about killing yourself because you could not find a solution to a personal problem?	1	2	3	4	5
8.	Felt excited because you were doing well at school or at work?	1	2	3	4	5
9.	Thought about killing yourself because you felt like a failure in life?	1	2	3	4	5
10.	Thought that your problems were so overwhelming that suicide was seen as the only option for you?	1	2	3	4	5
11.	Felt so lonely or sad you wanted to kill yourself so that you could end your pain?	1	2	3	4	5
12.	Felt confident about your ability to cope with most of the problems in your life?	1	2	3	4	5
13.	Felt that life was worth living?	1	2	3	4	5
14.	Felt confident about your plans for the future?	1	2	3	4	5

B

Reasons for Living Inventory for Adolescents

(RFL-A)

Name / Code Number_____ Gender: M / F Age _____ **RFL-A**

This questionnaire lists specific **reasons** that people sometimes have **for not committing suicide**, if the thought were to occur to them or if someone were to suggest it to them. Please read each statement carefully, and then choose a number that best describes how **important** each reason is to you for **not** committing suicide.

Use the scale below and circle the appropriate number in the space to the right of each statement. Please use the whole range of choices so as not to rate only at the middle (2, 3, 4, 5) or only at the extremes (1, 6).

How **important** to you is this **reason for not committing suicide?**

		1 = **Not** at all important	2 = Quite **unimportant**	3 = Somewhat unimportant	4 = Somewhat important	5 = Quite important	6 = Extremely important
1.	Whenever I have a problem, I can turn to my family for support or advice.	1	2	3	4	5	6
2.	It would be painful and frightening to take my own life.	1	2	3	4	5	6
3.	I accept myself for what I am.	1	2	3	4	5	6
4.	I have a lot to look forward to as I grow older.	1	2	3	4	5	6
5.	My friends stand by me whenever I have a problem.	1	2	3	4	5	6
6.	I feel loved and accepted by my close friends.	1	2	3	4	5	6
7.	I feel emotionally close to my family.	1	2	3	4	5	6
8.	I am afraid to die, so I would not consider killing myself.	1	2	3	4	5	6
9.	I like myself just the way I am.	1	2	3	4	5	6
10.	My friends care a lot about me.	1	2	3	4	5	6
11.	I would like to accomplish my plans or goals in the future.	1	2	3	4	5	6
12.	My family takes the time to listen to my experiences at school, work, or home.	1	2	3	4	5	6
13.	I expect many good things to happen to me in the future.	1	2	3	4	5	6
14.	I am satisfied with myself.	1	2	3	4	5	6
15.	I am hopeful about my plans or goals for the future.	1	2	3	4	5	6
16.	I believe my friends appreciate me when I am with them.	1	2	3	4	5	6
17.	I enjoy being with my family.	1	2	3	4	5	6
18.	I feel that I am an OK person.	1	2	3	4	5	6
19.	I expect to be successful in the future.	1	2	3	4	5	6
20.	The thought of killing myself scares me.	1	2	3	4	5	6
21.	I am afraid of using any method to kill myself.	1	2	3	4	5	6
22.	I can count on my friends to help if I have a problem.	1	2	3	4	5	6
23.	Most of the time, my family encourages and supports my plans or goals.	1	2	3	4	5	6
24.	My family cares about the way I feel.	1	2	3	4	5	6
25.	My future looks quite hopeful and promising.	1	2	3	4	5	6
26.	I am afraid of killing myself.	1	2	3	4	5	6
27.	My friends accept me for what I really am.	1	2	3	4	5	6
28.	I have many plans I am looking forward to carrying out in the future.	1	2	3	4	5	6
29.	I feel good about myself.	1	2	3	4	5	6
30.	My family cares a lot about what happens to me.	1	2	3	4	5	6
31.	I am happy with myself.	1	2	3	4	5	6
32.	I would be frightened or afraid to make plans for killing myself.	1	2	3	4	5	6

B–1

C

Self-Harm Behavior Questionnaire (SHBQ)

A lot of people do things which are dangerous and might get them hurt. There are many reasons why people take these risks. Often people take risks without thinking about the fact that they might get hurt. Sometimes, however, people hurt themselves on purpose. We are interested in learning more about the ways in which you may have intentionally or unintentionally hurt yourself. We are also interested in trying to understand why people your age may do some of these dangerous things. It is important for you to understand that if you tell us about things you've done which may have been unsafe or make it possible that you may not be able to keep yourself safe, we will encourage you to discuss this with a counselor or other confidant in order to keep you safe in the future. Please circle YES or NO in response to each question and answer the follow-up questions. For questions where you are asked who you told something, do not give specific names. We only want to know if it was someone like a parent, teacher, doctor, etc.

Things you may have actually done to yourself on purpose

1. Have you ever hurt yourself on purpose?   YES   NO
  (e.g., scratched yourself with finger nails or sharp object.)
    If **no**, go on to question #2.
    If **yes**, what did you do? _____

_____

  a. Approximately how many times did you do this?
  b. Approximately when did you first do this to yourself? (*write your age*) ____
  c. When was the last time you did this to yourself? (*write your age*) ____
  d. Have you ever told anyone that you had done these things?   YES   NO
    If **yes**, who did you tell? _____
  e. Have you ever needed to see a doctor after doing these things?   YES   NO

Times you hurt yourself badly on purpose or tried to kill yourself

2. Have you ever attempted suicide?   YES   NO
    If **no**, go on to question # 4.
    If **yes**, how? _____

_____

  (Note: if you took pills, what kind? _____ ; how many? ____ ;
  over how long a period of time did you take them? _____)
  a. How many times have you attempted suicide? ____
  b. When was the most recent attempt? (*write your age*) ____
  c. Did you tell anyone about the attempt?   YES   NO
    Who? _____

d. Did you require medical attention after the attempt? YES NO

    If yes, were you hospitalized overnight or longer? YES NO

    How long were you hospitalized?_____

e. Did you talk to a counselor or some other person like that after your attempt?
YES NO Who?_____

3. If you attempted suicide, please answer the following:

a. What other things were going on in your life around the time that you tried to kill yourself?_____

_____

_____

b. Did you actually want to die? YES NO

c. Were you hoping for a specific reaction to your attempt? YES NO

    If **yes**, what was the reaction you were looking for?_____

_____

d. Did you get the reaction you wanted? YES NO

    If you *didn't*, what type of reaction was there to your attempt?_____

_____

e. Who knew about your attempt? _____

Times you threatened to hurt yourself badly or try to kill yourself

4. Have you ever threatened to commit suicide? YES NO

    If **no**, go on to question # 5.

    If **yes**, what did you threaten to do?_____

_____

a. Approximately how many times did you do this?_____

b. Approximately when did you first do this? (*write your age*) _____

c. When was the last time you did this? (*write your age*) _____

d. Who did you make the threats to? (e.g., mom, dad) _____

e. What other things were going on in your life during the time that you were threatening to kill yourself?_____

_____

f. Did you actually want to die? YES NO

g. Were you hoping for a specific reaction to your threat? YES NO

    If **yes**, what was the reaction you were looking for?_____

_____

h. Did you get the reaction you wanted? YES NO

    If you didn't, what type of reaction was there to your attempt?_____

_____

_____

Times you talked or thought seriously about attempting suicide

5. Have you ever talked or thought about:

    –wanting to die   YES   NO

    –committing suicide   YES   NO

    a. What did you talk about doing? _____

_____

_____

    b. With whom did you discuss this? _____

    c. What made you feel like doing that? _____

_____

_____

    d. Did you have a specific plan for how you would try to kill yourself?   YES   NO

        If yes, what plan did you have? _____

_____

    e. In looking back, how did you imagine people would react to your attempt?

_____

_____

_____

    f. Did you think about how people would react if you did succeed
in killing yourself?   YES   NO

        If **yes**, how did you think they would react? _____

_____

_____

    g. Did you ever take steps to prepare for this plan?   YES   NO

        If **yes**, what did you do to prepare? _____

_____

_____

D

SHBQ Score Sheet

1   (SHB-Stat)   yes = 1   no = 0 _____ ____

a.   (SHB-Freq)   blank = 0   once = 1   twice = 2   3 times = 3   4 or more times = 4 ____

b.   (SHB-Hx)   blank = 0   0-1 year = 1   2-3 years = 2   4-5 years = 3   6 or more years = 4 ____

c.   (SHB-Rsk)   blank = 0   1 year or less = 4   1–2 years = 3   > 2 years = 2 ____

d.   (SHB-Dis)   yes = 1   no = 2 ____

e.   (SHB-Rx)   yes = 3   no = 2 ____

Total SHB _____

2   (SA-Stat)   yes = 1   no = 0 ____

   (SA-Mth)   blank = 0   OD on 1 small = 1   OD on 1 large = 2   OD on 2 or more = 3

                harm/injury = 4   traumatic/lethal = 5

a.   (SA-Freq)   blank = 0   once = 1   twice = 2   3 times = 3   4 or more times = 4 ____

b.   (SA-Rsk)   blank = 0   1 year or less = 4   1–2 years = 3   > 2 years = 2 ____

d.   (SA-MRx)   yes = 4   no = 2 ____

3

a.   (SA-Evn)   blank = 0   1 event = 1   2 events = 2   3 or more events = 4 ____

b.   (SA-Int)   yes = 3   no = 1 ____

Total SA _____

Score sheet continued   **D–1**

4   (ST-Stat)   yes = 1   no = 0

_____   _____

       (ST-Mth)   blank = 0   OD on 1 small = 1   OD on 1 large = 2   OD on 2 or more = 3

                            harm/injury = 4   traumatic/lethal = 5

_____   _____

a.   (ST-Freq)   blank = 0   1-2 times = 1   3-4 times = 2   4 or more times = 3

_____   _____

b.   (ST-Hx)   blank = 0   0-1 year = 1   2-3 years = 2   4-5 years = 3   6 or more years = 4

_____   _____

c.   (ST-Rsk)   blank = 0   1 year or less = 4   >1 year but < 2 years = 3   > 2 years = 2

_____   _____

e.   (ST-Evn)   blank = 0   1 event = 1   2 events = 2   3 or more events = 3

_____   _____

f.   (ST-Int)   yes = 2   no = 0

_____   _____

                                                        Total ST _____

5   (SI-Stat)   yes = 1   no = 0

_____   _____

a.   (SI-Mth)   blank = 0   OD on 1 small = 1   OD on 1 large = 2   OD on 2 or more = 3

                            harm/injury = 4   traumatic/lethal = 5

_____   _____

c.   (SI-Evn)   blank = 0   1 event = 1   2 events = 2   3 or more events = 3

_____   _____

d.   (SI-Pln)   yes = 2   no = 1

_____   _____

f.   (SI-Reac)   yes = 1   no = 2

_____   _____

g.   (SI-Pre)   yes = 2   no = 1

_____   _____

                                                        Total SI _____

E

Suicidal Behaviors Questionnaire (SBQ-R)

Name / Code Number _____ Gender: M / F   Age _____   **SBQ-R**

Ethnic Background (Please check only one)

1. Caucasian/White ☐   **4.** Hispanic/Latino American ☐   **6.** Other ☐   *Specify* _____

2. African American ☐   **5.** American Indian/Alaska Native ☐   **7.** Biracial ☐   _____

3. Asian American ☐

Education (Please check only one)

High School: 9th/10th grade ☐   11th Grade ☐   12th Grade ☐   High School Grad/GED ☐

College: Freshman ☐   Sophomore ☐   Junior ☐   Senior/Graduate ☐

Marital Status (Please check only one)

1. Single ☐   **3.** Separated ☐   **5.** Engaged ☐   *months* _____

2. Married ☐   **4.** Divorced ☐   **6.** Live-in partner ☐

Instructions: Please circle the number beside the statement or phrase that best applies to you.

1. Have you ever thought about or attempted to kill yourself? (Circle only one)

1 = Never

2 = It was just a brief passing thought

3a = I have had a plan at least once to kill myself but did not try to do it

3b = I have had a plan at least once to kill myself and really wanted to die

4a = I have attempted to kill myself, but did not want to die

4b = I have attempted to kill myself, and really hoped to die

2. How often have you thought about killing yourself in the past year? (Circle only one)

1 = Never   **3** = Sometimes (2 times)   **5** = Very Often (5 or more times)

2 = Rarely (1 time)   **4** = Often (3-4 times)

3. Have you ever told someone that you were going to commit suicide, or that you might do it? (Circle only one)

1 = No

2a = Yes, at one time, but did not really want to die

2b = Yes, at one time, and really wanted to do it

3a = Yes, more than once, but did not want to do it

3b = Yes, more than once, and really wanted to do it

4. How likely is it that you will attempt suicide someday? (circle only one)

0 = Never   **3** = Unlikely   **5** = Rather Likely

1 = No chance at all   **4** = Likely   **6** = Very Likely

2 = Rather Unlikely

F

Suicide Resilience Inventory-25 (SRI-25)

Name / Code Number _____ Gender: M / F   Age _____   **SRI-25**

Marital Status _____ Ethnic Background _____ Education _____

Please answer each statement as carefully and honestly as you can; your answers will be kept confidential. Circle a number to the right of each statement to indicate how much it describes your attitudes, beliefs, or feelings.

1 = Strongly Disagree
2 = Moderately Disagree
3 = Somewhat Disagree
4 = Somewhat Agree
5 = Moderately Agree
6 = Strongly Agree

		1	2	3	4	5	6
1.	There are many things that I like about myself.	1	2	3	4	5	6
2.	Most of the time, I see myself as a happy person.	1	2	3	4	5	6
3.	People close to me would find the time to listen if I were to talk seriously about killing myself.	1	2	3	4	5	6
4.	I can deal with the emotional pain of rejection without thinking of killing myself.	1	2	3	4	5	6
5.	I like myself.	1	2	3	4	5	6
6.	I could openly discuss thoughts of killing myself with people who are close to me, when it is necessary.	1	2	3	4	5	6
7.	I can find someone close to me to give me support (e.g., financial, shelter) if I find myself in a jam.	1	2	3	4	5	6
8.	I can resist thoughts of killing myself when I feel emotionally hurt.	1	2	3	4	5	6
9.	Most of the time I set goals that are reasonable for me to meet.	1	2	3	4	5	6
10.	I can resist the urge to kill myself when I feel depressed or sad.	1	2	3	4	5	6
11.	I am satisfied with most things in my life.	1	2	3	4	5	6
12.	I can resist thoughts of killing myself when faced with a difficult or life-threatening situation.	1	2	3	4	5	6
13.	I am proud of many good things about myself.	1	2	3	4	5	6
14.	I can control the urge to harm or hurt myself when I am criticized by someone.	1	2	3	4	5	6
15.	I can ask for emotional support from people close to me if I were to think about killing myself.	1	2	3	4	5	6
16.	Even if people close to me are angry with me, I can approach them if I want to talk about my personal problems.	1	2	3	4	5	6
17.	I can find someone (parent, friend, spouse, or relative) who can help me cope if I should think about killing myself.	1	2	3	4	5	6
18.	I can handle thoughts of killing myself when I feel lonely or isolated from other people.	1	2	3	4	5	6
19.	I feel that I am an emotionally strong person.	1	2	3	4	5	6
20.	Regardless of the problem situation I face, I can be happy with myself.	1	2	3	4	5	6
21.	If I am in trouble, I can ask for help from people close to me rather than attempt to kill myself.	1	2	3	4	5	6
22.	I have close friends or family members that I could turn to for emotional support if I were to think of killing myself.	1	2	3	4	5	6
23.	I can resist thoughts of killing myself when faced with humiliating or embarrassing situations.	1	2	3	4	5	6
24.	I can resist thoughts of killing myself when I feel hopeless about the future.	1	2	3	4	5	6
25.	I feel cheerful about myself.	1	2	3	4	5	6

F–1

References

Adam, K., Bouckoms, A., & Streiner, D. (1982). Parental loss and family stability in attempted suicide. *Archives of General Psychiatry, 39,* 1081-1085.

Adams, D., Overholser, J., & Lehnert, K. (1994). Perceived family functioning and adolescent suicidal behavior. *Journal of the American Academy of Child and Adolescent Psychiatry, 33,* 498-507.

Allison, S., Pearce, C., Martin, G., Miller, K., & Long, R. (1995). Parental influence, pessimism and adolescent suicidality. *Archives of Suicide Research, 1,* 229-242.

American Psychiatric Association. (1994). *Diagnostic and statistical manual of mental disorders* (4th ed.). Washington, DC: Author.

American Psychiatric Association. (2000). *Diagnostic and statistical manual of mental disorders* (4th ed., text rev.). Washington, DC: Author.

American Psychological Association. (2002). Ethical principles of psychologists and code of conduct. *American Psychologist, 57,* 1060-1073.

Andrews, J. A., & Lewinsohn, P. M. (1992). Suicidal attempts among older adolescents: Prevalence and co-occurrence with psychiatric disorders. *Journal of the American Academy of Child and Adolescent Psychiatry, 31,* 622-655.

Barnette, J. J. (2000). Effects of stem and Likert response reversals on survey internal consistency: If you feel the need, there is a better alternative to using these negatively worded stems. *Educational and Psychological Measurement, 60,* 361-370.

Baumeister, R. F. (1990). Suicide as escape from self. *Psychological Review, 99,* 90-113.

Baumeister, R. F., & Scher, S. J. (1988). Self-defeating behavior patterns among normal individuals: Review and analysis of common self-destructive tendencies. *Psychological Bulletin, 104,* 3-22.

Beautrais, A. L., Joyce, P. R., & Mulder, R. T. (1996). Risk factors for serious suicide attempts among youths aged 13 through 24 years. *Journal of the American Academy of Child and Adolescent Psychiatry, 35,* 1174-1182.

Beck, A. T., Davis, J. H., Frederick, C. J., Perlin, S., Porkorny, A. D., Schulman, R. E., et al. (1973). Classification and nomenclature. In H. L. P. Resnick & B. C. Hathorne (Eds.), *Suicide prevention in the seventies* (pp. 7-12). Washington, DC: US. Government Printing Office.

Beck, A. T., & Steer, R. A. (1990). *Manual for the Beck Anxiety Inventory.* San Antonio, TX: The Psychological Corporation.

Beck, A. T., & Steer, R. A. (1993). *Manual for the Beck Hopelessness Scale.* San Antonio, TX: Psychological Corporation.

Beck, A. T., Steer, R. A., & Brown, G. K. (1996). *Manual for the revised Beck Depression Inventory-II.* San Antonio, TX: Psychological Corporation.

Beck, A. T., Weissman, A., Lester, D., & Trexler, M. (1974). The measurement of pessimism: The Hopelessness Scale. *Journal of Consulting and Clinical Psychology, 42,* 861-865.

Benson, P. L. (1990). *The troubled journey: A portrait of 6th -12th grade youth*. Minneapolis, MN: Search Institute.

Bentler, P. M., & Wu, E. J. C. (2005). *EQS for Windows structural equation program manual*. Encino, CA: Multivariate Software, Inc.

Blumenthal, S., & Kupfer, D. (Eds.). (1990). *Suicide over the life cycle*. Washington, DC: American Psychiatric Press.

Bock, R. B., Gibbons, R., & Muraki, E. (1988). Full information item analysis. *Applied Psychological Measurement, 12*, 261-280.

Brent, D. A., Kolko, D. J., Wartella, M. E., Boylan, M. B., Moritz, G., Baugher, M., et al. (1993). Adolescent psychiatric inpatients' risk of suicide attempt at 6-month follow-up. *Journal of the American Academy of Child and Adolescent Psychiatry, 32*, 95-105.

Brent, D. A., Perper, J. A., Goldstein, C. E., Kolko, D. J., Allan, M. J., Allman, C. J., et al. (1988). Risk factors for adolescent suicide. A comparison of adolescent suicide victims with suicidal inpatients. *Archives of General Psychiatry, 45*, 581-588.

Brent, D. A., Perper, J., Moritz, G., Baugher, M., & Allman, C. (1993). Suicide in adolescents with no apparent psychopathology. *Journal of the American Academy of Child and Adolescent Psychiatry, 32*, 494-500.

Browne, M. N. (2001). An overview of analytic rotation in exploratory factor analysis. *Multivariate Behavioral Research, 36*, 111-150.

Browne, M. W., & Cudeck, R. (1993). Alternative ways of assessing model fit. In K. A. Bollen & J. S. Long (Eds.), *Testing structural equation models*. Thousand Oaks, CA: Sage.

Butcher, J. N., Williams, C. L., Graham, J. R., Archer, R. P., Tellegen, A., Ben-Porath, Y. S., & Kaemmer, B. (1992). *Minnesota Multiphasic Personality Inventory—Adolescents—MMPI-A: Manual for administration, scoring, and interpretation*. Minneapolis: University of Minnesota Press.

Canetti, L., Bachar, E., Galili-Weisstub, E., De-Nour, A., & Shalev, A. (1997). Parental bonding and mental health in adolescents. *Adolescence, 32*, 381-395.

Canino, G., & Roberts, R. E. (2001). Suicidal behavior among Latino youth. *Suicide and Life-Threatening Behavior, 31,* 122-131.

Cattell, R. B. (1966). The scree test for the number of factors. *Multivariate Behavioral Research, 1*, 245-276.

Centers for Disease Control (CDC). (2001). Suicide in the United States. CDC unpublished mortality data from the National Center for Health Statistics. *Mortality Data Trends*, Atlanta, GA: Author.

Centers for Disease Control and Prevention. (1998). Suicide among black youths—United States, 1980-1995. *Morbidity and Mortality Weekly Reports, 47,* 193-196.

Centers for Disease Control and Prevention. (Sept. 7, 1999). *Suicide Deaths and Rates per 100,000* [On-line]. Available: www.cdc.gov/ncipc/data/us9794/suic.htm.

Chance, S. E., Kaslow, N. J., Summerville, M. B., & Wood, K. (1998). Suicidal behavior in African American individuals: Current status and future directions. *Cultural Diversity and Mental Health, 4,* 19-37.

Chang, E. C. (2002). Predicting suicide ideation in an adolescent population: Examining the role of social problem solving as a mediator and a moderator. *Personality and Individual Indifferences, 32*, 1279-1291.

Cicchetti, D. V. (1994). Guidelines, criteria, and rules of thumb for evaluating normed and standardized assessment instruments in psychology. *Psychological Assessment, 6*, 284-290.

Cicchetti, D. V., & Sparrow, S. S. (1990). Assessment of adaptive behavior in young children. In J. J. Johnson and J. Goldman (Eds.), *Developmental assessment in clinical child psychology: A handbook* (pp. 173-196). New York: Pergamon Press.

Clark, D. C. (1993). Suicidal behaviors in childhood and adolescence: Report studies and clinical implications. *Psychiatric Annals, 23,* 271-283.

Clark, L. A., & Watson, D. (1995). Constructing validity: Basic issues in objective scale development. *Psychological Assessment, 7*, 309-319.

Cohen, S., & Hoberman, H. M. (1983). Positive events and social supports as buffers of life change stress. *Journal of Applied Social Psychology, 13*, 99-125.

Colle, L., Belair, J., DiFeo, M., Weiss, J., & LaRoche, C. (1994). Extended open-label fluoxetine treatment of adolescents with major depression. *Journal of Child and Adolescent Psychopharmacology, 4*, 225-232.

Committee on Cultural Psychiatry. (1989a). Suicide among Blacks in the US. In Group for the Advancement of Psychiatry (Eds.), *Suicide and ethnicity in the United States* (pp. 11-29). New York: Brunner/Mazel.

Committee on Cultural Psychiatry. (1989b). Suicide among Hispanic-Americans. In Group for the Advancement of Psychiatry (Eds.), *Suicide and ethnicity in the United States* (pp. 72-94). New York: Brunner/Mazel.

Comrey, A. L., & Lee, H. B. (1992). *A first course in factor analysis* (2nd ed.). Hillsdale, NJ: Lawrence Erlbaum Associates, Inc.

Coopersmith, S. (1967). *The antecedents of self-esteem.* San Francisco: WH Freeman.

Corwyn, R. F. (2000). The factor structure of global self-esteem among adolescent and adults. *Journal of Research in Personality, 34*, 357-379.

Cowell, J. M., Gross, D., McNaughton, D., Ailey, S., & Fogg, L. (2005). Depression and suicidal ideation among Mexican American school-aged children. *Research and Theory for Nursing Practice: An International Journal, 19*, 77-90.

Cronbach, L. J. (1951). Coefficient alpha and the internal structure of tests. *Psychometrika, 16*, 297-334.

Crowley, S. L. (1998). A psychometric investigation of the FACES-III: Confirmatory factor analysis with replication. *Journal of Social Service Research, 15*, 131-147.

Cull, J. G., & Gill, W. S. (1982). *Suicide Probability Scale.* Los Angeles: Western Psychological Services.

D'Attilio, J. P., Campbell, B. M., Lubold, P., Jacobson, T., & Richard, J. A. (1992). Social support and suicide potential: Preliminary findings for adolescent populations. *Psychological Reports, 70*, 76-78.

Davis, R., & Short, J. F. (1977). Dimensions of Black suicide: A theoretical model. *Suicide and Life-Threatening Behavior, 8*, 161-173.

Dean, P. J., & Range, L. M. (1996). The escape theory of suicide and perfectionism. *Death Studies, 20*, 415-424.

De Man, A. F., & Leduc, C.P. (1995). Suicidal ideation in high school students: Depression, and other correlates. *Journal of Clinical Psychology, 51*, 173-180.

Derogatis, L. R. (1992). *The Brief Symptom Inventory (BSI): Administration, scoring, and procedures manual II.* Townson, MD: Clinical Psychometric Research.

DeVellis, R. F. (2003). *Scale development: Theory and applications* (2nd ed.). Thousand Oaks: Sage.

De Wilde, E., Kienhorst, I., Diekstra, R., & Wolters, W. (1992). The relationship between adolescent suicidal behavior and life events in childhood and adolescence. *American Journal of Psychiatry, 149*, 45-51.

Diekstra, R. F. W., Kienhorst, C. W. M., & DeWilde, E. J. (1995). Suicide and suicidal behavior among adolescents. In M. Rutter & D. J. Smith (Eds.), *Psychosocial Disorders in young people*: Time trends and their causes (pp. 686-761). Chichester, England: Wiley.

Diener, E., Emmons, R. A., Larsen, R. J., & Griffin, S. (1985). The Satisfaction with Life Scale. *Journal of Personality Assessment, 49*, 71-75.

Dieserud, G., Roysamb, E., Braverman, M. T., Dalgard, O. S., & Ekeberg, O. (2003). Predicting repetition of suicide attempt: A prospective study of 50 suicide attempters. *Archives of Suicide Research, 7*, 1-15.

DiFilippo, J. M., & Overholser, J. C. (2000). Suicidal ideation in adolescent psychiatric inpatients as associated with depression and attachment relationships. *Journal of Clinical Child Psychology, 29,* 155-166.

Doherty-Schmid, K., Rosenthal, S. I., & Brown, E. D. (1988). A comparison of self-report measures of two family dimensions: Control and cohesion. *American Journal of Family Therapy, 16,* 73-77.

Dori, G. A., & Overholser, J. C. (1999). Depression, hopelessness, and self-esteem: Accounting for suicidality in adolescent psychiatric inpatients. *Suicide and Life-Threatening Behavior, 29,* 309-318.

Dozois, D. (2003). The psychometric characteristics of the Hamilton Depression Inventory. *Journal of Personality Assessment, 80,* 31-40.

DuBois, D. L., Felner, R. D., Brand, S., Phillips, R. S. C., & Lease, A. M. (1996). Early adolescent self-esteem: A developmental-ecological framework and assessment strategy. *Journal of Research on Adolescence, 6,* 543-579.

Dubow, E. F., & Ullman, D. G. (1989). Assessing social support in elementary school children: Survey of Children's Social Support. *Journal of Clinical Child Psychology, 18,* 52-64.

Durkheim, E. (1951). *Suicide: A study in sociology.* (J. A. Spaulding & G. Simpson, Trans.). Glencoe, IL: Free Press. (Original work published 1897).

D' Zurilla, T. J., & Maydeu-Olivares, A. (1995). Conceptual and methodological issues in social problem-solving assessment. *Behavior Therapy, 26,* 409-432.

D' Zurilla, T. J., & Nezu, A. (1990). Development and preliminary evaluation of the Social Problem-Solving Inventory. *Psychological Assessment: A Journal of Consulting and Clinical Psychology, 2,* 156-163.

D' Zurilla, T. J., & Nezu, A., & Maydeu-Olivares, A. (1994). *Manual for the Social Problem-Solving Inventory-Revised.* Unpublished manuscript, State University of New York at Stony Brook.

Early, K. E. (1992). *Religion and suicide in the African American community.* Westport, CT: Greenwood Press.

Early, K. E., & Akers, R. L. (1993). "It's a White thing": An exploration of beliefs about suicide in the African American community. *Deviant Behavior: An Interdisciplinary Journal, 14,* 277-296.

Eggert, L. L., Herting, J. R., & Thompson, E. A. (1994). *High school questionnaire: Profile of Experiences.* Seattle: University of Washington School of Nursing.

Eggert, L. L., Thompson, E. A., Herting, J. R., & Nicholas, L. J. (1995). Reducing suicide potential among high-risk youth: Tests of a school-based prevention program. *Suicide and Life-Threatening Behavior, 25,* 276-296.

Epstein, N. B., Baldwin, L. M., & Bishop, D. S. (1983). The MacMaster Family Assessment Device. *Journal of Marital and Family Therapy, 9,* 171-180.

Erdman, H. P., Greist, J. H., Gustafson, D. H., Taves, J. E., & Klein, M. H. (1987). Suicide risk prediction by computer interview: A prospective study. *Journal of Clinical Psychiatry, 48,* 464-467.

Esposito, C. L., & Clum, G. A. (2003). The relative contribution of diagnostic and psychosocial factors in prediction of adolescent suicidal ideation. *Journal of Clinical Child and Adolescent Psychology, 32,* 386-395.

Evans, E., Hawton, K., & Rodham, K. (2004). Factors associated with suicidal phenomena in adolescents: A systematic review of population-based studies. *Clinical Psychology Review, 24,* 957-979.

Evans, E., Hawton, K., Rodham, K., & Deeks, J. (2005). The prevalence of suicidal phenomena in adolescents: A systematic review of population-based studies. *Suicide and Life-Threatening Behavior, 35,* 239-250.

Eyman, J. R., & Eyman, S. K. (1990). Suicide risk and assessment instruments. In P. Cimbolic & D. A. Jobes (Eds.), *Youth suicide: Issues, assessment, and intervention.* (pp. 9-32). Springfield, IL: Charles C. Thomas.

Fabrigar, L. R., Wegener, D. T., MacCallum, R. C., & Strahan, E. J. (1999). Evaluating the use of exploratory factor analysis in psychological research. *Psychological Methods, 4,* 272-299.

Fan, X., & Thompson, B. (2001). Confidence intervals about score reliability coefficients, please: An EPM guidelines editorial. *Educational and Psychological Measurement, 61,* 517-531.

Felix-Ortiz, M., & Newcomb, M. D. (1992). Risk and protective factors for drug use among Latino and White adolescents. *Hispanic Journal of Behavioral Sciences, 14,* 291-309.

Fisher, C. B. (2003). *Decoding the ethics code: A practical guide for psychologists.* Thousand Oaks: Sage.

Fitzpatrick, A. R. (1983). The meaning of content validity. *Applied Psychological Measurement, 7,* 3-13.

Fliege, H., Kocalevent, R., Walter, O. B., Beck, S., Gratz, K. L., Gutierrez, P. M., et al. (2006). Three assessment tools for deliberate self-harm and suicide behavior: Evaluation and psychopathological correlates. *Journal of Psychosomatic Research, 61,* 113-21.

Flouri, E., & Buchanan, A. (2002). The predictive role of parental involvement in adolescent suicide. *Crisis: the Journal of Crisis Intervention and Suicide Prevention, 23,* 17-22.

Floyd, F. J., & Widaman, K. F. (1995). Factor analysis in the development and refinement of clinical assessment instruments. *Psychological Assessment, 7,* 286-299.

Fowler, R. C., Rich, C. L., & Young, D. (1986). San Diego suicide study II. Substance abuse in young cases. Archives of General Psychiatry, *43,* 962-965.

Frankl, V. (1959). *From death-camp to existentialism.* Boston: Beacon.

Fremouw, W., Callahan, T., & Kashden, J. (1993). Adolescent suicidal risk: Psychological, problem solving, and environmental factors. *Suicide and Life-Threatening Behavior, 23,* 46-54.

Garland, A., Shaffer, D., & Whittle, B. (1989). A national survey of school-based, adolescent suicide prevention programs. *Journal of the American Academy of Child and Adolescent Psychiatry, 28,* 931-934.

Garroutte, E. M., Goldberg, J., Beals, J., Herrell, R., Manson, S. M., & the AI-SUPERPFP team. (2003). Spirituality and attempted suicide among American Indians. *Social Science & Medicine, 56,* 1571-1579.

Gavazzi, S. M. (1994). Perceived social support from family and friends in a clinical sample of adolescents. *Journal of Personality Assessment, 62,* 465-471.

Gibbs, J. T., & Hines, A. M. (1989). Factors related to sex differences in suicidal behavior among Black youth: Implications for interventions and research. *Journal of Adolescent Research, 4,* 152-172.

Goldberg, L. R. (1972). Parameters of personality inventory construction and utilization: A comparison of prediction strategies and tactics. *Multivariate Behavioral Research Monographs, 7,* 2.

Golden, C. J., Sawicki, R. F., & Franzen, M. D. (1984). Test construction. In G. Golden & M. Hersen (Eds.), *Handbook of psychological assessment* (pp. 19-37). New York: Pergamon Press.

Goldman, S., & Beardslee, W. R. (1999). *Suicide in children and adolescents.* In D. G. Jacobs (Ed.), The Harvard Medical School Guide to suicide assessment and intervention (pp. 417-422). San Francisco: Jossey-Bass.

Goldston, D. B. (2003). *Measuring suicidal behavior and risk in children and adolescents.* Washington, DC: American Psychiatric Association.

Gould, M. S., Fisher, P., Parides, M., Flory, M., & Shaffer, D. (1996). Psychosocial risk factors of child and adolescent completed suicide. *Archives of General Psychiatry, 53,* 1155-1162.

Gould, M. S., & Kramer, R. A. (2001). Youth suicide prevention. *Suicide and Life-Threatening Behavior, 31* (Supplement), 6-31.

Gould, M. S., Marrocco, F. A., Kleinman, M., Thomas, J. G., Mostkoff, K., Cote, J., et al. (2005). Evaluating iatrogenic risk of youth suicide screening programs: A randomized controlled trial. *Journal of the American Medical Association, 293,* 1635-1643.

Gray, N. S., Hill, C., McGleish, A., Timmons, D., MacCulloch, M. J., & Snowden, R. J. (2003). Prediction of violence and self-harm in mentally disordered offenders: A prospective study of the efficacy of HCR-20, PCL-R, and psychiatric symptomatology. *Journal of Consulting and Clinical Psychology, 71,* 443-451.

Greening, L., & Stoppelbein, L. (2002). Religiosity, attributional style, and support as psychosocial buffers for African American and White adolescents' perceived risk for suicide. *Suicide and Life-Threatening Behavior, 32,* 404-417.

Greist, J. H., Gustafson, D. H., Stauss, F. F., Rowse, G. L., Laughren, T. P., & Chiles, J. A. (1973). A computer interview for suicide-risk prediction. *American Journal of Psychiatry, 130,* 1327-1332.

Grunbaum, J. A., Kann, L., Kinchen, S., Ross, J., Lowry, R., et al. (2004). Youth risk behavior surveillance—United States, 2003. *Morbidity and Mortality Weekly Reports, 53,* 1-96.

Grunbaum, J. A., Kann, L., Kinchen, S. A., Williams, B., Ross, J. G., Lowry, R., et al. (2002). Youth risk behavior surveillance—United States, 2001. *Morbidity and Mortality Weekly Reports, 54,* 1-64.

Guiao, I. Z., & Thompson, E. A. (2004). Ethnicity and problem behaviors among adolescent females in the United States. *Health Care for Women International, 25,* 296-310.

Gutierrez, P. M. (1998). Self-Harm Behavior Questionnaire (SHBQ). Unpublished manuscript. Northern Illinois University, DeKalb.

Gutierrez, P. M. (1999). Suicidality in parentally bereaved adolescents. *Death Studies, 23,* 359-379.

Gutierrez, P., King, C. A., & Ghaziuddin, N. (1996). Adolescent attitudes about death in relation to suicidality. *Suicide and Life-Threatening Behavior, 26,* 8-18.

Gutierrez, P. M., Muehlenkamp, J. J., Konick, L. C., & Osman, A. (2005) What role does race play in adolescent suicidal ideation? *Archives of Suicide Research, 9,* 177-192.

Gutierrez, P. M., Osman, A., Barrios, F. X., & Kopper, B. A. (2001). Development and initial validation of the Self-Harm Behavior Questionnaire. *Journal of Personality Assessment, 77,* 475-490.

Gutierrez, P. M., Osman, A., Kopper, B. A., Barrios, F. X., & Bagge, C. L. (2000). Suicide risk assessment in a college student population. *Journal of Counseling Psychology, 47,* 403-413.

Gutierrez, P. M., Osman, A., Kopper, B. A., & Barrios, F. X. (2000). Why young people do not kill themselves: The Reasons for Living Inventory for Adolescents. *Journal of Clinical Child Psychology, 29,* 177-187.

Gutierrez, P. M., Osman, A., Kopper, B. A., & Barrios, F. X. (2004). Appropriateness of the Multi-Attitude Suicide Tendency Scale for non-white individuals. *Assessment, 11,* 73-84.

Gutierrez, P. M., Watkins, R., & Collura, D. (2004). Suicide risk screening in an urban high school. *Suicide and Life-Threatening Behavior, 34(4),* 421-428.

Hagstrom, A. H., & Gutierrez, P. M. (1998). Confirmatory factor analysis of the Multi-Attitude Suicide Tendency Scale. *Journal of Psychopathology and Behavioral Assessment, 20,* 173-186.

Harkavy-Friedman, J. M., & Asnis, G. M. (1989). Assessment of suicidal behavior: A new instrument. *Psychiatric Annals, 19,* 382-387.

Harrington, R., Kerfoot, M., Dyer, E., McNiven, F., Gill, F., Harrington, V., et al. (1998). Randomized trial of a home-based family intervention for children who have deliberately poisoned themselves. *Journal of the American Academy of Child and Adolescent Psychiatry, 37,* 512-518.

Harrington, R., Kerfoot, M., Dyer, E., McNiven, F., Gill, F., Harrington, V., et al. (2000). Deliberate self-poisoning in adolescence: Why does a brief family intervention work in some cases and not others. *Journal of Adolescence, 23,* 13-20.

Harris, T. L., & Molock, S. D. (2000). Cultural orientation, family cohesion and family support in suicide ideation and depression among African American college students. *Suicide and Life-Threatening Behavior, 30,* 341-353.

Hawton, K., Appleby, L., Platt, S., Foster, T., Cooper, J., Malmberg, A., et al. (1998). The psychological autopsy approach to studying suicide: A review of methodological issues. *Journal of Affective Disorders, 50,* 269-276.

Hay, J. A., Hawes, R., Faught, B. E., & Hay, J. A. (2004). Evaluation of a screening instrument for developmental coordination disorder. *Journal of Adolescent Health, 34,* 308-313.

Haynes, S. N., & Lench, H. C. (2003). Incremental validity of new clinical assessment measures. *Psychological Assessment, 15,* 456-466.

Haynes, S. N., Richard, D., & Kubany, E. (1995). Content validity in psychological assessment: A functional approach to concepts and methods. *Psychological Assessment, 7,* 238-247.

Heacock, D. R. (1990). Suicidal behavior in Black and Hispanic youth. *Psychiatric Annals, 20,* 134-142.

Heisel, M. J., & Flett, G. L. (2004). Purpose in life, satisfaction with life, and suicide ideation in a clinical sample. *Journal of Psychopathology and Behavioral Assessment, 26,* 127-135.

Hewitt, P. L., Newton, J., Flett, G. L., & Callander, L. C. (1997). Perfectionism and suicide ideation in adolescent psychiatric patients. *Journal of Abnormal Child Psychology, 25,* 95-101.

Hill, R. W., Huelsman, T. J., Furr, M. R., Kibler, J., Vicente, B. P., & Kennedy, C. (2004). A new measure of perfectionism: The Perfectionism Inventory. *Journal of Personality Assessment, 82,* 80-91.

Hoijtink, H., Rooks, G., & Wilmink, F. W. (1999). Confirmatory factor analysis of items with a dichotomous response format using the multidimensional Rasch model. *Psychological Methods, 4,* 300-314.

Horn, J. L. (1965). A rationale and technique for estimating the number of factors in factor analysis. *Psychometrika, 30,* 179-185.

Hovey, J. D., & King, C. A. (1997). Suicidality among acculturating Mexican Americans: Current knowledge and directions for research. *Suicide and Life-Threatening Behavior, 27,* 92-103.

Hu, L., & Bentler, P. M. (1999). Cutoff criteria for fit indices in covariance structure analysis: Conventional criteria versus new alternatives. *Structural Equation Modeling, 6,* 1-55.

Hu, L., Bentler, P. M., & Kano, Y. (1992). Can test statistics in covariance structure be trusted? *Psychological Bulletin, 112,* 351-362.

Hunter, E. C., & O'Connor, R. C. (2003). Hopelessness and future thinking in parasuicide: The role of perfectionism. *British Journal of Clinical Psychology, 42,* 355-365.

Jacobs, D., & Klein-Benheim, M. (1995). The psychological autopsy: A useful tool for determining proximate causation in suicide cases. *Bulletin of the American Academy of Psychiatry and the Law, 23,* 165-182.

Jobes, D. A., & Drozd, J. F. (2004). The CAMS approach to working with suicidal patients. *Journal of Contemporary Psychotherapy, 34,* 73-85.

Jobes, D. A., & Mann, R. E. (1999). Reasons for living versus reasons for dying: Examining the internal debate of suicide. *Suicide and Life-Threatening Behavior, 29,* 97-104.

Joiner, T. E., Petti, J. W., Perez, M., Burns, A. B., Gencoz, T., Gencoz, F., et al. (2001). Can positive emotion influence problem-solving attitudes among suicidal adults? *Professional Psychology: Research and Practice, 32,* 507-512.

Juon, H. S., & Ensminger, M. E. (1997). Childhood, adolescent, and young adult predictors of suicidal behaviors: A prospective study of African Americans. *Journal of Child Psychology and Psychiatry, 38,* 553-563.

Kandel, D. B., Raveis, V. H., & Davies, M. (1991). Suicidal ideation in adolescence: Depression, substance use, and other risk factors. *Journal of Youth and Adolescence, 20,* 289-309.

Kann, L., Kinchen, S. A., Williams, B. I., Ross, J. G., Lowry, R., Grunbaum, J. A., et al. (2000). Youth risk behavior surveillance – United States, 1999. *Morbidity and Mortality Weekly Reports, 49 (SS-5),* 1-51.

Kaplan, M. L., Asnis, G. M., Sanderson, W. C., Keswani, L., DeLecuona, J. M., & Joseph, S. (1994). Suicide assessment: Clinical interview vs. self-report. *Journal of Clinical Psychology, 50,* 294-298.

Kashani, J. H., Goddard, P., & Reid, J. C. (1989). Correlates of suicidal ideation in a community sample of children and adolescents. *Journal of the American Academy of Child and Adolescent Psychiatry, 28,* 912-917.

Kashden, J., Fremouw, W., Callahan, T., & Franzen, M. (1993). Impulsivity in suicidal and nonsuicidal adolescents. *Journal of Abnormal Child Psychology, 21,* 243-248.

Kaslow, N. J., Thompson, M. P., Brooks, A. E., & Twomey, H. B. (2000). Ratings of family functioning of suicidal and nonsuicidal African American women. *Journal of Family Psychology, 14,* 585-599.

Kazdin, A. E. (1995). Preparing and evaluating research reports. *Psychological Assessment, 7,* 228-237.

Kazdin, A. E. (2003). *Research design in clinical psychology,* (4th ed.). Boston: Allyn and Bacon.

Kazdin, A. E. (2005). Evidence-based assessment for children and adolescents: Issues in measurement development and clinical application. *Journal of Clinical Child and Adolescent Psychology, 34,* 548-558.

Kazdin, A. E., French, N., Unis, A., Esveldt-Dawson, K., & Sherick, R. (1983). Hopelessness, depression, and suicidal intent among psychiatrically disturbed inpatient children. *Journal of Consulting and Clinical Psychology, 51,* 504-510.

Kelly, T. M., Lynch, K. G., Donovan, J. E., & Clark, D. B. (2001). Alcohol use disorders and risk factors interaction for adolescent suicidal ideation and attempts. *Suicide and Life-Threatening Behavior, 31,* 181-193.

Kendall, P. C., Cantwell, D. P., & Kazdin, A. E. (1989). Depression in children and adolescents: Assessment issues and recommendations. *Cognitive Therapy and Research, 13,* 109-146.

King, C. A., Franzese, R., Gargan, S., McGovern, L., Ghaziuddin, N., & Naylor, M. W. (1995). Suicide contagion among adolescents during acute psychiatric hospitalization. *Psychiatric Services, 46,* 915-918.

King, C. A., Hovey, J. D., Brand, E., & Ghaziuddin, N. (1997). Prediction of positive outcomes for adolescent psychiatric inpatients. *Journal of the American Academy of Child and Adolescent Psychiatry, 36,* 1434-1442.

King, C. A., Raskin, A., Gdowski, C., Butkus, M., & Opipari, L. (1990). Psychosocial factors associated with urban adolescent female suicide attempts. *Journal of the American Academy of Child and Adolescent Psychiatry, 29,* 289-294.

King, C. A., Segal, H., Naylor, M., & Evans, T. (1993). Family functioning and suicidal behavior in adolescent inpatients with mood disorders. *Journal of the American Academy of Child and Adolescent Psychiatry, 32,* 1198-1206.

King, J. D., & Kowalchuk, B. (1994). *Manual for the Inventory of Suicide Orientation-30.* Minneapolis: National Computer Systems, Inc.

Klein, D. N., Dougherty, L. R., & Olino, T. M. (2005). Toward guidelines for evidence-based assessment of depression in children and adolescents. *Journal of Child and Adolescent Psychology, 34,* 412-432.

Klimes-Dougan, B. (1998). Screening for suicidal ideation in children and adolescents: Methodological considerations. *Journal of Adolescence, 21,* 435-444.

Klimes-Dougan, B., Free, K., Ronsaville, D., Stilwell, J., Welsh, C.J., & Radke-Yarrow, M. (1999). Suicidal ideation and attempts: A longitudinal investigation of children of depressed and well mothers. *Journal of the American Academy of Child and Adolescent Psychiatry, 38,* 651-659.

Kline, P. (1993). *The handbook of psychological testing.* New York: Routledge.

Kline, P. (1998). *Principles and practices of structural equation modeling.* New York: Guilford Press.

Knight, G. P., & Hill, N. E. (1998). Measurement equivalence in research involving minority adolescents. In V. C. McLoyd & L. Steinberg (Eds.), *Studying minority adolescents: Conceptual, methodological, and theoretical issues* (pp. 183-210). Mahwah, NJ: Lawrence Erlbaum Associates.

Kosky, R. (1983). Childhood suicidal behavior. *Journal of Child Psychology and Psychiatry, 24,* 457-468.

Kosky, R., Silburn, S. & Zubrick, S.R. (1990). Are children and adolescents who have suicidal thoughts different from those who attempt suicide? *Journal of Nervous and Mental Disease, 178,* 38-43.

Kovacs, M., Goldston, D., & Gatsonis, C. (1993). Suicidal behaviors and childhood-onset depressive disorders: A longitudinal investigation. *Journal of the American Academy of Child and Adolescent Psychiatry, 32,* 8-20.

Kuchar, P. S., & DiGuiseppi, C. (2003). Screening for suicide risk. In *Guide to clinical preventive services, (2nd ed.): Mental disorders and substance abuse.* U. S. Preventive Services Task Force, <http://cpmcnet.columbia.edu/texts/gcps/gcps0060.html>, accessed April 15, 2003.

Leenaars, A. A., & Wenckstern, S. (1990). Suicide prevention in schools: An introduction. *Death Studies, 14,* 297-302.

Lewinsohn, P. M., Rohde, P., & Seeley, J. R. (1994). Psychosocial risk factors for future adolescent suicide attempts. *Journal of Consulting and Clinical Psychology, 62,* 297-305.

Lewinsohn, P.M., Rohde, P., & Seeley, J. R. (1996). Adolescent suicidal ideation and attempts: Prevalence, risk factors, and clinical implications. *Clinical Psychology: Science and Practice, 3,* 25-46.

Lewinsohn, P. M., Seeley, J. R., & Gotlib, I. H. (1997). Depression-related psychosocial variables: Are they specific to depression in adolescents? *Journal of Abnormal Psychology, 106,* 365-375.

Linehan, M. M., Goodstein, L. J., Nielsen, S. L., & Chiles, J. A. (1983). Reasons for staying alive when you are thinking of killing yourself: The Reasons for Living Inventory. *Journal of Consulting and Clinical Psychology, 51,* 276-286.

Lord, F. M. (1980). *Applications of item response theory to practical testing problems.* Hillsdale, New Jersey: Erlbaum.

Lyons, J. S., Perrotta, P., & Hancher-Kvam, S. (1988). Perceived social support from family and friends: Measurement across disparate samples. *Journal of Personality Assessment, 52,* 42-47.

Marano, C. D., Cisler, R. A., & Lemerond, J. (1993). Risk factors for adolescent suicidal behavior: Loss, insufficient familial support and hopelessness. *Adolescence, 28,* 851-865.

Marciano, P. L., & Kazdin, A. E. (1994). Self-esteem, depression, hopelessness, and suicidal intent among psychiatrically disturbed inpatient children. *Journal of Clinical Child Psychology, 23,* 151-160.

Marion, M., & Range, L. M. (2003). African American college women's suicide buffers. *Suicide and Life-Threatening Behavior, 33,* 33-43.

Maris, R. W. (1991a). The developmental perspective of suicide. In A. Leenaars (Ed.), *Life span perspectives of suicide: Time-lines in the suicide process* (pp. 25-38). New York: Plenum Press.

Maris, R. W. (1991b). Special issue: Assessment and prediction of suicide: Introduction. *Suicide and Life-Threatening Behavior, 21,* 1-17.

Maris, R. W., Berman, A. L., Maltsberger, J. T., & Yufit, R. I. (Eds.). (1992). *Assessment and prediction of suicide.* New York: Guilford.

Markson, S., & Fiese, B. H. (2000). Family rituals as a protective factor for children with Asthma. *Journal of Pediatric Psychology, 25,* 471-479.

Mash, E. J., & Hunsley, J. (2005). Evidence-based assessment of child and adolescent disorders: Issues and challenges. *Journal of Child and Adolescent Psychology, 34,* 362-379.

Maydeu-Olivares, A., & D'Zurilla, T. J. (1996). A factor-analytic study of Social Problem-Solving Inventory: An integration of theory and data. *Cognitive Therapy and Research, 20,* 115-133.

Mazza, J. J. (2000). The relationship between posttraumatic stress symptomatology and suicidal behavior in school-based adolescents. *Suicide and Life-Threatening Behavior, 30,* 91-103.

Mazza, J. J., & Reynolds, W. M. (1998). A longitudinal investigation of depression, hopelessness, social support, and major and minor life events and their relation to suicidal ideation in adolescents. *Suicide and Life-Threatening Behavior, 28,* 359-374.

Mazza, J. J., & Reynolds, W. M. (2001). An investigation of psychopathology in nonreferred suicidal and nonsuicidal adolescents. *Suicide and Life-Threatening Behavior, 31,* 282-302.

McKeown, R. E., Garrison, C. Z., Cuffe, S. P., Waller, J. L., Jackson, K. L., & Addy, C. L. (1998). Incidence and predictors of suicidal behaviors in a longitudinal sample of young adolescents. *Journal of the American Academy of Child and Adolescent Psychiatry, 37,* 612-619.

Miller, D. N. & DuPaul, G. J. (1996). School-based prevention of adolescent suicide: Issues, obstacles, and recommendations for practice. *Journal of Emotional and Behavioral Disorders, 4,* 221-230.

Miller, I. W., Norman, W. H., Bishop, S. B., & Dow, M. G. (1986). The Modified Scale for Suicidal Ideation: Reliability and validity. *Journal of Consulting and Clinical Psychology, 54,* 724-725.

Molock, S. D., Kimbrough, R., Lacy, M. B., McClure, K. P., & Williams, S. (1994). Suicidal behavior among African American college students: A preliminary study. *Journal of Black Psychology, 20,* 234-251.

Moretti, M. M., Fine, S., Haley, G., & Marriage, K. (1985). Childhood and adolescent depression: Child-report versus parent-report information. *Journal of the American Academy of Child Psychiatry, 24,* 298-302.

Morrison, L. L., & Downey, D. L. (2000). Racial differences in self-disclosure of suicidal ideation and reasons for living: Implications for training. *Cultural Diversity and Ethnic Minority Psychology, 6,* 374-386.

Muehlenkamp, J. J., Gutierrez, P. M., Osman, A., & Barrios, F. X. (2005). Validation of the Positive and Negative Suicide Ideation (PANSI) Inventory in a diverse sample of young adults. *Journal of Clinical Psychology, 61,* 431-445.

Murphy, K. R., & Davidshofer, C. O. (1994). Psychological testing: Principles and applications (3rd ed.). Englewood Cliffs, NJ: Prentice-Hall.

Muthén, L. K., & Muthén, B. (2004). *Mplus statistical analysis with latent variables: User's guide.* Los Angeles: Author.

National Center for Health Statistics. (NCHS: 2000). *Health, United States, 2000, with adolescent health chartbook* (DHHS Publication No. PHS 2001-1232-1). Hyattsville, MD: Author.

National Council on Measurement in Education. (1999). *Standards for educational and psychological testing*. Washington, DC: Author.

Neeleman, J., Wessely, S., & Lewis, G. (1998). Suicide acceptability in African- and White Americans: The role of religion. *Journal of Nervous and Mental Disease, 186,* 12-16.

Nezu, A. M., Ronan, G. F., Meadows, E. A., & McClure, K. S. (Eds.). (2000). *Practitioner's guide to empirically based measures of depression*. Hingham, MA: Kluwer/Plenum.

Nunnally, J. C., & Bernstein, I. H. (1994). *Psychometric theory*. (3rd ed.). New York: McGraw-Hill.

O'Carroll, P. W., Berman, A. L., Maris, R. W., Moscicki, E. K., Tanney, B. L., & Silverman, M. M. (1996). Beyond the Tower of Babel: A nomenclature for suicidology. *Suicide and Life-Threatening Behavior, 26,* 237-252.

O'Donnell, L., Stueve, A., Wardlow, D., & O'Donnell, C. (2003). Adolescent suicidality and adult support: The reach for health study of urban youth. *American Journal of Health Behavior, 27,* 633-644.

Olson, D. H., Portner, J., & Bell, R. (1982). FACES-II. In D. Olson et al. (Eds.), *Family inventories*. St. Paul, MN: Family Social Service.

Olson, D. H., & Tiesel, J. (1991): *FACES-II: Linear scoring and interpretation*. Minneapolis: Life Innovations, Family Inventories Project.

Olsson, C. A., Bond, L., Burns, J. M., Vella-Brodricks, D. A., & Sawyer, S. M. (2003). Adolescent resilience: A concept analysis. *Journal of Adolescence, 26,* 1-11.

Oquendo, M. A., Dragatsi, D., Harkavy-Friedman, J., Dervic, K., Currier, D., Burke, A. K., et al. (2005). Protective factors against suicidal behavior in Latinos. *The Journal of Nervous and Mental Disease, 193,* 438-443.

Orbach, I. (1988). *Children who don't want to live*. San Francisco: Jossey-Bass Publishers.

Orbach, I. (1997). A taxonomy of factors related to suicidal behavior. *Clinical Psychology: Science and Practice, 4,* 208-224.

Orbach, I., Lotem-Peleg, M., & Kedem, P. (1995). Attitudes toward the body in suicidal, depressed, and normal adolescents. *Suicide and Life-Threatening Behavior, 25,* 211-221.

Orbach, I., & Milkulincer, M. (1998). The Body Investment Scale: Construction and validation of a body experience scale. *Psychological Assessment, 10,* 415-425.

Orbach, I., Milstein, E., Har-Even, D., Apter, A., Tiano, S., & Elizur, A. (1991). A Multi-Attitude Suicide Tendency scale for adolescents. *Psychological Assessment: A Journal of Consulting and Clinical Psychology, 3,* 398-404.

Orbach, I., Stein, D., Palgi, Y., Asherov, J., Har-Even, D., & Elizur, A. (1996). Perception of physical pain in accident and suicide attempt patients: Self-preservation vs. self-destruction. *Journal of Psychiatric Research, 30,* 307-320.

Orbach, I., Stein, D., Shani-Sela, M., & Har-Even D. (2001). Body attitudes and body experiences in suicidal adolescents. *Suicide and Life-Threatening Behavior, 31,* 237-249.

Osman, A. (1998). *The Reasons for Living Inventory for Young Adults*. Unpublished manuscript. Department of Psychology, University of Northern Iowa.

Osman, A., Bagge, C. L., Gutierrez, P. M., Konick, L. C., Kopper, B. A., & Barrios, F. X. (2001). The Suicidal Behaviors Questionnaire-Revised (SBQ-R): Validation with clinical and nonclinical samples. *Assessment, 8,* 443-454.

Osman, A., Barrios, F. X., Grittmann, L. R., & Osman, J. R. (1993). The Multi-Attitude Suicide Tendency Scale: Psychometric characteristics in an American sample. *Journal of Clinical Psychology, 49,* 701-708.

Osman, A., Barrios, F. X., Gutierrez, P. M., Wrangham, J. J., Kopper, B. A., Truelove, R. S., et al. (2002). The Positive and Negative Suicide Ideation (PANSI) inventory: Psychometric evaluation with adolescent inpatient samples. *Journal of Personality Assessment, 79,* 512-530.

Osman, A., Barrios, F. X., Osman, J. R., Hoffman, J., & Hammer, R., & Panak, W. F. (1994). Validation of the Multi-Attitude Suicide Tendency Scale in adolescent samples. *Journal of Clinical Psychology, 50,* 847-855.

Osman, A., Downs, W. R., Kopper, B. A., Barrios, F. X., Besett, T. M., Linehan, M. M., et al. (1998). The Reasons for Living Inventory for Adolescents (RFL-A): Development and psychometric properties. *Journal of Clinical Psychology, 54,* 1063-1078.

Osman, A., Gilpin, A. R., Panak, W. F., Kopper, B.A. Barrios, F. X., Gutierrez, P.M., et al. (2000). The Multi-Attitude Suicide Tendency Scale: Further validation with adolescent psychiatric inpatients. *Suicide and Life-Threatening Behavior, 30,* 377-385.

Osman, A., Gutierrez, P. M., Barrios, F. X., Bagge, C. L., Kopper, B. A., & Linden, S. (2005). The Inventory of Suicide Orientation-30: Further validation with adolescent psychiatric inpatients. *Journal of Clinical Psychology, 61,* 481-497.

Osman, A., Gutierrez, P. M., Jiandani, J., Kopper, B.A., Barrios, F. X., Linden, S.C., et al. (2003). A preliminary validation of the positive and negative suicide ideation (PANSI) inventory with normal adolescent sample. *Journal of Clinical Psychology, 59,* 493-512.

Osman, A., Gutierrez, P. M., Kopper, B. A., Barrios, F. X., & Chiros, C. E. (1998). The Positive and Negative Suicide Ideation Inventory: Development and validation. *Psychological Reports, 28,* 783-793.

Osman, A., Gutierrez, P. M., Muehlenkamp, J. J., Dix-Richardson, F., Barrios, F. X., & Kopper, B.A. (2004). Suicide Resilience Inventory-25: Development and preliminary psychometric properties. *Psychological Reports, 94,* 1349-1360.

Osman, A., Kopper, B. A., Barrios, F. X., Gutierrez, P. M., & Bagge, C. L. (2004). Reliability and validity of the Beck Depression Inventory—II with adolescent psychiatric inpatients. *Psychological Assessment, 16,* 120-132.

Osman, A., Kopper, B. A., Linehan, M. M., Barrios, F. X., Gutierez, P. M., & Bagge, C. L. (1999). Validation of the Adult Suicidal Ideation Questionnaire and the Reasons for Living Inventory in an adult psychiatric inpatient sample. *Psychological Assessment, 11,* 115-123.

Overholser, J. C., Adams, D. M., Lehnert, K. L., & Brinkman, D. C. (1995). Self-esteem deficits and suicidal tendencies among adolescents. *Journal of the American Academy of Child and Adolescent Psychiatry, 34,* 919-928.

Overholser, J. C., Freiheit, S. R., & DiFilippo, J. M. (1997). Emotional distress and substance abuse as risk factors for suicide attempts. *Canadian Journal of Psychiatry, 42,* 402-408.

Paloutzian, R. F., & Ellison, C. W. (1982). Loneliness, spiritual well-being and quality of life. In L. A. Peplau, & D. Perlman (Eds.) *Loneliness: A sourcebook of current theory, research, and therapy* (pp. 224-237). New York: Miley-Interscience.

Payne, B. J., & Range, L.M. (1995). Attitudes toward life and death and suicidality in young adults. *Death Studies, 19,* 559-569.

Pearce, C. M., & Martin, G. (1994). Predicting suicide attempts among adolescents. *Acta Psychiatrica Scandinavica, 90,* 324-328.

Pelcovitz, D., van der Kolk, B. A., Roth, S., Mandel, F., & Kaplan, S. (1997). Development and validation of the structured interview for measurement of disorders of extreme stress. *Journal of Traumatic Stress, 10,* 3-16.

Perez, V. W. (2005). The relationship between seriously considering, planning, and attempting suicide in the Youth Risk Behavior Survey. *Suicide and Life-Threatening Behavior, 35,* 35-49.

Perkins, D. F., & Hartless, G. (2002). An ecological risk-factor examination of suicide ideation and behavior of adolescents. *Journal of Adolescent Research, 17,* 3-26.

Pfeffer, C., Normandi, L., & Kakuma, T. (1994). Suicidal children grow up: Suicidal behavior and psychiatric disorders among relatives. *Journal of the American Academy of Child and Adolescent Psychiatry, 33,* 1084-1097.

Pinto, A., Whisman, M. A., & McCoy, K. J. M., (1997). Suicidal ideation in adolescents: Psychometric properties of the Suicidal Ideation Questionnaire in a clinical sample. *Psychological Assessment, 9,* 63-66.

Prinstein, M. J., Boergers, J., Spirito, A., Little, T. D., & Grapentine, W. L. (2000). Peer functioning, family dysfunction, and psychological symptoms in a risk factor model for adolescent inpatients' suicidal ideation severity. *Journal of Clinical Child Psychology, 29,* 392-405.

Procidano, M. E., & Heller, K. (1983). Measures of perceived social support from friends and from family: Three validation studies. *American Journal of Community Psychology, 11,* 1-24.

Radloff, L. S. (1991). The use of the Center for Epidemiologic Studies Depression Scale in adolescents and young adults. *Journal of Youth and Adolescence, 20,* 149-166.

Randell, B. P., Eggert, L. L., & Pike, K. C. (2001). Immediate post intervention effects of two brief youth suicide prevention interventions. *Suicide and Life-Threatening Behavior, 31,* 41-61.

Reinecke, M. A., Du Bois, D. L., & Schultz, T. M. (2001). Social problem solving, mood, and suicidality among inpatient adolescents. *Cognitive Therapy and Research, 25,* 743-756.

Reinherz, H. A., Giaconia, R. M., Silverman, A. B., Friedman, A., Pakiz, B., Frost, A. K., et al. (1995). Early psychosocial risks for adolescent suicidal ideation and attempts. *Journal of the American Academy of Child and Adolescent Psychiatry, 34,* 599-611.

Rew, L., Thomas, N., Horner, S. D., Resnick, M. D., & Beuhring, T. (2001). Correlates of recent suicide attempts in a triethnic group of adolescents. *Journal of Nursing Scholarship, 33,* 361-367.

Reynolds, W. M. (1987). *Reynolds Adolescent Depression Scale: Professional Manual.* Odessa, FL: Psychological Assessment Resources, Inc.

Reynolds, W. M. (1988). *Suicidal Ideation Questionnaire: Professional manual.* Odessa, FL: Psychological Assessment Resources.

Reynolds, W. M. (1990). Development of a semistructured clinical interview for suicidal behavior in adolescents. *Psychological Assessment, 2,* 382-390.

Reynolds, W. M. (1991a). A school-based procedure for the identification of adolescents at risk for suicidal behaviors. *Family Community Health, 14,* 64-75.

Reynolds, W. M. (1991b). Psychometric properties of the Adult Suicidal Ideation Questionnaire in college students. *Journal of Personality Assessment, 56,* 289-307.

Reynolds, W. M. (1998). *Adolescent Psychopathology Scale: Administration and interpretation manual.* Odessa, FL: Psychological Assessment Resources, Inc.

Reynolds, W. M. (2002). *Reynolds Adolescent Depression Scale: Professional Manual,* (2nd ed.). Odessa, FL: Psychological Assessment Resources, Inc.

Reynolds, W. M., & Mazza, J. (1994, June). *Use of the Suicidal Behaviors Interview for screening of school-based adolescents for risk of suicidal behaviors.* Paper presented at the meeting of the national conference on risk taking behaviors among children and adolescents. Arlington, VA.

Reynolds, W. M., & Richmond, B. O. (1978). What I think and feel: A revised measure of Children's Manifest Anxiety. *Journal of Abnormal Child Psychology, 6,* 271-280.

Reynolds, W. M., & Waltz, J. (1986, August). *Life events, social support and suicidal ideation in adolescents.* Paper presented at the annual meeting of the American Psychological Association, Washington, DC.

Rich, A. R., Kirkpatrick-Smith, J., Bonner, R. L., & Jans, F. (1992). Gender differences in the psychosocial correlates of suicidal ideation among adolescents. *Suicide and Life-Threatening Behavior, 22,* 364-373.

Ritter, D. R. (1990). Adolescent suicide: Social competence and problem behaviors of youth at high risk and low risk for suicide. *School Psychology Review, 19,* 83-95.

Roberts, R. E. (2000). Depression and suicidal behaviors among adolescents: The role of ethnicity. In I. Cuéllar & F. A. Paniagua (Eds.), *Handbook of multicultural mental health: Assessment and treatment of diverse populations* (pp. 359-388). San Diego: Academic Press.

Roberts, R. E., Chen, Y. R., & Roberts, C. R. (1997). Ethnocultural differences in prevalence of adolescent suicidal behaviors. *Suicide and Life-Threatening Behavior, 27,* 208-217.

Rosenberg, M. (1965). *Society and the adolescent self-image.* Princeton, NJ: Princeton University Press.

Rotheram-Borus, M. J., Trautman, P. D., Dopkins, S. C., & Shrout, P. E. (1990). Cognitive style and pleasant activities among female adolescent suicide attempters. *Journal of Consulting and Clinical Psychology, 58,* 554-561.

Rubenstein, J. L., Heeren, T., Housman, D., Rubin, C., & Stechler, G. (1989). Suicidal behavior in "normal" adolescents: Risk and protective factors. *American Journal of Orthopsychiatry, 59,* 59-71.

Rudd, M. D. (1990). An integrative model of suicidal ideation. *Suicide and Life-Threatening Behavior, 20,* 16-31.

Rudd, M. D., & Joiner, T. (1998). The assessment, management, and treatment of suicidality: Toward clinically informed and balanced standards of care. *Clinical Psychology: Science and Practice, 5,* 135-150.

Rutter, M. (1987). Psychosocial resilience and protective mechanisms. *American Journal of Orthopsychiatry, 57,* 316-331.

Ryff, C. D. (1989). Happiness is everything, or is it? Explorations on the meaning of psychological well-being. *Journal of Personality and Social Psychology, 57,* 1069-1081.

Sadowski, C., & Kelley, M. L. (1993). Social problem solving in suicidal adolescents. *Journal of Consulting and Clinical Psychology, 61,* 121-127.

Sadowski, C., Moore, L. A., & Kelley, M. L. (1994). Psychometric properties of the Social-Problem Solving Inventory (SPSI) with normal and emotionally-disturbed adolescents. *Journal of Abnormal Child Psychology, 22,* 487-500.

Sanchez, H. G. (2001). Risk factor model for suicide assessment and intervention. *Professional Psychology: Research and Practice, 32,* 351-358.

Sandoval, J., London, M. D., & Rey, T. (1994). Status of suicide prevention in California schools. *Death Studies, 18,* 595-608.

Sayer, N. A., Spoont, M., Nelson, D. B., & Nugent, S. (2004). Development and psychometric properties of the Disability Application Inventory. *Psychological Assessment, 16,* 192-196.

Schulein, M. J., & Switaj, N. (2005). *Normative data for the Reasons for Living Inventory for Adolescents.* Unpublished manuscript, Marshfield: Department of Psychiatry and Behavioral Health.

Seligman, M. E. P., & Csikszentmihalyi, M. (2000). Positive psychology. *American Psychologist, 55,* 5-14.

Shaffer, D., Garland, A., Vieland, V., Underwood, M., & Busner, C. (1991). The impact of curriculum-based suicide prevention programs for teenagers. *Journal of the American Academy of Child and Adolescent Psychiatry, 30,* 588-596.

Shaffer, D., Scott, M., Wilcox, C., Maslow, C., Hicks, R., Lucas, C. P., et al. (2004). The Columbia Suicidescreen: Validity and reliability of a screen for youth suicide and depression. *Journal of the American Academy of Child and Adolescent Psychiatry, 43,* 71-79.

Shain, B. N., Naylor, M., & Alessi, N. (1990). Comparison of self-rated and clinician-rated measures of depression in adolescents. *American Journal of Psychiatry, 147,* 793-795.

Shiang, J. (1998). Does culture make a difference? Racial/ethnic patterns of completed suicide in San Francisco, CA 1987-1996 and clinical applications. *Suicide and Life-Threatening Behavior, 28,* 338-354.

Shneidman, E. S. (1981). The psychological autopsy. *Suicide and Life-Threatening Behavior, 11,* 325-340.

Shneidman, E. (1993). *Suicide as psychache: A clinical approach to self-destructive behavior.* Northvale, NJ: Jason Aronson, Inc.

Smith, G. (1999). Resilience concepts and findings: Implications for family therapy. *Journal of Family Therapy, 21,* 154-158.

Smith, G. T., & McCarthy, D. M. (1995). Methodological considerations in the refinement of clinical assessment instruments. *Psychological Assessment, 7,* 300-308.

Smith, P. B., Buzi, R. S., & Weinman, M. L. (2001). Mental health problems and symptoms among male adolescents attending a teen health clinic. *Adolescence, 36,* 323-332.

Sorenson, S. B., & Rutter, C. M. (1991). Transgenerational patterns of suicide attempt. *Journal of Consulting and Clinical Psychology, 59,* 861-866.

Speckens, A. E. M., & Hawton, K. (2005). Social problem solving in adolescents with suicidal behavior: A systematic review. *Suicide and Life-Threatening Behavior, 35,* 365-387.

Spirito, A., Valeri, S., Boergers, J., & Donaldson, D. (2003). Predictors of continued suicidal behavior in adolescents following a suicide attempt. *Journal of Clinical Child and Adolescent Psychology, 32,* 284-289.

Stack, S., & Wasserman, I. (1992). The effects of religion on suicide ideology: An analysis of the networks perspectives. *Journal for the Scientific Study of Religion, 31,* 457-466.

Stack, S., & Wasserman, I. (1995). The effect of marriage, family, and religious ties on African American suicide ideology. *Journal of Marriage and the Family, 57,* 215-223.

Steiger, J. H., & Lind, J. (1980, May). *Statistically based tests for the number of common factors.* Paper presented at the annual meeting of the Psychometric Society, Iowa City, IA.

Stewart, S. M., Lam, T. H., Betson, C., & Chung, S. F. (1999). Suicide ideation and its relationship to depressed mood in a community sample of adolescents in Hong Kong. *Suicide and Life-Threatening Behavior, 29,* 227-240.

Stouthamer-Loeber, M., Loeber, R., Farrington, D. P., Zhang, Q., van Kammen, W., & Majuin, E. (1993). The double edge of protective and risk factors for delinquency: Interventions and developmental patterns. *Developmental and Psychopathology, 5,* 683-701.

Sue, D. W., & Sue, D. (1990). *Counseling the culturally different: Theory and practice* (2nd ed.). New York: Wiley.

Takane, Y., & de Leeuw, J. (1987). On the relationship between item response theory and factor analysis of discretized variables. *Psychometrika, 56,* 393-408.

Tanney, B. (1992). Mental disorders, psychiatric patients, and suicide. In R. Marks., A. Berman, J. Maltsberger, & R. Yufit. (Eds.), *Assessment and prediction of suicide* (pp. 277-320). New York: Guilford.

Thompson, E. A., Mazza, J. J., Herting, J. R., Randell, B. P., & Eggert, L. L. (2005). The mediating roles of anxiety, depression, and hopelessness on adolescent suicidal behaviors. *Suicide and Life-Threatening Behavior, 35,* 14-34.

Tortolero, S. R., & Roberts, R. E. (2001). Differences in nonfatal suicide behaviors among Mexican and European American middle school children. *Suicide and Life-Threatening Behavior, 31,* 214-223.

Velez, C. N., & Cohen, P. (1988). Suicidal behavior and ideation in a community sample of children: Maternal and youth reports. *Journal of the American Academy of Child and Adolescent Psychiatry, 27,* 349-356.

Velting, D. M., Rathus, J. H., & Miller, A. L. (2000). MACI personality scale profiles of depressed adolescent suicide attempters: A pilot study. *Journal of Clinical Psychology, 56,* 1381-1385.

Wagman, B., Resnick, M. D., Ireland, M., & Blum, R. W. (1999). Suicide attempts among American Indian and Alaska native youth. *Archives of Pediatrics and Adolescent Medicine, 153,* 573-580.

Watkins, R. L., & Gutierrez, P. M. (2003). The relationship between exposure to adolescent suicide and subsequent suicide risk. *Suicide and Life-Threatening Behavior, 33,* 21-32.

Watt, T. T., & Sharp, S. F. (2002). Race differences in strains associated with suicidal behavior among adolescents. *Youth & Society, 34,* 232-256.

Weissman, M. M., Bruce, M. L., Leaf, P. J., Florio, L. P., & Holzer, C. E. III. (1991). Affective Disorders. In L. N., Robins & D. A. Regier (Eds.). *Psychiatric Disorders in America: The Epidemiological Catchment Area Study* (pp. 53-80). New York: Free Press.

Werlang, B.S.G., & Botega, N. J. (2003). A semistructured interview for psychological autopsy: An inter-rater reliability study. *Suicide and Life-Threatening Behavior, 33,* 326-333.

Wild, L. G., Flisher, A. J., & Lombard, C. (2004). Suicidal ideation and attempts in adolescents: Associations with depression and six domains of self-esteem. *Journal of Adolescence, 27,* 611-624.

Windle, M., & Miller-Tutzauer, C. (1992). Confirmatory factor analysis and concurrent validity of the Perceived Social Support-Family measure among adolescents. *Journal of Marriage and the Family, 54,* 777-787.

Yoder, K. A., & Hoyt, D. R. (2005). Family economic pressure and adolescent suicidal ideation: Application of the family stress model. *Suicide and Life-Threatening Behavior, 35,* 251-264.

Yudofsky, S. C., Silvaer, J. M., Jackson, W., Endicott, J., & Williams, D. (1986). The Overt Aggression Scale for the objective rating of verbal and physical aggression. *American Journal of Psychiatry, 143,* 35-39.

Yuen, N., Andrade, N., Nahulu, L., Makini, G., McDermott, J. F., Danko, G., et al. (1996). The rate and characteristics of suicide attempts in the Native Hawaiian adolescent population. *Suicide and Life-Threatening Behavior, 26,* 27-36.

Zayas, L. H., Fortuna, L. R., Lester, R. J., & Cabassa, L. J. (2005). Why do so many Latina teens attempt suicide? A conceptual model for research. *American Journal of Orthopsychiatry, 75,* 275-287.

Zayas, L. H., Kaplan, C., Turner, S., Romano, K., & Gonzales-Ramos, G. (2000). Understanding suicide attempts by adolescent Hispanic females. *Social Work, 45,* 53-63.

Zwick, W. R., & Velicer, W. F. (1986). Comparison of five rules for determining the number of components to retain. *Psychological Bulletin, 17,* 253-269.

Index